Vision and Reality

Changing Education and Training in South Africa

EDITED BY

WALLY MORROW AND KENNETH KING

VISION AND REALITY – CHANGING EDUCATION AND TRAINING
IN SOUTH AFRICA

University of Cape Town Press (Pty) Ltd
Private Bag, Rondebosch, 7701,
Cape Town, South Africa

First published 1998

© University of Cape Town Press and W Morrow and K King

ISBN 1-919713-27-1

Cover design: Jos Thorne
Typesetting and reproduction: RHT desktop publishing cc, Durbanville, 7550,
    South Africa. Set in 11 on 13 pt AGaramond.
Printing and binding: Creda Communications, Epping 11, Cape Town

Contents

SECTION ONE: POLICY AND IMPLEMENTATION: RHETORIC AND REALITY

SECTION TWO: INTEGRATING EDUCATION AND TRAINING

SECTION FIVE: DIVERSITY AND SOCIAL COHESION IN EDUCATION

List of tables and figures

List of editors and contributors

Nelleke Bak – Dr Bak is one of the editors of Section Four and the author of Chapter 15. She is a Senior Lecturer in the Department of Philosophy of Education, University of the Western Cape.

Mignonne Breier – Mignonne Breier is the author of Chapter 9. She is a Senior Researcher in the Education Policy Unit at the University of the Western Cape and, until recently, was the Acting Director of the Unit.

Zubeida Desai – Zubeida Desai is one of the editors of Section Five and a joint author of Chapter 18. She is a Senior Lecturer in the Department of Didactics, University of the Western Cape.

Gari Donn – Dr Donn is one of the editors of Section Two, and the author of Chapter 5. She is a Lecturer in the Institute for the Study of Education and Society at Edinburgh University.

Levi Engelbrecht – Levi Engelbrecht is a joint editor of Section Three and one of the authors of Chapter 11. He is a Senior Lecturer in the Department of Educational Psychology, University of the Western Cape.

Noel Entwistle – Professor Entwistle is one of the editors of Section Four and the author of Chapter 13. He is the Bell Professor of Education at Edinburgh University.

Jonathan Geidt – Jonathan Geidt is the author of Chapter 16. He is a Lecturer in the Centre for Adult and Continuing Education, University of the Western Cape.

André Gouws – Professor Gouws is one of the authors of Chapter 11. He is Professor of Educational Psychology in the Faculty of Education, University of the Western Cape.

Brian Gray – Brian Gray is the author of Chapter 10. He is a Senior Lecturer in the Department of Didactics, University of the Western Cape, and the Director of the Science Through Applications Project.

Zelda Groener – Dr Groener is the author of Chapter 6. She is a Senior Lecturer, and the Acting Director of the Centre for Adult and Continuing Education, University of the Western Cape.

Harold Herman – Professor Herman is the author of Chapter 3. He is the Professor of Comparative Education and Dean of the Faculty of Education, University of the Western Cape.

Edith Jantjes – Professor Jantjes is the author of Chapter 12. Until her retirement in 1997 she was a Professor in the Faculty of Education, University of the Western Cape.

Ruth Jonathan – Professor Jonathan is the editor of Section Five and the author of Chapter 20. She is the Professor of Educational Theory and Policy at Edinburgh University, and the Director of the Graduate School in the Social Sciences.

Peter Kallaway – Professor Kallaway is the author of Chapter 2. He is the Professor of History of Education in the Faculty of Education, University of the Western Cape.

Kenneth King – Professor King is one of the general editors of the book, the editor of Section One and the author of Chapter 1. He is Professor of International and Comparative Education and the Director of the Centre of African Studies at Edinburgh University.

Glenda Kruss – Dr Kruss is one of the editors of Section Two and the author of Chapter 7. She is a Senior Lecturer in the Department of Comparative Education, University of the Western Cape.

Cedric Linder – Professor Linder is the joint author of Chapter 14. He is a Professor in the Department of Physics, University of the Western Cape.

Lilian Lomofsky – Lilian Lomofsky is one of the authors of Chapter 11. She is a Lecturer in the Department of Educational Psychology, University of the Western Cape.

Delia Marshall – Dr Marshall is one of the joint authors of Chapter 14. She is a Research Assistant in the Department of Physics, University of the Western Cape.

Simon McGrath – Dr McGrath is the author of Chapter 8. He is a Research Fellow in the Centre of African Studies and the Institute for the Study of Education and Society at Edinburgh University.

Dirk Meerkotter – Professor Meerkotter is the editor of Section Three and the author of Chapter 4. He is a Professor in the Department of Didactics and Deputy Dean of the Faculty of Education, University of the Western Cape.

Suzette Meerkotter – Suzette Meerkotter is the author of Chapter 19. She was previously a language teacher and Deputy Principal at Guguletu Comprehensive Secondary School.

Wally Morrow – Professor Morrow is one of the general editors of the book, and the author of Chapter 17. He is the Professor of Philosophy of Education and was, previously, the Dean of the Faculty of Education, University of the Western Cape.

George Thomson – Professor Thomson is one of the authors of Chapter 11. He is the Professor of Educational Psychology at Edinburgh University.

Prevot van der Merwe – Dr van der Merwe is one of the authors of Chapter 18. He is a Lecturer in the Department of Didactics, University of the Western Cape.

List of abbreviations

ABET   adult basic education and training
ANC   African National Congress
B.Ed   Baccalaureus Educationis
CACE   Centre for Adult and Continuing Education
CBO   community-based organisation
COMSEC   Community Self-Employment Centre
COSATU   Congress of South African Trade Unions
DET   Department of Education and Training
DFE   Department for Education (UK)
DFID   Department for International Development (UK)
ETDP   Education, Training and Development Practitioners
GTC   General Teaching Council for Scotland
HOR   House of Representatives
HSRC   Human Sciences Research Council
LSEN   Learners with Special Educational Needs
NCESS   National Committee on Education
NCSNET   National Commission on Special Needs in Education and Training
NECC   National Education Co-ordinating Committee
NEPI   National Education Policy Investigation
NGO   non-governmental organisation
NQF   National Qualifications Framework
NTB   National Training Board
NTSI   National Training Strategy Initiative
NUMSA   National Union of Metalworkers of South Africa
NZQA   New Zealand Qualifications Authority
OAU   Organisation for African Unity
OBE   outcomes-based education
OECD   Organisation for Economic Co-operation and Development
PRP   Participatory Research Project (COSATU)
RDP   Reconstruction and Development Programme

RSA	Republic of South Africa
SAIRR	South African Institute for Race Relations
SAQA	South African Qualifications Authority
SCOTVEC	Scottish Vocational and Educational Council
SCRE	Scottish Council for Research and Education
SEB	Scottish Examination Board
SME	small and micro-enterprise
SMME	small, medium and micro-enterprise
SOED	Scottish Office Education Department
SOEID	Scottish Office Education and Industry Department
SQA	Scottish Qualifications Authority
THRIP	Technology and Human Resources for Industry Programme
UCT	University of Cape Town
UDF	United Democratic Front
UK	United Kingdom
UNDP	United Nations Development Programme
UNESCO	United Nations Educational, Scientific and Cultural Organisation
UWC	University of the Western Cape
WCED	Western Cape Education Department

Acknowledgements

Many people made major contributions in putting this volume together, and a few deserve special mention.

Dirk Meerkotter initiated the project and made an irreplaceable contribution in following the idea through over a period of two years.

The groundwork for the book was done by the section editors, who were as follows:

Section 1: Kenneth King
Section 2: Glenda Kruss and Gari Donn
Section 3: Dirk Meerkotter and Levi Engelbrecht
Section 4: Noel Entwistle and Nelleke Bak
Section 5: Ruth Jonathan

The enormous task of technically preparing the final manuscript and bibliography, and co-ordinating the chapters of the twenty-five authors with their disparate styles of presentation and referencing was undertaken by Anneke and Suzette Meerkotter.

The British Council, through its higher education links scheme, which is funded by the Department for International Development, made a direct contribution to the production of this book. They also funded the academic link between the University of the Western Cape and Edinburgh University, which made this book possible. Tracy Michel and Lynne Aschman of the Cape Town Office of the British Council deserve particular thanks for their sustained support and encouragement of the link project and its several published outcomes.

Rosemary Meny-Gibert of the University of Cape Town Press provided valuable professional and technical advice and has guided the production of the book.

Preface

The government which came to power as a result of the democratic elections of 1994 in South Africa inherited a situation in which as a high priority it had to change public education in some decisive way. At the same time, however, education and training were already being changed by other agencies and influences such as students, non-governmental organisations (NGOs), for-profit providers and the fundamental changes in direction in education policy internationally. Now, four years later, it is timely to analyse the current situation and assess progress in this field. This is the principal purpose of this book. During the years of Apartheid, even before the watershed year of 1976, denunciations of Apartheid education were prominent in the rhetoric of the struggle for liberation, and educational institutions became the sites of some of the most bitter and effective resistance to oppression. The Apartheid education system was rightly seen as one of the mainstays in the maintenance of the injustices of Apartheid, and a fundamental change away from that system was seen as one of the keys to achieving liberation. In this highly polemical context the wholesale and uncritical repudiation of virtually anything from the past, especially those standards of excellence and structures of authority which were not essentially embedded in Apartheid education, became common-place, and major system-wide supports to the culture of schooling and learning unravelled. The new government had to be seen to be dramatically changing the education system.

By the early 1990s high hopes had been raised about what changing education could be expected to deliver. It was hoped that change would simultaneously benefit the previously disenfranchised and marginalised and improve the quality of education for all. There was the perception that the culture of teaching and learning had broken down in many black, and especially urban, sectors of society and it was hoped that radical changes to the education system would restore it and revitalise the whole field after the disaster of Apartheid education. In the context of such hopes and perceptions, and the strident popular demands in terms of which they were expressed, it was understandable that the new government would launch an ambitious programme of developing human resource policy at a breakneck pace.

In an earlier phase there was what, with the benefit of hindsight, can now be seen as a myopic concentration on governance structures and systems of control, with little attention to the substance of education. More recently, attention has shifted to curriculum issues and qualifications' frameworks. These policy developments have been inspired by multiple aims, from redressing the injustices of the past and the redistribution of educational resources, to attempts to reconceptualise what is meant by educational quality and the simultaneous achievement of equity, development and global competitiveness.

However, this already enormously complex and strenuous national agenda for change has been even further complicated by the profound changes taking place in education and training systems internationally. In many OECD (Organisation for Economic Co-operation and Development) countries conventional understandings of public education were being challenged by a groundswell of disillusionment with the mass systems of education and training that had been developed earlier this century. There were thus dynamic currents of change abroad, including a fascination with new labour processes, which bore in strongly on attempts in South Africa to craft new policies to change and shape the education and training system.

During this period the intensifying dissatisfaction with established education and training systems in many countries was accompanied by a deepening penetration of market mechanisms for the distribution of education, reinforced by an instrumental conception of the goals of education and a sense that unified systems of education and training were appropriate to the work of the new knowledge society. One aspect of these changes was the shrinking of public funding for education, which had led to policies of 'rightsizing' and 'rationalisation' and an emphasis on the exchange value of education and training. Questions about the 'relevance' of education have been pressed more and more insistently and the 'merging' of education and training systems has become more common, and what is called the 'commodification' of education has rapidly come to dominate public understanding of education, and to shape the programmes on offer. The rapid growth of global economic systems, with the transnationalisation of production and internationalisation of markets, and the accelerating penetration of powerful information and communication technology into work, and other aspects of daily life, have profoundly impacted on the ways in which education and training are conceived and conducted.

These developments have handed education policy, practice and theory a complex set of demands, challenges and goals which, in many cases, are in serious conflict with each other, conflicts which are exacerbated by resource restraints. Neither this, nor critical debate about how policy, practice and theory can be coherently related to each other are issues which are specific to South Africa; but in South Africa, with its particular history of division and oppression, and with the insistent demand on education authorities to be seen to be changing education and training, and to do so essentially and rapidly, these issues come into sharp and raw focus.

The global change agenda coincides with, but may well conflict with, the national change agenda. The integration of the systems of education and training in South Africa faces in two directions – towards redress and towards globalisation – which are in some respects incompatible with each other. In a similar way, the unification of the previously separated systems of education in South Africa might have been expected to lead to financial savings as overlaps were eliminated, and this would have coincided with the global change agenda. However, to avoid the resource depletion of institutions which had already been disadvantaged under Apartheid required massive equity and re-dress funding expenditures – a requirement which is in conflict with the global change agenda.

Public education is everywhere a social practice that is the primary site of simultaneous national and personal aspirations that are often in tension with each other, and it stands at the intersection of a broad range of demands and a nexus of theoretical and political problems. This contradictory web of demands, aspirations and problems is nakedly exposed in South Africa during this phase in which a national priority is to establish a society in which justice, equality, human rights, dignity, quality of life and economic empowerment are all simultaneously advanced.

The conflict between global and national change agendas could have been expected to give rise to difficulties and there are those who claim that the education and training system in South Africa is currently in serious crisis. The disappointing matriculation results at the end of 1997 are cited as one symptom, but the inflation of qualifications, and the deterioration of 'standards' which this is regarded as signalling, the migration out of the system of some of the most experienced teachers, and the deep demoralisation of the teaching profession (which is in the front line of accomplishing fundamental educational transformation) are cited as additional symptoms of the depth and extent of the crisis. In some ways it might have been expected that the major project of changing a whole national system of education would be unlikely to run along a smooth path, but the government and its Department of Education run the serious risk of losing the goodwill which was one of their main advantages as they came to power, on the wave of popular legitimacy inherited from the struggle against Apartheid.

This volume takes a step back from the polemics of the day and reflects carefully and critically on the multiplicity of influences changing education and training systems in South Africa. It takes up several of the major themes which can be seen as emerging and re-emerging in a variety of discursive contexts. Each of the five sections focuses on a particular web of related questions. Sections one and two address questions of policy, the former in broad brushstrokes, and the latter in terms of a critical analysis of some more specific current policy initiatives. Sections three and four turn the spotlight on issues of practice, the former in relation to the professional regeneration of teachers, the latter in relation to the crucial problems of how teaching and learning can be systematically organised in a situation which is endemic in much of the developing world, in which the number of learners increases exponentially while the material and human resources for education shrink. Section five looks at an issue which is at the heart of educational debate, not only in South Africa but in plural societies everywhere – the question of cultural and linguistic diversity, and the expectation that education will contribute to social cohesion and a sense of national identity.

This collection of papers demonstrates the ways in which policy, practice and theory are interdependent, and in which the complexity of the challenges to the project of changing education and training require a multi-faceted approach. The authors approach the issues from a range of disciplinary perspectives, and the resulting richness shows the advantages of collaborative efforts to understand and come to grips with the challenges faced in changing education and training systems in the contemporary world.

This book is an outcome of the institutional collaboration between the universities of the Western Cape and Edinburgh under the auspices of a project administered by the British Council and funded by the Department for International Development (DFID) in Britain. The authors from both institutions have experienced the radical restructuring and reshaping of their education and training systems, and worked together at the point at which the globalising, market-driven agenda intersected in South Africa with a more local and national agenda, inspired by concerns with redress and the advance of social justice through education. In addition, this book was a means of enhancing the international experience of both sets of staff, contributing to capacity-building and pursuing new research agendas that could emerge from these forms of long-term institutional partnerships. Over the first three years of this academic collaboration there have emerged a series of valuable contributions to our understanding of what is involved in changing education and training in South Africa.

Wally Morrow and Kenneth King

SECTION ONE

Policy and implementation: rhetoric and reality

Introduction

This section touches on some of the largest and most challenging issues in South African education and training at the end of the 1990s. The concerns are with equity, access, inclusion, quality, professional morale and the transition to work. These may, at first, seem to be the very ordinary challenges to every education system in the world at this period; but as the first generation of post-Apartheid reforms are rolled into place, and promise to affect every level of education and training, the authors urge that there is a particular need for the research and policy constituencies to face up to a series of very difficult questions that go to the very heart of the planned reform process.

The first of these concerns differentiation versus uniformity. It is understandable, given South Africa's bitter history of separate and unequal curricula for different groups, that the impetus of reform should be towards integrated systems of education and skills training, open to all. Historically, South Africans concerned with equity (and indeed many others in the rest of Africa during the colonial period) fought against notions that there should be curricula 'adapted' to their situation or to their cultures or geographical location, for example in rural areas. The motto of those defending Africa from these ideas could be summed up as 'No differentiation in education before political equality' (King 1971). For several decades there was, of course, major differentiation in South Africa. The chapters which follow raise some fundamental questions about how, now that majority rule has been achieved, the nation can best address some of the massive deficits in skills and knowledge that have been acquired over the many past decades.

If the culture of learning and teaching in many urban black schools has in addition been undermined by almost twenty years of struggle and boycott, will a new curriculum, based on new assumptions about the organisation of knowledge, assist in bringing that sector back into the mainstream? Unless there are special measures to address the deficits in quality, morale and student commitment, is it not possible that any single comprehensive reform will be much more readily accommodated by those schools that were not directly involved in the struggle?

May the same not be said of many rural and farm schools, whether located in former homelands or not? The application of a single national curriculum model will by itself not necessarily remedy the special requirements of the rural poor. Equally, in the domain of skills acquisition, we can ask if the imposition of a single learnership system, covering both formal and informal employment, will be able adequately to offer pathways to good quality training and to meaningful work opportunities.

In the fields of formal education and skills training, there can be little doubt that, faced with the legacy of fragmentation, there is an enormous attraction in presenting bold, national systems open to all. The implementation challenge may, however, be that these national initiatives will need to be delivered in fundamentally different ways in different areas and with different groups if the unequal starting points of various communities are not to be simply reinforced by the introduction of the new curricula.

A second thread running through this section is the recognition that the present does have a history. Terms such as 'apprenticeship', 'skill', 'technical' and 'matriculation', or even the names of particular institutions, have had a certain resonance as symbols of achievement even when they have been inaccessible to the majority. The re-categorisation of levels and processes of learning in the reforms of the education and training systems is enormously ambitious since it must project new symbols of excellence, and seek rapidly to secure commitment to them across the population. The dangers in this re-categorisation of learning are that the past is framed as fundamentally different from the vision of the reform, and that previous excellence becomes questionable.

A last theme suggested both implicitly and explicitly by these chapters is that research on education and training will itself need to be refocused. It was natural in the era of Apartheid for scholars to work on the policies themselves that were being generated by the government. Correspondingly, there was very little empirical work done on the character of rural or urban education; indeed, it was positively discouraged by the state. Now, by contrast, there is a real research challenge to get behind terms such as 'the culture of learning', 'outcomes-based education' and 'learnership', and to analyse the process whereby these new categories and approaches begin to be disseminated and acquire value in ordinary communities of pupils, teachers and parents.

Kenneth King

1

Policy coherence in education, training and enterprise development in South Africa: the implementation challenge of new policies

KENNETH KING

This chapter is concerned with analysing the tension between the development of policy and the challenge of implementation. It is also concerned with what could be termed policy coherence. By this we mean importance of policy in one sphere being reinforced by policies elsewhere. Examples could have been taken from many different sectors in South Africa. In this instance, however, where we are primarily concerned with education and training, the emphasis will be on those policies concerned with employment and enterprise development on the one hand, and those concerned with human resource development through schools, higher education and training institutions on the other. Since South Africa entered its post-Apartheid era in 1994 as one of the most unequal societies in the world according to available data (Standing *et al.* 1996:19) particular attention will be given to those enterprise, education and training policies that set out deliberately to do something about these stark contrasts. It is of special significance to Chapter 2 by Kallaway, on rural education, that with the advent of majority rule in 1994, it was acknowledged that Africans in rural areas were the worst affected by poverty. It must also be recalled that South Africa entered this new policy environment with a human development situation (according to the United Nations Development Programme's Human Development Index) in which the black population was on a par with the Democratic Republic of Congo and the white population on a par with Canada (Standing *et al.* 1996:20).

The dual concerns of this chapter with enterprise development and human resource development need to be seen against the wider economic challenges to the new majority government. On the one hand the country has appeared to espouse the conventional wisdom that in an increasingly competitive world, the South African economy must be increasingly removed from the greenhouse of protection and hardened up in the chilly winds of trade liberalisation and export-led industrialisation. At the same time, and unlike most of the other countries which in the 1980s and 1990s were engaging with these kinds of macroeconomic adjustment measures, the African National Congress (ANC) government has shown a strong obligation to develop policies for the redress of over a century of discrimination against the majority of its people.

The tension between equity and growth, between greater competitiveness and redistribution, is part of the backcloth to this chapter. But the particular threads that will be followed, at the policy level, are those that may give some insight into how these concerns with equity, poverty and growth can be detected in the education and training arenas. Education and training policy spheres have carried a double burden in respect of this equity-growth challenge. Historically, education and training have been prime examples of racially determined inequity, and hence the systems are seen as prime targets for radical change; at the same time, these human resource development fields have been identified as powerful vehicles for change in other sectors.

We shall look especially closely at the threads in the education and training policy papers which are concerned with the linkages between education and work, and we shall be particularly interested in whether the education and training policy environment of the new government seeks explicitly to relate to the huge contrasts in the labour market. A valuable indicator of such a concern may well be the extent to which education and training policies are concerned with different post-school and post-training livelihoods, and in particular whether they project a vision of preparation for employment and self-employment in both urban and rural settings. In other words, is there evidence in the education and training policy papers of a particular version of the labour market, and is specific consideration given to approaches to employment and enterprise development?

Because this chapter is concerned with the development of an inclusive policy for education, training and enterprise, and with policy coherence amongst government departments, we are less interested in examining small, medium and micro-enterprise (SMME) policies in the obvious places – in *The President's Conference on Small Business* (June 1994), in the Department of Trade and Industry's *White Paper on National Strategy for Development and Promotion of Small Business in South Africa* (20 March 1995), and in the

National Small Business Act (November 1996), which provided for the establishment of the National Small Business Council (NSBC)[1] and the Ntsika Enterprise Promotion Agency (NEPA). Rather, we see micro-enterprise and self-employment as elements in a much larger, hitherto neglected policy arena of the informal economy, with links to informal education and informal training in both urban and rural areas. For the purposes of this chapter, we are concerned with the attempt to fashion an inclusive strategy for education, training and enterprise development, and will examine this through the prism of two government departments – Education and Labour.

The starting point for the analysis is 1993, just before majority rule (though it could be taken back to 1991[2]). Currently, it is much too early to be clear how the inclusive vision will fare as the new policies on education, training and enterprise are progressively implemented, but even at the level of policy coherence there are at least some grounds for concern.

The pre-majority rule frameworks on education and training

With the history of stark and discriminatory separation of provision of all social services in South Africa, it should not be surprising that the keywords in the new thinking about equitable access and redress of dualism should be 'integrated' and 'unified'. Thus, in the June 1993 document *Framework for Lifelong Learning* (ANC/COSATU 1993) the ANC envisioned a triple integration: first, of the racially divided education systems; second, of the fragmented and under-resourced provision of training; and third, of the two hitherto separate systems of education and training.[3]

While the first of these integrations could have been anticipated, on the basis of post-colonial history in the rest of Africa, the second and third would appear to have been influenced by the desire of South African policy-makers to fashion a new system that would be more in step with the changing nature of work, technology and labour process. The integration of education and training (and of their respective departments) seems also to have been influenced by a judgement that it would assist social exclusion and the millions of South Africans who had benefited only minimally from initial, formal schooling. An integrated system, open to all, through the whole of life, had very powerful backing in a country with so many different types of 'lost generations'.

It is clear that this first radical framework of June 1993 assumed that redress was inseparable from re-entry to education and training opportunities, and re-entry should mean recourse to a common national qualification system. In a country whose history of separate areas, schools and training systems had long emphasised different standards, it was not surprising that a new single set of standards for all was proposed. The attraction of the new scheme was that it was

6

a mechanism both for educational and employment mobility. Most important, it had a vision of a national system, not just for those who might be in unionised jobs, in the government service or in what has been called the formal sector of the economy, but also for those who were in the rural areas and in the informal economy:

> The problem still remains – how to ensure that people do not get trapped into dead end jobs or unemployment or find themselves unable to make employment shifts … The answer lies in career pathing defined within a national framework.
>
> The challenge is to ensure that every branch of income generating activity is covered by the new system. If, as at present, different branches of economic activity do not speak to each other – or some are completely left out (for example, training for self-employment or rural development projects), then it will follow that mobility between the sections will be restricted if not prohibited. The opportunity for progression should be possible in all areas of productive and service sector work (ANC/COSATU 1993:8).

The novel aspect of the new vision was that, although it emerged from particular elements of the formal labour movement, notably the metalworkers' union (NUMSA), it saw all economic activity in South Africa as falling into thirteen broad areas and within each of these, there would be Sector Education and Training Boards (SETBs) which would take responsibility for career paths. Again, the *Framework* paper was careful to make it clear that SETBs 'should cover all areas of income-related activity – formal and "informal" – within their scope and to the end of pre-tertiary level' (ANC/COSATU 1993:9). In its own words, the *Framework* emphasised that the new system would cover 'formal industry, self-employment and development projects' *(ibid.)*.

This may seem a very centralising aspiration, but in a country where there had been all manner of unrecognised training by non-governmental organisations (NGOs), or within the firm, the farm or the household, the sheer ambition and inclusiveness of the new scheme must have been very persuasive. Unlike most policy outlines on education and training, the thread that we are following in this chapter – of provision for the huge but neglected informal economy – is very clear.

There is, in fact, a separate section of the *Framework* paper on micro-enterprises and self-employment, and it is firmly stated that 'a web of institutional arrangements will be needed to give support to communities and individuals who generate their own employment' *(ibid.* p.10). It was underlined and very strongly emphasised that appropriate education and training would be made available and would be accredited as part of the new national system. Amongst the particular 'special target groups' that are identified for attention, it is worth noting the priority for women, rurally based groups and the disabled.

7

Just over six months later, a good deal of the vision was projected again in the *Policy Framework for Education and Training* document published by the Education Department of the ANC (January 1994). Just four months before May 1994 and majority rule, there was still a strong emphasis on the planned integration of education and training. Indeed, it appeared that the ANC believed that the very separation of education from training had, like Apartheid itself, 'contributed significantly to the situation where most of our people are under-educated, under-skilled, and under-prepared for full participation in social, economic and civic life' (ANC 1994:10). In other words, if the Apartheid labour market was not to continue, there would need to be transformation of all types and levels of skill and knowledge.

In this key document, there is still the expectation of a unified Ministry of Education and Training, and there is still a strong emphasis on the need for opportunities to be identified for the out-of-school-youth, under-educated employees, the unemployed and people in the rural areas. There is even a separate section on rural and farm schools. However, there is no explicit attention given to the education and training needs of the self-employed nor of the informal economy, nor of the particular challenge of integrating them into a national framework. Understandably, as the document emerged from the still separate Education Department of the ANC, it was primarily concerned with the different subsectors of education, both formal and non-formal. In the ten policy initiatives that the ANC thought it 'likely' would be taken over the next five years (1994–9), the integration of education and training, linked to a South African qualifications authority, remains the one that is most closely connected to our concern with the millions who have sought to create their own work, and by necessity have sought their own training. They are promised that: 'Learning and skills which people have acquired through experience and informal training will be formally assessed and credited towards qualifications' (*ibid.*).

In summary, the very strong view that emerges from this framework, or manifesto, is that the historical separateness of education and training has been, in effect, a human resources Apartheid; the very words used of political Apartheid are applied to these two spheres: 'The education and training systems follow separate and unequal paths which limit career choice and belittle vocational education' (*ibid.* p.109). The planned integration was going to deal not only with the low status of the vocational institutions; it was also going to bring in to a single national fold, the millions of unskilled, low-skilled and informally skilled citizens of South Africa.[4]

The search for national inclusiveness through separate Departments of Education and Labour

Soon after the ANC was installed as a major player in the Government of National Unity (GNU), the *White Paper on the Reconstruction and Development Programme* (September 1994) was published. It was intended, fundamentally, to restructure the economy and alleviate the legacy of poverty and inequality. High on rhetoric and low on implementation, the Reconstruction and Development Programme (RDP) Office would eventually be wound up in April 1996. It was not surprising that the *Draft White Paper on Education and Training* (appearing the same month as the RDP paper) should have borrowed the keywords 'reconstruction and development' from the RDP paper and applied them to no less than two of the five parts of its own text.[5] Arguably, the *Draft White Paper* (and to a considerable extent the White Paper that followed it in March 1995) was much more concerned with the restructuring of the education system than it was with the wider linkages to the economy, the labour market and those categories of the self-employed, underemployed and the rural poor with which the original unified *Framework* paper of 1993 had been preoccupied. Apart, therefore, from a few sentences lifted virtually intact from the earlier ANC policy – about accrediting and assessing those who have had informal training – there was a distinct sense of the Department of Education being concerned principally with the education side of the proposed integration of education and training.

Over the next four years, 1994 through 1997, there was the Interministerial Working Group on Education and Training (IMWG), but the two key ministries (of Education and Labour) continued to be separate. There was, of course, collaboration on the development of the National Qualifications Framework (NQF), but the two departments remained separate, and hence that inclusiveness (and ease of movement back and forth amongst education, training and the economy, which was so evident in the original *Framework for Lifelong Learning*, 1993) was lost.

This 1993 education and training 'project' had also been very concerned with equity; with how an integrated education and training system could draw in huge groupings like the informally trained and the inadequately schooled, as well as other vulnerable groups in the rural and urban areas. However, in both departments the tension has continued between policy development for 'existing clients' who are already in institutional settings that have always recognised qualifications, and that for the large body of the population who are at the opposite end of the much-discussed ideal 'high skill', 'high wage' economy.

The great temptation in the construction and development of a new qualifications system in South Africa is that its implementers in the departments both of Education and Labour are likely to find themselves preoccupied with the demands (and even the resistance) of 'the insiders' – those who already have qualifications or who hope to have within existing institutions – rather than those who were quite outside the scope of Apartheid provision of education and training, and who are still outsiders today. In other words, the energies and financial resources of the implementing agencies could well go into exchanging one qualifications system for another, *for the kinds of clients who would have had access to the previous formal qualifications system anyway.*

The real challenge, by contrast, is to offer South Africans a new national system in which those categories of outsiders we have targeted in this chapter are, for the first time, made to feel that they are natural clients. No one should under-estimate the difficulty of this national project of qualification inclusiveness, and it is clear that even one of its main architects, Adrienne Bird, has been aware of precisely this outsider dimension of the NQF:

> Being a non-holder of a qualification within a qualifications framework represents an invidious position – not because of a decrease in social status, but crucially because one then has to operate without a recognised source of quality specification increasingly required by clients and markets. This applies to those employed by others and to those who are self-employed. One of the strong arguments against an NQF is that, if you're self-employed, why on earth do you need qualifications? (Bird & Gamble 1996:107)

Different departmental approaches to our 'target groups' in the period 1996–7

Once the decision had been taken not to merge Education and Labour into a single Ministry of Education and Training, it was not surprising that there emerged from the two departments somewhat separate versions of the relationship between the target groups and the respective education and training systems. There was, for example, a whole series of documents published in the sphere of education during the period 1996–7, most notably, the *Green Paper on Higher Education Transformation* (Department of Education 1996b), the 'Preliminary Report' of the National Committee on Further Education (Department of Education 1997a), and *Curriculum 2005: Lifelong Learning for the 21st Century* (Department of Education 1997b). In the sphere of training policy, the major report in the same period was the *Green Paper: Skills Development Strategy for Economic and Employment Growth in South Africa* (Department of Labour 1997). We shall note briefly the extent to which they take on board our concern with those outside the formal economy and the formal education and training sectors.

In the higher education *Green Paper*, the most explicit discussion about the labour market is in fact much less about the employment options for higher education graduates within the existing South African work environment than it is about orientating the South African system of higher education within the competitive, globalising world. This is not to say that there is no concern with the agenda of redress for the historically disadvantaged black institutions, but the overarching discourse about higher education and the economy is about 'knowledge workers with globally equivalent skills' and the challenge of 'continuous technological improvement and competitiveness' (Department of Education 1996b:14). The vision of the globalised world of knowledge production is well captured in the following: 'Knowledge, information and culture increasingly inhabit a borderless world with new computer and communication technologies transforming the way people work, produce and consume' *(ibid.)*.

The concern with globalisation is a critical issue in the planning of higher education for South Africa, but it is interesting to note that there is virtually no discussion in the Green Paper about the implications for employment (or unemployment) in South Africa of this particular vision, and certainly little attempt to translate the broad terms of the globalisation logic into local consequences for courses, employment planning, etc. There is, for example, no discussion of enterprise orientation for undergraduates and no mention of graduates who could expect to find themselves in various kinds of self-employment. Nor is the discussion on open learning concerned with non-traditional constituencies such as the self-employed.[6]

By contrast, the 'Preliminary Report' of the National Committee on Further Education (Department of Education 1997a) has a good deal more to say about the linkage between further education and the world of SMMEs, as well as about the critical state of unemployment facing graduates more generally. The 'Preliminary Report' judges, like the *Green Paper on Higher Education*, that there will need to be an active training concern for improvements in productivity and output in order to maintain international competitiveness. However, it goes on to identify the SMME sector as one of the key players in producing the present dynamism and it underlines enterprise development as a crucial linkage for further education: '... the dynamic parts of the economy which are labour creating are in the semi-formal and service sectors, including small businesses... .Thus programmes to prepare people for entrepreneurship, to support small businesses to train for the service sectors will be functions of Further Education and Training in the future' *(ibid.* p.47).

11

The third sector where there was significant development in the same period was in the conceptualisation of the compulsory education segment of schooling. During February and March 1997, documentation emerged for the new Curriculum 2005 in the following materials:

- *Curriculum 2005: Lifelong Learning for the 21st Century* (Department of Education 1997b).
- *Curriculum 2005: Lifelong Learning for the 21st Century: A User's Guide* (Department of Education 1997c).
- *Curriculum 2005: Discussion Document* (Department of Education 1997d).

It has become commonplace for reforms of basic education to pay more attention to the work environment (for example, the curriculum emphasis on self-employment preparation in Kenya) (King 1996). Particularly in South Africa where reform seeks to unify education and training systems and emphasises relevant, applied competencies, it would be surprising if there were not frequent reference to how the curriculum has implications for work and employment. This is not the place for an exhaustive review of the documentation from this perspective. However, it may be worth illustrating from a few of the eight new 'learning areas' whether there are particular themes that exemplify the new concern to equip learners 'with the knowledge, competencies and orientations needed for success after they leave school or have completed their training' (Bengu, in Department of Education 1997b:1).

First, from the new learning area of Technology, there is an explicit commitment that pupils should understand and apply the technological process to solve problems, and should be able to apply a range of technological knowledge and skills ethically and responsibly. It is also anticipated that the curriculum will create 'more positive attitudes, perceptions and aspirations towards technology-based careers' (Department of Education 1997d:83).

In the new curriculum for Grades 1 to 9 there is a much more direct relationship with post-school involvement in SMME in the learning area termed Economic and Management Sciences. Following the practice of all the other learning areas, Economic and Management Sciences has a small number of specific outcomes that capture the core expectations from this field over the nine years of basic education. It is probably significant that the first of these appears to be central to the whole field: 'Engage in entrepreneurial activities'. It should be noted that the specific outcome suggests active involvement in enterprise, and it is further explained in the following way:

> This Specific Outcome should be at the heart of the learning programmes of the Economic and Management Sciences. It encapsulates all the elements of economic and financial activities and is admirably suited to be developed, from Grade 1

12

onwards, in a cyclical spiral of increasing depth and complexity. This Specific Outcome has a significant role to play in preparing the learner for the world of work (Department of Education 1997d:196).

There follows, in the various assessment criteria associated with this outcome and some of the other outcomes, a whole series of what are called range statements (to indicate the coverage of the criteria) such as 'starting a business (real or simulated)' and 'Managerial expertise is demonstrated'.

However, along with the specific outcome mentioned above, there is another which suggests the importance of a very positive orientation to sustained economic growth. It is phrased as follows: 'Actions which advance sustained economic growth, reconstruction and development in South Africa are demonstrated'. The gloss on this outcome suggests that the attitudes of young people towards economic growth are themselves considered crucial:

> This Specific Outcome focuses on the essentials that will advance sustainable growth, reconstruction and development in the national economy. As a constructive and positive approach from individuals and organisations is needed, the values and attitudes which could hamper/help the achievement of these goals should be identified and critically analysed (Department of Education 1997d:212).

What is intriguing about the way that this whole area of Economic and Management Sciences is treated is that there is absolutely no acknowledgement that the skills and knowledge may prove more directly useful to pupils after school, given the shortage of formal sector jobs in the economy.[7] In other words, it is not suggested anywhere in this particular sphere of outcomes-based education (OBE) that a very possible outcome may be self-employment. With South Africa's specific history of imposed differentiation, this hesitation about linking school skills to rural or urban livelihoods is understandable. The very inclusiveness of the vision is compelling, but the reality for more than a quarter of young people is that they will be obliged to enter some form of self-employment or informal economic activity, and that number may be as high as 50 per cent in some of the poorer rural areas (Standing *et al.* 1996:86).

New skills policies and the challenge of inclusion

During March 1997, there emerged the Department of Labour's *Green Paper: Skills Development Strategy for Economic and Employment Growth in South Africa*. To a very much greater extent than the Education documents just discussed, this Green Paper is alert to the several different constituencies who must be the beneficiaries of reforms. The emphasis (right from the first page) is accordingly not just on the formally employed, but on the self-employed, those in micro-enterprises and what are termed 'target groups' – 'including the unemployed, retrenched workers, youth, women, people with disabilities and people in rural areas' (Department of Labour 1997:1). The paper does look outwards to the requirements of global competitiveness, but it looks as often inwards at those millions who have not profited from formal schooling, formal skills acquisition or the formal labour market.

One of the core elements in this ambitious Green Paper is a new system of learnerships. Equally, one of the challenges it issues is to ensure that the new training instruments no longer operate primarily in the traditional industrial sector, for example in seeking to halt the declining number of apprenticeships, but apply across a variety of employment and self-employment sites, including the small and micro-enterprise sectors (SME) sectors.[8] This has meant thinking about how to deliver to SMEs the crucially important work experience and other requirements of these new learnerships.

There are certain to be difficulties in arranging this; but what is clear about the South African proposals, even from the discussion in the Green Paper alone, is that in contrast to many other countries in Africa where there are effectively two training systems (the so-called traditional or informal apprenticeship and the so-called modern) the intention is clearly to have a single national system, if at all possible.

There is thus the aim to develop learnerships in all the twelve learning fields – from Agriculture to Construction. It is then necessary for the Green Paper to anticipate that there will need to be 'special arrangements for target groups' if they are to be satisfactorily included in the national scheme. This means that those specially disadvantaged by South Africa's peculiar history, or by gender or location or disability, can look to intervention by the state in the form of leverage of the planned levy funds to ensure their participation in the emerging national system of training.[9]

The Green Paper is also unusual in that it gives attention to those who are expecting to become new entrepreneurs. Again, this is evidence of a desire to fashion, in the new learnership system, a scheme that is genuinely national. The aim is to avoid the rigours of the German system where entrepreneurship may only follow full skill acquisition but also to recognise that many tens of thousands will annually have to become self-employed because there is no other option. Seeking to accommodate in the national system their particular requirements and experiences of work may well prove difficult, but at least the intention is to make them candidates for learnerships and thus national qualifications.

The SME dimension of learnerships is therefore much more than an awkward category to accommodate in the emerging national skill development system. The SME sector itself, with its obvious emphasis on self-employment, has also had the effect of underlining the importance of entrepreneurship orientation as a possible element in all learnerships (Department of Labour 1997:35).

It is too early to be clear about how the ambition to create a 'massively expanded and diversified qualification framework' will work out (*ibid.* p. 29). The first piloting of the learnership system in two sectors (Hospitality and Construction) in one province, KwaZulu-Natal, started in 1997 with the assistance of Danida. Significantly, the indications were that the pilot would focus on one of the more challenging aspects of the new learnerships – their availability to disadvantaged groups such as the unemployed, retrenched workers and rural women. Preliminary results, however, suggest that the learnership has been facing a number of quite serious obstacles. (Provincial Skills Development Pilot Project 1998:1).

The emphasis at the national level on the learnership covering three very different constituencies – the traditional industry-based apprentices, the new micro-entrepreneurs and the target (disadvantaged) groups – and on its being related to identified job opportunities, whether for employees or the self-employed, will be enormously challenging, and not least because the pilot learnerships will have to be acceptable to sector education and training organisations and to their national training standards.

What will be effectively on trial in this and other pilots is whether higher levels of training, linked to the possibility of real jobs or work, can be developed for the huge numbers of South African youth who have been ill served by schools and the skewed historical priorities of their society. In many countries, including OECD (Organisation for Economic Co-operation and Development) countries, disadvantaged young people have been provided with crash courses, special programmes and bouts of community or work experience, much of which has been regarded as second-rate, low-status training by its recipients. By contrast, South Africa is setting out to make them participants in the new national qualifications framework.

The imperative of fashioning a single national system of skills development where there has been a deeply divided skills profile is understandable, but few are pretending that it will be easy. Even the most basic issues, such as determining the conditions of the new learnership contract and negotiating the kind of training wage that should be offered by different industrial and commercial sectors, are likely to be absolutely critical to the take-up of the learnership. Especially in the formal industrial sector, there is the danger that the training scheme will be seen by the unions as a cheaper replacement for regular workers and by employers as an enforced spending on trainees who are not even their own employees.

For South Africa, with its tradition of deeply fragmented training opportunities between rural and urban communities, between modern sector firms and survivalist and subsistence enterprises, and between white and non-white definitions of skilled, semi-skilled and unskilled labour, there is every reason to have a 'skills revolution' – to use the phrase from the Green Paper. However, the supreme challenge will be to develop a national skills and qualifications service that really does manage to be inclusive. If it is to be truly national, then the hugely demanding tasks of standard setting, accreditation and assessment will need to encompass skilled work carried out in the household economy, in the micro-enterprises in townships and villages, as well as in the dynamic informal sector that is becoming more evident in the very centre of South Africa's cities. However, the challenge to the new skills revolution is not so much the assessing and accrediting functions, though they will be very considerable. The real test will be whether the system can include the qualitative changes in skill levels that are fundamental to the assumptions about South Africa's competitiveness in this Green Paper, and whether these can be extended to SMEs as well as to larger formal sector firms:

> But, given the demands of a more complex and changing economy, characterised by increasing use of information, more complex technologies and a general rise in the skill requirements of jobs, *people must also have rising levels of applied competence.* The focus on skills development in this Green Paper is about this process of deepening individuals' specialised capabilities in order that they are able to access incomes through formal sector jobs, through small micro enterprise or community projects which in turn positively contribute to the economic success and social development of our country (Department of Labour 1997:6, emphasis added).

What will be the mechanisms that will encourage this radical vision of up-skilling in the informal economy, in the smaller, formal sector firms and in the large modern firms and the public sector? In a country that lacks a long-standing indigenous tradition of apprenticeship, will it be easy to persuade the tens of thousands pursuing forms of self-employment to take on young people with learnership contracts rather than as casual, on-the-job labourers? What leverage will there be to encourage such micro-enterprises to undertake programmes of structured learning and diversified work experience for their trainees?

One of the few very powerful mechanisms that appears to be available is that, historically, South Africans do have very popular and powerful aspirations towards qualifications. Consequently, the country has a major infrastructure for acquiring qualifications in part-time or distance mode in the form of institutions such as UNISA, Technikon SA and VISTA (with almost a quarter of a million students). Both traditionally and currently, this 'qualifications economy' has operated because of the close link between qualifications and improved wage and salary, and it has been particularly evident in the widespread interest by teachers in increasing their incomes through higher qualifications.

What is obviously uncertain at this stage in the development of a nation-wide framework of qualifications is how attractive qualifications will prove to be where there are major retrenchments in the formal sector of the economy, including in teaching, and where there may be growing resistance in industry to the idea that there should be 'payment for what you know as opposed to what you do'. A great deal depends on whether the qualifications economy has been reinforced primarily by the link to improved wages, or whether there are other factors, such as status and job satisfaction, associated with it.

In that sector with which we are principally concerned – the self-employed and micro-entrepreneurs – there has in other countries been a resistance to schemes, such as the levy grant, which are designed to encourage higher levels of training. In the South African setting, no decision has yet been taken about what threshold should be set below which companies are not compelled to pay the levy, but it is clear that the Green Paper takes very seriously the importance of retaining SMEs within the frame of learnerships and associated qualifications, through special measures (see the Small Enterprise Training Support Scheme [SETS], Department of Labour 1997:70–1).

In concluding this section on the Green Paper on skills development and its concern with SME, it should by now be clear that the paper itself makes many bold attempts to argue that there should be a single national system of new learnerships covering the entire spectrum of productive work in South Africa. It is difficult to exaggerate the scale and complexity of the task of extending the new traineeships into quite new fields both in the formal and informal economies; it is especially difficult to do so at a time when the whole basis of training itself is being recast, against a new set of national standards. However, as the Green Paper admits, the critical lubricant of change is likely to be monetary:

> The reward system attached to formal qualification entry requirements, grading systems and occupational segmentation within firms, as well as the level of competitive pressure and the rate of investment in new technology, all impact on the response of employers and employees toward training (Department of Labour 1997:14).

In a situation where the new framework will allow for recognition of prior learning and of existing, unacknowledged skills, it is possible that the unionised sections of the economy will be in a much more powerful position to change the official training status of their members than will trainees in the informal and micro-enterprise sectors. For the one-person firms making burglar bars with two helpers in a township, for example, the intention of the Green Paper is that they should identify with the same learning field (Manufacturing or Construction) as the large corporates, and that levy funds could come their way to support training. If that is to happen in any meaningful sense, however, it will probably be important for trade associations of micro-entre-preneurs to emerge with influence parallel to those in the commercial trading and hawking area (Mosdell 1991:329ff.) or in the taxi industry (Khosa 1991).

However, if levy funds are going to help leverage learnerships in the SME sectors, it will take more than the emergence of strong trade associations and of a popular desire to acquire qualifications; it will need strong state policies – almost a state project – to develop a meaningful national framework of participation. Without this pressure, there is even the danger that the ambitious exercise of changing the whole basis of the education, training and enterprise development systems could end up, as we have suggested earlier, accrediting the efforts of those who are already best placed to profit from the qualifications economy.

Conclusion

Running behind this whole concern with fashioning an inclusive human resource development project are the tensions that have become much sharper since majority rule – between global competitiveness and local economic development, or between growth and equity.

The radical changes that are just about to impact on all aspects of human resource development are also, we have said, both global and local. Globally they connect with unified systems in several OECD countries, but locally the reforms have been projected as necessary to end Apartheid in the spheres of education, training and enterprise.

We have noted that in the reform of the skills strategy, it is made very clear that there are a whole series of vulnerable 'target' groups that must be incorporated into the national framework of opportunities if reform is to be successful. In Curriculum 2005, the notion of constituencies of young people at risk is much less sharply developed. Both departments, however, project their own elements in what in each case is a single national scheme. This was inevitable given the legacy of separate but unequal programming from the Apartheid years.

The fact that the Apartheid legacy made it almost inescapable for a new policy to offer a single, integrated and inclusive system of education and training should not blind us to the possibility that the self-employed may actually prefer short, sharp tailor-made training, and especially if the acquisition of a national qualification is an unwieldy and complicated process. Equally, in the matter of rural education and training, there can be no denying the attention given to this sector that the Green Paper on skills development is determined to provide. However, unlike Kallaway's concern in Chapter 2, it is assumed that redress to the rural sector must be within single nationally agreed qualifications.

Be that as it may, the separate but co-ordinated support of Education and Labour in the implementation of the NQF will be the test case of inclusiveness over the next ten years. As implementation starts at the national level and through pilot schemes, it would be a good moment to mount a long-term evaluation of the process whereby the target groups in this chapter are identified, and become part of a more unified learning society.

Endnotes

1. NSBC was disbanded in 1998
2. Elements of this inclusive vision can be detected in the National Union of Metal-workers' (NUMSA) Vocational Training Project (1991) and in the National Education Policy Investigation (NEPI 1993b:59–62). See also McGrath (1996: chapter 4).
3. The ANC/COSATU document was just 28 pages long, but it contained the essence of what would later appear as the Green Paper (Department of Labour 1997).
4. It must be recalled that terms such as unskilled and semi-skilled were themselves racially biased in countries such as Zimbabwe and South Africa prior to majority rule.
5. Namely, 'The reconstruction and development of the education and training pro-ramme' and 'The reconstruction and development in the school system'.
6. By contrast the National Commission on Higher Education's *Discussion Document: A Framework for Transformation* (1996) would appear to pay greater attention to the challenge of these new 'outsider' constituencies (pp. 34–9).
7. Statistics on unemployment in South Africa continue to be highly unreliable, but a rate of 20–25 per cent or more is regarded as a minimum estimate (Standing *et al.* 1996).
8. The Green Paper uses the acronym SME rather than the usual SMME in order to make the point that the first M (for medium-sized industry) tends to have training arrangements closer to large-scale industry than to small and micro-enterprise. We shall use SME when discussing the Department of Labour's Green Paper, but otherwise the more usual SMME.
9. The Green Paper argues that the South African tradition of serving target groups such as the poor, unemployed and rural youth has too often meant a variety of providers offering stand-alone courses with little skill and employment impact (Department of Labour 1997:10).

2

Whatever happened to rural education as a goal for (South) African development?

Peter Kallaway

The re-ordering of the international discourse on education in the 1990s has led to an alarming trend of defining the South's educational objectives in terms of the global discourse of the North in the age of neo-liberalism. A major hallmark of these educational reforms is their orientation towards 'human resource development' capable of delivering 'successful' economic systems akin to those that are held to be characteristic of the newly industrialised countries of the Pacific Rim. The 'new imperialism' of educational policy discourses appears to have been very effective in subordinating many countries of the South to a new domination of educational codes and assumptions imported from the industrialised world. The globalisation of the language and practices of the qualifications frameworks, learning profiles and outcomes-based education (OBE) – sometimes appended to older (and rather vaguer) formulations that have a Third World lineage, such as life-long learning[1] – now constitute a new international and almost hegemonic set of policies and practices. These are defended as being somehow intrinsic to the extension of democratic rights to the poor of the Third World and the key to economic freedom in the context of the global economy.

A major aspect of these new formulations of policy is that they represent the epitomy of technicism in the field of education – a renewal of the worst aspects of the 'manpower' planning strategies of the 1960s relating to a crude approach to individual rates of return in education. They also frequently reflect a behaviouristic notion of educational outcomes. These proposals often emerge in the form of a private language which can only be accessed by a limited number of officials and innovators, leaving the vast majority of educators, parents and students disempowered and disabled in a time of diminishing resources and dwindling morale in the educational sector in Africa. The general impression conveyed is that if you are not operating within these precise parameters you cannot possibly be a concerned, progressive or democratic educator; yet many of the assumptions regarding the scientific nature of these innovations are increasingly being questioned in contexts where they have a longer history (for example, Scandinavia, New Zealand, Britain and Australia). The particular effect of such developments in Africa, where there has already been a drastic decline in the provision and the quality of education, is of considerable note.

These policy recommendations appear to ignore the links between the provision of education and the social and economic needs of the rural poor. The exclusive emphasis of the new policy formulations on the problems that arise from the global economy and the need for particular kinds of 'human resource development' that will encourage effective integration into the global economy effectively ignore the 80 per cent of the population whose lives will never be part of the global economy in any direct way and whose skills will be used in the village, the farm, the local factory or plantation. The demise of dual-labour market theory seems to have been taken to mean that there are no educational problems that are specific to rural populations.

The purpose of this chapter is to note that strategies for vocational education in Africa, with particular regard to rural communities, which were highlighted as a key aspect of development strategies in the 1960s and 70s – such as 'education for self reliance' or the 'Brigades of Botswana' (Nyerere 1967, Foster 1969), and the World Bank programmes in support of 'Non-Formal Education' (Coombs & Ahmed 1974) – have never been replaced with a viable alternative. Whatever the reasons for the failure or demise of such programmes, which aimed at linking the school curriculum to the world of (rural) work in the past, the need for careful attention to that linkage has increased rather than decreased in the interim, given the overall decline in access to secondary and tertiary education and the prospects for finding alternative employment in the formal sector. Yet, the debate on these issues has been extremely muted in recent years.[2]

What are the explanations for the demise of this educational discourse that has its roots deep in the colonial past? Is it not time for educators and educational planners to renew their interest in the area?

These comments arise out of the experience of the South African context in the years since 1994 when the new democratic government came to power. Despite a wide-ranging debate on the future of education after Apartheid, there has been little sign of a willingness or inclination to learn from the African experience of education in the post-colonial era. This is perhaps partly a result of a deep-seated legacy within resistance politics of viewing the South African experience as unique; it is also the consequence of the market-led nature of policy development since 1995, where the rationale for educational change has been massively located in the field of skills development for the modern sector of the labour market in the context of the need for global economic competitiveness and 'efficiency'. In a context where labour, state and industry have reached a large measure of agreement over the goals which have been crafted from the educational innovations of the United Kingdom, New Zealand and Australia since the 1980s, there is little room for policy priorities which emphasise African rural development (see papers in Kallaway *et al.* 1997; National Training Strategy Board 1994; *South African Qualifications Authority Acts* 1995; Department of Education, 1995b; National Training Board and GTZ 1997).

This neglect of the African experience is also probably the result of a widely held perception that educational innovation in Africa – along the lines associated with 'education for self reliance, – was not only hopelessly romantic but also hopelessly delinked from the realities of the marketplace. It is the socialist baggage of the innovations as well as the perceived lack of success of such programmes that gives rise to this neglect. It is also in part a consequence of the elitist bent of policy-making that has been characteristic of much of African development planning in recent years, which has tended to neglect the specific interests of the rural poor in favour of market-related policy development. In that context the issue of equity or redress is often ignored.[3]

The question therefore arises: is there any point in raising questions about the viability of a massively discredited educational experiment in the Third World? What could South Africa or any other African or Third World country learn from such an investigation?

Hints of an answer are suggested by a recent World Bank study by Kevin Cleaver (1997),[4] which once again highlighted the fact that 'the poorest are often ignored in development programmes' and asserted the need to establish 'safety nets for the rural and urban poorest'. Cleaver identifies one of the key adjustments needed for the development strategy as the expansion of national health, education, population and nutrition programmes that include services to the rural population, and a focus on primary services at a time when most of the services established in the post-independence era have been run down to breaking point. This situation is in part the outcome of a 'lack of commitment to agricultural development in many African countries' which has the effect of inhibiting 'the quality and quantity of donor efforts'. In addition, 'one of the most debilitating weaknesses has been the widespread failure of structural adjustment programmes (favoured by the World Bank and other aid agencies during the 1980s–90s) to create an enabling environment for private investment in the rural sector'.

This report has signalled that the Bank might play a role in supporting the modified rural development strategy outlined in the Cleaver report. Despite doubtful references to the need for '*appropriate* agricultural policy and invest-ment' and the need for 'governments to generate widespread *commitment* by their citizenry', this report signals that the Bank will be 'more selective in targeting countries for assistance in rural development programmes, focus-ing on those that demonstrate commitment to appropriate agricultural policy and development. Through well-articulated country assistance strategies, the Bank will ensure that national education, health, nutrition, transport, water and economic policy programs provide support for rural and agricultural development'.

Leaving aside, here, the whole question of the kind of development or growth that is to be promoted through these strategies, it is of some signifi-cance that the Bank sees fit to highlight these issues at the time when the long freeze of structural adjustment policies appears to be showing signs of a thaw.

It seems ironic that just at the time when the new South African govern-ment appears to be abandoning the Reconstruction and Development Pro-gramme (RDP), which underscored the need for a development strategy designed to meet the needs of the poor and rural communities, the World Bank should be tabling policies that affirm the significance of such initiatives for poverty relief and rural development in Africa.

In that light it seems a significant moment to reassess the role of education in African development and, in particular, to revive the old debate on the link between vocationalism and education in the rural areas of Africa, with refer-ence to the globalisation priorities of the present time, and the process of reconstructing rural education after Apartheid.

The global picture: vocational education and development in post-colonial Africa

During the 1960s and 1970s a great deal of emphasis was laid upon the im-portance of education as a tool of rural development in Africa and the Third World. Post-independence discourse on democracy, equity, development and human rights presented a powerful case for the empowerment of the rural poor as a primary goal of economic and social policy.

Rural development was identified variously with economic growth, with modernisation, with increased agricultural production, with socialist forms of organisation, and with services for basic needs such as health, education, transport and water supply, yet development thinking of outsiders shifted in due course from the view that economic growth and modernisation was enough, with benefits trickling down to the poor, to the more realistic if depressing view that sometimes growth and modernisation make the poor poorer; that the main gains from increased agricultural production often go to the urban populations or the rural rich, and the well off and the powerful benefit more from rural services than do the poor and the weak (Chambers 1983:146–7, see also Chambers 1997).

In that context there was a systematic focus on the provision of vocational and agricultural education as a tool for development at the primary, secondary and adult level. There were numerous initiatives to support that view reflected in policy and practice in states as ideologically disparate as Tanzania, Zambia, Mozambique, Kenya and Botswana. The popularity of strategies for non-formal education was predicated upon this view and agencies like the World Bank did much to encourage the development of vocational rural education in schools and post-secondary colleges (Coombs & Ahmed 1974).[5]

The Addis Ababa conference on African Education in May 1961 gave a lead to these trends. The conference set the tone for much subsequent debate and policy development by framing the priorities of African education in terms of an emphasis on the 'need to orientate the content of education towards serving the economic and technological development requirements of Africa and providing a proper place for traditional cultural values of the continent' (UNESCO 1961). There was an emphasis on shifting from general to vocational and technical education with particular emphasis on the development of science, language study and technical education. At secondary level, vocational and technical education was promoted as a key aspect of the curriculum. In subsequent years, examples of initiatives in keeping with the emphasis on rural education were given considerable publicity by the media and by academics, and were often reported on in a rather romantic and uncritical manner.[6]

Yet, despite all these declarations of intent and the thousands of pages of policy and research print expended on the issue, progress was slow. At the Nairobi conference (July 1968) to assess the progress of these recommendations it was noted once again that the 'inadequacy of the educational system in meeting the real needs of communities and the reorganisation of primary education in rural areas' presented a problem that had not yet been adequately addressed (Jolly 1969:23–4). By 1965, at the height of the popularity of the vocational education trend worldwide, very small numbers of secondary school students were seen to have opted for the vocational route in Africa (see Table 2.1 below). Out of forty-one reporting countries only three regarded agricultural education as the number one priority for school education, while five chose technical education.

Table 2.1

Number of teachers and students in secondary level vocational education in Africa, south of the Sahara, 1955–65

Teachers				Pupils		
Year	Total	1955 = 100	Number of countries	Total	1955 = 100	Number of countries
1955	1 300	100	22	36 300	100	30
1960	2 400	185	22	62 700	173	30
1965	3 300	254	22	105 000	289	30

Source: Jolly (1969:38).

World Bank data over the period 1964 to 1994 demonstrates the fall in the significance of vocational secondary education in the World Bank's development funding. This also meant a decline in the emphasis on rural development, the improvement of the quality of rural life and economic efficiency of rural peoples. There is a constant decline in the significance of this factor from 1964 onwards, as indicated in Table 2.2.

These developments underscored the seminal statement by Philip Foster in the 1960s regarding the 'vocational school fallacy' and the problematic nature of vocational education in the African context (Foster 1966:396–423; Foster 1969:81–101). Kenneth King has more recently reviewed the evidence for Foster's assumptions regarding the limits of vocational education, and noted that, despite the received wisdom derived from Foster in academic circles, there has been sustained interest in the potential of vocational education right up to the 'new interventionism' of the present time. He notes that the ILO's (International Labour Organisation) JASPA programme (Jobs and Skills Programme for Africa) highlighted the importance and potential of the area once again in the mid-1980s (ILO 1986). The subsequent publication of the collection *Vocationalising Education* by Jon Lauglo and Kevin Lillis in 1988 renewed debate on these issues (Lauglo & Lillis 1988).

Table 2.2

World Bank education lending by subsector, 1964–94

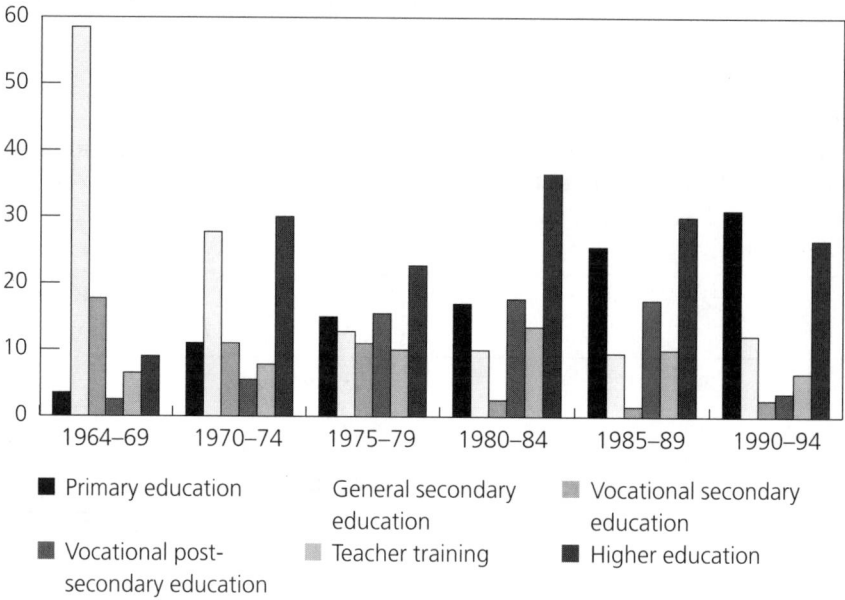

- Primary education
- General secondary education
- Vocational secondary education
- Vocational post-secondary education
- Teacher training
- Higher education

Source: World Bank (1995:148).

King's assessment of the current situation is that there is still considerable caution regarding these policies. They can be justified as a valued extension of general education, but should not be seen as a magic solution for the school-leaver or to youth unemployment problems. It should always be borne in mind that such programmes are much more expensive than conventional general education, and that there is a range of constraints militating against large-scale implementation of such policies even in the most promising circumstances (King 1991:125–9).

In an attempt to assess the significance of these educational initiatives in post-colonial Africa, there is a need to avoid romantic and idealistic trips back into the heady sixties visions of ideal peasant societies in China or Tanzania or Nicaragua. To recognise the continuing need for attention to the problems of rural education for development is not simply to assert that the same policies should be revived. At the same time, it is of the utmost importance to take a realistic look at the appalling neglect that now seems to characterise international educational policy needs for the poor in the field of rural education. The whole question of the specificity of the educational needs of the poor and rural inhabitants is increasingly ignored. To put it in other terms, the problem is simply discarded by international agencies and national governments and off-loaded onto impoverished rural communities in the name of political devolution. These communities invariably do not have the resources to make decisive and meaningful interventions.

It has been pointed out repeatedly by historians of education that the question of 'the relevance of education' and the need to link the curriculum of the school to the needs of the marketplace represents a recurring theme in the field of education. In some contexts it represents a cyclical debate that re-emerges in congruence with downturns in the economy (Reeder 1981:177–204).

The precise nature of those debates is not relevant to this paper. It is sufficient here simply to point to those trends and to link them to the question of educational policy and provision in South Africa at the present time.

The South African situation

Rural education from Union to Apartheid, 1910–1948

The history of African education in South Africa from colonial times to the Apartheid era had much in common with the history of colonial and post-colonial education in Africa. In both contexts there was a constant emphasis on the need for special attention to be given to the education of rural peoples and the orientation of the curriculum to the needs of rural societies. A great deal has been written about the ideological and political content of these seemingly humanitarian and disinterested curriculum objectives in the colonial context, and there has been much evidence of indigenous resistance to such attempts to impose an 'adapted' form of education on African rural communities from the time of the Phelps-Stokes Commission in the 1920s to the run-up to independence in British Africa.[7]

In South Africa there were many parallels to the broader process and every commission on African education this century more or less underlined the need for vocational, agricultural and rural education for Africans (Loram 1917; British Government 1903–5; Brookes 1930; Dodd 1938; Martinius 1922; Malherbe 1977).[8]

During the Apartheid era the idea of promoting a special kind of 'Bantu education' specifically tailored to the 'needs' of indigenous cultures and to the rural context of the Bantustans provided the official gloss for policy, but in effect very little was done to change the formal content of secondary school education. Even at the level of language of instruction, the official languages (Afrikaans and English) remained the only official media of instruction for high school education between 1948 and 1994. Little if anything was done to

27

implement Verwoerd's dream of providing a formal educational system that was distinctly 'Bantu' or 'rural' in its essence, despite repeated formal commitments to the ideal.

A common denominator of all the policies followed from the time of Union to the era of Apartheid reform in the 1980s was that a practical, vocational education was held to be the appropriate form of education for 'the native', and that it was held to have particular relevance for rural people.[9]

As with colonial, missionary education in Africa, the early attempts at 'adapted education' in South Africa, pioneered by C T Loram and the Natal Native Education Department, were not particularly successful in changing the nature of education from formal, academic education to vocational education. There were many attempts to adapt the curriculum, but overall that adaptation of the content of the curriculum was no closer to being achieved in South Africa than it was in colonial Kenya or Rhodesia (for example, Loram 1917).

One of the major reasons for this in both contexts was that any form of technical education, however modest, be it wagon building, leather-work, carpentry, masonry or agricultural science in the old mission days, or training to be a motor mechanic, electrician, plumber or computer operator in recent times, required expensive workshops and laboratories which were just not available for the underprivileged sector of the population.

One of the key indicators of policy development in the Depression years was the Native Economic Commission (1932), which set the tone for policy in this field for many years to come. (Rheinallt Jones & Saffrey 1933–4) The similarities in the language of the 'Majority Report' of the Commission and that of the Eiselen Commission on Native Education twenty years later is striking. It also reveals clear resonances with the debates taking place elsewhere in colonial Africa at the time.

Two types of education are recommended, a 'social education for the mass', and 'a type of technical education having the object of qualifying its recipients in certain valuable accomplishments – of teachers, clerks, interpreters, medical practitioners' (Native Economic Commision 1930–2). Picking up themes that had been initiated by Sir Langham Dale in the Cape at the end of the nineteenth century, the report opposed the provision of education which 'has the effect of turning out natives who seek non-manual work'. It argued that 'Native education should not pursue a course which makes the Native dissatisfied with everything in his background. But it should proceed from the foundation of Native society, and build up, giving the Native a pride in his own people, and a desire to develop what is good...in his own institutions,' particularly with regard to the development of rural economic and social institutions.

28

The Commission argued that 'the education ... provided is largely ineffective' and recommended the kind of 'adapted education' that Loram had advocated and implemented in the context of the Native Affairs Commission and the Natal Native Education Department during the 1920s. More specifically, it recommended a limited number of Native high schools designed to train men as farm demonstrators, to train women as home demonstrators, and 'to offer vocational education to a limited number of Natives' to work among their people. State funding was needed to encourage the improvement of Native agricultural methods and it was noted that it was of the utmost importance to 'gain Native cooperation for these moves'.[10]

The Eiselen Commission, the Tomlinson Commission and Bantu education,[11] 1948 to the 1980s

The advent of Apartheid reinforced this trend in policy development from the days of the United Party. The idea of a separate education for Africans, backed by the idea of the need to promote racial/cultural identity, was complemented by the idea of a separate curriculum that was appropriate to the rural context of the homelands. Yet, despite all the rhetoric, very little of this materialised. Whatever the rhetoric of Bantu education regarding a separate education for the development of Africans in their 'own' (rural) areas, the practical reality never reflected this shift. Although whites and blacks had very different educational experience under Apartheid, this was dictated by the unequal allocation of resources to the various racially or geographically defined sections of the system rather than through the differentials imposed by varieties of curricula. The reason for this lack of curriculum change, in spite of the spirited statements by Verwoerd and others to the contrary, has not yet been adequately explained. At the very least, the secondary school curriculum remained formally the same for all groups throughout the Apartheid era.

In reviewing the legacy of Native education in 1952, the Eiselen Commission found 'that varieties of vocational and technical education were being offered at primary schools, industrial and handcraft centres in some towns, and industrial departments attached to mission schools' (Eiselen 1951: 89–90). But there was no uniformity in the duration of the courses offered and the Commission commented on 'the slow growth of industrial education of a really vocational nature' (Eiselen 1951: 89–90). There were only 2170 places in such schools for Africans in 1949. The Commission recommended the expansion of technical education with the objective of 'training in vocations and polytechnic schools for all those who can be absorbed by the development plan or the present Bantu society'. The vocational education and training had to be promoted but kept within the limits of an Apartheid labour market where 'white skills would be protected'. The Minister of Bantu Education explained in 1959 that: '…the intention is in the first place to concentrate vocational training mainly in the Bantu areas, in order to meet the need which exists for people with vocational training in the development of the Bantu communities themselves' (Hansard 1959. Col. 8314).

Eiselen's report provided a major critique of the 'Native Education' of the earlier age and defined the 'outstanding characteristics of education in the Bantu Areas', identifying the key to the Apartheid project as the development of rural education. 'In the planning of the schools, the syllabi and methods of education, special attention was never paid to the socio-economic needs of the Bantu Areas. The Bantu child was trained for the labour market of the European and not for service to his own Bantu community and area' (Eiselen 1951). In addition 'the training of teachers does not take the problems of the Bantu Areas into account. It is necessary that teachers should be trained for this task so that they can give guidance. Most Bantu who received a good education did not employ their energies for constructive work for their own people and the Bantu Areas' (Eiselen 1951). It was therefore necessary in keeping with this philosophy to ensure 'that the schools should develop *from* the Bantu and *for* the Bantu' (Eiselen 1951). Education must not be divorced from the overall economic and social needs of the community. On the contrary 'education must be the large driving wheel which starts the machinery of development and keeps it going' (Eiselen 1951). In order to ensure 'real development, as against pseudo-development, real education must engage with the life of the community – culturally, socially, and economically' (Eiselen 1951). The Tomlinson Report recommended the 'speedy training of artisans, tradesmen, and technicians for the development of the Bantu areas' (Tomlinson 1955:24).

Despite these intentions the UNESCO report on education under Apartheid in 1972 (UNESCO 1972:89–95) indicated that only thirteen trade schools, including five secondary schools that provided some trade training, had been established. There were also ten vocational schools for girls offering dressmaking and home-management courses. A school certificate in vocational training had been initiated but it was only valid in the Homelands.

The irony was that despite the avowed intention of Apartheid ideologues regarding the promotion of agriculture and rural development, courses in animal husbandry, agriculture or farming are not mentioned in any of these contexts. By 1968 the total enrolment of Africans in technical subjects was 626.

Table 2.3 gives a picture of the slow progress in the field of vocational and technical education for Africans under Apartheid. The number of students enrolled for courses in agriculture at African university colleges in 1968 was five.

30

Table 2.3
African enrolment in vocational and technical classes under Apartheid

Year	Number of places recommended by Eiselen Commission	Actual African enrolment in vocational and technical classes
1949	2 170	–
1955	4 000	2 237
1957	4 900	2 952
1959	6 000	1 379
1963	–	2 035

Source: SAIRR (RR97/65:93–95).

During the 1980s the National Party made dramatic reforms in the rhetoric and reality of educational policy for Africans through a series of moves which were captured by the change in the title of the relevant authority from the 'Department of Bantu Education' to the 'Department of Education and Training'. Instead of mass education with a racial twist avowedly aimed at keeping anyone who was not white in an inferior position in the job market, the reform rhetoric of the 1970s borrowed from the Manpower Services Commission in Britain to strengthen the links between education and work.

On the basis of recommendations from the Human Sciences Research Council (HSRC) (De Lange Commission) in 1981 (HSRC 1981), [12] the expansion of vocational guidance and the extension of vocational and technical education took place at both the secondary and tertiary level. Although the success of these initiatives was uneven (Bot 1988), [13] the effort to change the direction of policy was significant. The previous assumptions that vocational education and training for blacks was either to be discouraged as posing a threat to the monopoly of skills for whites or that blacks were only to be trained for skilled work in the 'homeland' areas were both abandoned as the whole issue of skills shortage entered into the centre of the debate about economic growth (Chisholm 1984).

Big business and the state, along with a range of other pressure groups, applauded these changes as a significant break with the past of labour market racial discrimination and a fundamental step towards addressing problems of human resource development in South Africa.

31

The National Education Policy Investigation (NEPI) and subsequent policy developments, 1990s

The response from anti-Apartheid groups and educationalists to National Party initiatives to reform education, was predicated on the vision of a new education constructed by the Peoples' Education movement of the 1980s. This was distilled in the report of the National Education Policy Investigation (NEPI) in 1993 (NEPI 1993a). The investigation drew on the skills and experience of a variety of researchers who were keen to provide a radical vision of educational change in keeping with the social democratic principles that had been a fundamental feature of both the internal and external wings of the liberation movements.

The four reports of NEPI that were concerned with issues relating to this paper were those entitled *Human Resources Development, Adult Basic Education, Adult Education* and *Post-Secondary Education.* Although there is much emphasis on the issue of adult literacy, there is little or no mention of rural education or agricultural education. The NEPI Report was one of the only examples of a South African policy investigation in which the African post-colonial educational experience is considered with a view to learning about the educational transition in South Africa. Yet, even here the amount of attention given to the African experience in this field is minimal – confined to a few remarks about the 'Botswana Brigades' and 'Education with Production' (NEPI 1993b:63–4).

NEPI noted that development education in the 1960s was closely tied to the issue of modernisation and the need for newly independent countries to follow the 'modernisation' path of the West. One of the key factors in that 'catch-up' strategy was seen to be the issues of literacy and numeracy and this led to many campaigns to address these issues. Faced with only partial success in this field, UNESCO developed its 'functional literacy' approach, which aimed at a carefully targeted literacy work teaching work-specific skills together with literacy skills to farmers, operators and technicians, and cottage and craft industry workers. This Experimental World Literacy Programme (EWLP) was implemented in eleven countries during the 1960s but UNESCO's own evaluation in 1976 was very critical. Attempts to combine literacy acquisition with hard skill development were thought to be a failure '…and lessons from this work have helped to shape assumptions about the criteria for success for the next generation of literacy workers' (NEPI 1993c:33–4).

Knowledge production and the kinds of knowledge that are inscribed on the school curriculum along with the dangers that globalisation discourses hold for the eradication of indigenous knowledge were noted. The NEPI

Report pointed to the need for fresh initiatives to draw upon local knowledge to empower rural peoples, no matter how difficult that might be in practice. 'The way in which knowledge is produced and transmitted determines to a large extent the basic organising principles of [educational institutions] and the relationship which holds between these institutions and society' (NEPI 1993e:11). If all the knowledge to be transmitted to rural children in Africa is to be determined outside the village or the community or even the nation, and the means of evaluating that knowledge is framed in terms of external outcomes relevant to the modern sector of the society, how will it be possible to frame curricula which empower rural children and societies (Greenstein 1997a)?

There is no space here to look in detail at how these recommendations have been taken up in the new generation of policy documents, commissions, White Papers, Green Papers and legislation in the post-1994 era, but it is, in general, significant that the recommendations of the NEPI Report have been largely ignored in the reconstruction of education in South Africa. The aspects of the Report that have been significant have been those recommendations that relate to the need for active labour market policies and state intervention in the field of training and qualifications. The key concepts here have been 'certification', 'flexibility' and 'transformability'. These recommendations were initially piloted by the Congress of South African Trade Unions (COSATU) in the NEPI context and the National Training Board, and then taken forward to form the basis of the National Qualifications Framework (NQF), the South Africans Qualifications Authority (SAQA), the *White Paper on Education and Training* (WPET) and the most recent document, *Curriculum 2005*, which is dominated by the assumptions of outcomes-based education (OBE). In every instance these innovations have been drafted under severe pressure of time and with less than ideal consultation with educators, though the training aspect has probably been more consultative.

The dominant mode of consultation that is used to justify these processes is that of 'stakeholder' consultation, a mode of operations inherited from the times of the struggle, where all parties to a discussion are seen to have a democratic right to equal say and influence – even in areas where expertise of a high level is needed to make informed educational judgements (Morrow 1996a).

What has emerged at the end was a process of educational transformation that is often defended in terms of democratic change. The reality is that very little real consultation is taking place with the educators, teachers, communities and students who will be the recipients of the new system. In particular, those who are the least powerful – the inhabitants of the rural areas or those engaged in agriculture and farming – will apparently have had little or no say in the changes that are about to be implemented in the educational system.

What is significant is that the changes are being driven by an international discourse that is well nigh hegemonic. It is very difficult for individual teachers, or schools or communities or teacher organisations to mount a critique of the educational transformation that is being carried out in the name of democracy and the empowerment of the disadvantaged.

Contemporary realities and challenges

The strategies for rural development education had much to recommend them during the 1960s for anyone interested in the increase of democracy and equity in Africa, despite the legacy of resistance to such reforms during the colonial era. The earlier link with strategies for socialist transformation is also not in itself a disqualifying factor in reconsidering these approaches. In similar fashion, it would be wrong to dismiss the importance of addressing the specific needs of rural education in a South Africa after Apartheid on the grounds that the ideologues of Bantu education had seen in this policy a fundamental building block for Apartheid.

An apparent contradiction in the present policies of the South African government in the field of education is the insistence on equality of all in the field of education (i.e. an equalisation and redress of opportunities to ensure a more equal distribution of educational resources), without the recognition that at the same time the need for ever more sophisticated technical and educational skills to supply the human resources for the Growth, Employment and Redistribution (GEAR) strategy potentially pulls in precisely the opposite direction – of specialisation and selection rather than the construction of a high quality system for all. The imperatives of GEAR require an educational system that is able to produce an élite of graduates, technicians and managers of 'world class' who are able to compete in the international sphere. Members of this group will no longer be defined by their white skins as they were in the past, but their skills and their jobs will place them in a position in the job market that will mean that they will by definition be privileged in relation to the rest of the population. That new élite – both in terms of the skills they possess and in terms of the status that secures them in modern society – will ensure that those who have such skills will be able to move easily in the job market of the new global economy.

As Lynn Ilon has pointed out, 'for the new élite employment opportunities will now be global'. This group will have an inordinate influence over the framing of educational policy directions in the future because of their strategic location in the new social and economic structure of society. But in an era of structural adjustment and free trade,

... the global economy is clearly delineating very different rates of return to education for different groups. Outside of the new élite, and a small middle class who will use their resources and influence to make sure that their schools retain a measure of quality, the poor will be left with an educational system that is adequate only to retaining them as members of a larger system and preparing them for low level employment. Their lack of private resources and access to good jobs means that educational quality for these people will become a lower priority for the state (Ilon 1994:102–3).

The acknowledgement of these issues implies that it is important to clarify what happens to the majority of the population who do not form the new skilled élite – who are not part of the 'fortunate few' who will be able to enter the brave new world of marketing their skills in the context of the world market. To insist on the equality function of schooling and ignore the function of selection, is, as Phillip Foster pointed out years ago in relation to the reform of education in the post-colonial era, to miss the whole point about the role of education-society relations in twentieth-century Africa, and fail to grasp the motivation that lies behind the quest for access to schooling or the dynamic behind the reforms of education at the present time. As Lynn Ilon has put it:

> The skills needed for this new breed of (international élite) are very different from the typical curriculum for educational professionals. It will involve systems analysis, economics, a basis in the various social sciences, courses on global trends, computer modelling, and management. Education is entering an era where much of its success will be based on its ability to fit within a global system, to direct resources efficiently, and to trouble-shoot effectively. Perhaps more daunting is the notion that the benefits to be derived from the human resources explosion will not benefit all. In fact the globalisation of the economy will mean that many people become even more marginal [to the core modern economy]. Denying this fact of the global economic system and continuing to train all students as if they had equal non-school resources, equal starting places and equal educational opportunities, and equal job and career possibilities means that education will become even less useful for these populations. Serving these populations will mean identifying their particular circumstances and needs and detailing plans that move them forward rather than selling them the myth of their equal chances of global success. While some may emerge at the upper scales of education, selling the myth that this is a possibility for all can be likened to the logic that promotes the purchase of lottery tickets (Ilon 1994:105).

The education which will serve the citizens of a democratic state most adequately, which will promote equity and empower the young most effectively, will be the curriculum that manages to bridge the gap between developing 'primary, analytic and critical thinking skills' which teach students 'through a curriculum which teaches people how to recognise, analyse, and criticise the larger system' of economic, social and political relations and at the same time allows for the empowerment of those who are marginal to the modern economy, like rural youth. Although the precise nature of the new policy direction is difficult to dictate or specify in general terms, because the precise nature of what needs to be done will vary from place to place and time to time, what emerges from this enquiry is that 'a total concentration on modern sector job-related skills development' is inadequate for an educational system which seeks to promote equity and democratic citizenship (Ilon 1994:105).

The danger that emerges from this investigation is that predicating contemporary educational reforms for Third World contexts on the human resource imperatives of a modern high skill economy or on the assumption of a post-Fordist world are highly problematic. In Africa in general the decline or demise of education curricula which sought to directly address the development needs of rural communities represents an alarming failure to meet the goals of equity through education. While it would be foolish to ignore the lessons of the past with regard to the limitations of education as a tool of development, it is equally foolish to ignore totally the potential contribution that is possible if the correct use is made of imaginative curriculum innovations.

The tendency to dismiss educational initiatives that sought to make direct interventions into issues of development as attempts to control and subordinate rural peoples to the colonial order or dismiss them as an aspect of failed socialist experiments, or even to see in them only in the light of machinations of Apartheid social engineering, is to throw out the baby with the bathwater. Even the World Bank has recently suggested that it is important to revisit these issues in a more positive light if adequate educational curricula are to be investigated for the majority of Africa's poor.

South African government recommendations for the transformation of education in the post-Apartheid era have bought into the global trend of educational reform premised on the needs for certain kinds of human resource development. It might be of some significance to review the achievements of post-independence African and Third World experiments in rural education with regard to rural upliftment. In the light of the tradition of radical questioning of the kinds of knowledge appropriate to the school and the needs for specific kinds of African development, it seems worthwhile to pose questions about the appropriateness of this massive initiative to buy into the global formulas without adequate investigation of indigenous needs, specifically with regard to the development of the rural sector. It is not suggested that changes in the school curriculum could in themselves lead to significant changes in the lot of rural youth, but there are at least significant indications that some link-ages of this kind should form part of a serious attempt to investigate a plan for reconstruction and development in post-Apartheid South Africa.

Endnotes

1. Life-long learning is 'a comprehensive and visionary concept which includes formal, non-formal and informal learning extended throughout the lifespan of an individual to attain the fullest possible development in personal, social and professional life. It views education in its totality, and includes learning that occurs at home, school, community and work-place...' (NEPI 1993d:9). Life-long learning is potentially an umbrella under which rural development education can occur but it is so wide that it is not useful here in defining specific policy directions.

2. One of the few projects that has kept this vision alive up to the present time in Africa is the Foundation for Education with Production (FEP), which operates in Botswana and Zimbabwe. See the journal *Education with Production*.

3. In the African context the selective amnesia referred to in this chapter concerns the question of the role of education in rural development or the field of rural vocational education. In the South African case there is another kind of selective amnesia which is linked to this, but which cannot be taken up here – this is the neglect of the whole tradition of educational resistance and People's Education inherited from the struggle years in the process of educational reconstruction. For reference to this issue see articles by Saleem Badat, Peter Kallaway and Linda Chisholm in Kallaway *et al.*(1997).

4. The work is entitled *Rural Development, Poverty Reduction and Environmental Growth in Sub-Saharan Africa* and is cited in FINDINGS 92 (August 1997). All quotations are from this summary.

5. A key document in this regard was the World Bank *Education Sector Working Paper* (1971) which argued for 'a reorientation of the education and training systems, with greater emphasis on vocational education and on non-formal training for agriculture and industry' to 'redress present imbalances' cited in K King (1991:125).

6. Prominent examples of these policies were those undertaken in Tanzania (Education for Self Reliance), Kenya (Rural Polytechnics) and, outside of government, by the Brigades in Botswana. These experiments should also be seen against the background of the dramatic initiatives regarding rural education in China, Cuba and Nicaragua at that time (see Arnove 1986; Torres 1990; Price 1979).

7. See King (1974) and the whole range of reports by the British Colonial Office; Phelps-Stokes Reports; Murray (1937)

8. See also 1908 Cape Report on Native Education; 1935–6 Commission on Native Education. The issue of rural education was not only related to the question of educational provision for the colonised. Rural whites and 'poor whites' were the subjects of a set of initiatives on the topic, drawing heavily on the American experience. See UG 29–1934, Report of a Conference on Rural Education; Malherbe (1977:208–9; 227–32).

9. In the early years of the century the distinction between manual education and vocational education was important. The former was simply a form of induction into manual work on the farm; the curriculum for the latter did include training in specific skills like masonry, leatherwork, carpentry, wagon-making (for boys) and housework, sewing and dressmaking (for girls).

10. See Native Economic Commission (1930–32), para. 603–10; para. 628; para. 611–13; para. 638. There was also a Minority Report of Lucas and Roberts, representing the liberal Cape tradition, which rejected the idea of a different or 'adapted' education for Africans (para. 654–55).

11. Union of South Africa (UG 53/1951) *The Report of the Commission on Native Education in South Africa* (Eiselen Commission) (Pretoria, Government Printer); Union of South Africa (1955) (UG 61/1955) Commission for the Socio-Economic Development of the Bantu Areas within the Union of South Africa (Tomlinson Report) Pretoria, Government Printer.

12. This influential report was followed up in 1992 by the last report of the National Party government on education, the *Educational Renewal Strategy*.

13. For example, the attempt to introduce comprehensive schools for Africans in the Western Cape (that is, schools that offered technical and vocational education) proved to be a complete failure and the schools were closed down after a few years. At the tertiary level, the expansion of the technikon and technical college sector to include students from all racial groups was a significant departure from the policies of Apartheid.

3

Access and equity: major challenges to universities in South Africa

HAROLD HERMAN

Many African countries suffer from the worst conditions of poverty coupled with the highest population growth rates in the world. According to Saint (1992), these conditions when combined with a high degree of student activism have made managing access to higher education extremely difficult. African traditions of kinship solidarity also place further demands on access to higher education, while government interference in university policy has often resulted in disastrous outcomes, such as when the President of Kenya, during the early 1990s, ordered the country's four universities to enrol all of the 13 832 qualifying applicants instead of the intended 25 per cent of the pool. Similar pressures have contributed to Kenya's higher education enrolments, which increased from 8 900 in 1984 to 41 000 in 1991. Nigeria's already high total school and student population is expected to grow from 10 134 000 (1991) to 14 508 000 by the year 2000. Saint (1992) suggests that many African universities will be compelled to introduce selection criteria as they will be unable to accommodate the exploding student numbers.

Whichever way access has been widened, it has almost always created some degree of conflict and tension, either within the institution or between the institution and other stakeholders, such as the state, the community, employment agencies or donors. In many circles it has become an accepted fact that the goals of equality and efficiency are incompatible. Strong arguments are being raised in academic circles that universities should rather concentrate on output (the number of students completing in the shortest time possible) instead of getting involved in all sorts of social engineering experiments which are not only costly, but which do not yield the expected results.

Structural limits to access and equity in higher education

Liberal and socialist educational reformers understandably argue that maximal access to universities is desirable in the interests of equity and justice, even more so in the case of those who have historically been discriminated against, such as minorities and the economically disadvantaged. There may, however, be an argument for a more realistic and focused expansion of university enrolments in countries with a capitalist economic system. Judging from the economic policy of the new democratically elected government, South Africa is aspiring to full participation in the competitive modern industrial world, where universities in countries with high economic growth rates have increasingly adopted more selective admissions policies. Hence the argument for a rethink of unlimited access and open admissions policies at universities.

The argument is similar to the one advanced by Henry Levin (1982) on the dilemmas of comprehensive secondary school reforms in Western Europe. The schooling systems of capitalist countries serve dual functions. On the one hand, they must contribute to reproducing wage labour for the system of monopoly capitalism that dominates the economies; on the other, they must act as the primary agent for providing equality and mobility to the vast majority of the population of such countries. But, according to Levin, there is a basic incompatibility between these two roles. The reproduction needs of capitalist production require highly unequal educational outcomes while the ideology of the educational system tends to inspire expectations and policies of greater equality, and to satisfy the aspirations for social mobility. As long as the structural inequalities of capitalist production persist, the total system of schooling must contrive to reproduce those inequalities. This means that greater equality in educational treatment at the secondary and post-secondary levels must necessarily be compensated by increasing inequalities in the translation of education into occupational positions in the labour market, if the capitalist workforce is to be reproduced. The unequal preparation and allocation of workers for the work hierarchy will require compensating inequalities at some higher level if egalitarian educational reforms are introduced at a lower level.

If schools do not do the required selection, this function is passed on to higher levels of education, such as universities, and to social-class biased selection for occupational roles. This reality should be considered even if the goals for university selection are egalitarian. Levin argues that as more and more students become eligible for higher education through alternative routes, the occupational stratification role must fall increasingly on the system of higher education and the labour market. This is clearly shown by the proliferation of selective admissions policies in Western Europe, and Japan and other capitalist countries in Asia with high growth rates. In countries such as Germany, university admissions for lucrative professions are dominated by *numerus clausus*, a policy based upon the ranking of students according to grade point average in secondary schools (Herman 1995).

In the drive for access and equity at South African universities, these arguments have to be taken into account. It is necessary to proceed with caution and realism when planning to remove past disparities. Uncoordinated open admissions and affirmative action policies could lead to massive enrolments of educationally disadvantaged students, which may create unforeseen problems if the needs of students cannot be addressed in the teaching and learning programmes of universities.

Universities in South Africa and access

In terms of the *Universities Act*, No. 60 of 1955, universities in South Africa are at liberty to set their own admission requirements in addition to a matriculation exemption. A matriculation exemption is usually given to a student who has successfully completed twelve years of schooling and on condition he/she meets the prescribed requirements laid down by the South African Certification Council (previously the Matriculation Board), such as passing certain courses on the higher grade. This is similar to the A-level passes required in the United Kingdom and some other countries. Historically white universities (HWUs) have always set high entrance requirements because they catered for white students with high matric grades. Historically black universities (HBUs) catered mainly for marginal achievers and subsequently they do not set high admissions criteria. The few black students with high matric passes are usually attracted to HWUs because the type of disciplines they offer are often in demand and generate high returns on their academic investments. Also, in the minds of parents and teachers, these institutions have good reputations.

HWUs have had little difficulty in selecting 'their' students. For decades whites had privileged access to a free and compulsory schooling system; in addition, many were able to afford prestigious private schooling. This is evident in the high pass rates that have been obtained at primary and high school level and the large number of white matriculants that enter university and other tertiary institutions. It stands to reason that a group that has had such privileged access to schooling will also reap the benefits it generates, such as securing the best higher education opportunities the country has to offer as well as competing from a stronger base for lucrative bursaries to continue advanced studies. By contrast, poor teaching conditions, under-qualified teachers, inadequate facilities and no compulsory education system, coupled with educational boycotts and revolts in black education, have contributed to poor matriculation results for students formerly under the Department of Education and Training (the department which controlled African schooling prior to 1994). Ultimately, HBUs stood at the receiving end of the inequalities and results of such a system. This is clearly captured in the Research Report on the HBUs (Education Policy Unit, UWC 1997) which emphasises the provision of high quality and appropriately focused undergraduate programmes as longer-term necessary pre-conditions for widening access to postgraduate studies for disadvantaged and under-achieving students. The Report recommends ways of increasing the pool of suitable postgraduate students at HBUs. However, it also cautions that in order to ensure higher student success and completion rates and cost effectiveness, more selective admissions to postgraduate programmes will be necessary, accompanied by effective alternative admissions procedures to identify potential ability (*ibid.* p. 458).

In South Africa, admission to university, especially at HWUs, has for many years been based fundamentally on meritocracy. Previous research to test the reliability of matric results as indicators of success at university was done almost exclusively on white students. It was only in the 1980s that any meaningful research was undertaken in respect of black students. The results indicated that there was a weak correlation between their matric results and their performance at university (Herman 1995; Strebel 1987). It must, however, be borne in mind that these studies were considering marginally qualifying students (D and E aggregates). Contrary to these findings, a recent analysis of first year pass rates for the University of the Western Cape (UWC) for 1993 and 1994 has revealed a strong relationship overall between matriculation results and university success. The study suggests that the entry requirement for courses should be set at a D aggregate matric pass (Kreel & Low 1995).

Many universities in South Africa which have admitted black students have also embarked on some form of academic support system in an attempt to increase their students' chances of successfully completing their programmes. The state has refused to subsidise such initiatives and universities have found it extremely difficult either to sustain their programmes or to extend them further. HBUs and the University of South Africa (UNISA, a mainly correspondence university) have made a considerable contribution towards making university education for black students possible. At some of the English-medium universities, black student enrolment at first year level has now increased to over 40 per cent. Afrikaans-medium HWUs, which previously did not admit black students at all, have over the past few years dropped the racial barriers, but they have admitted only a limited number of black students, mostly those with good matric results.

A number of other attempts have been made by some universities to make university education more accessible for historically disadvantaged students. These include work-study programmes and special loan schemes for those who cannot normally afford to pay for tuition, academic support programmes and bridging courses (especially in science) for those who entered university with marginal matric results or who have problems with language proficiency in English, and revised admissions criteria and selection procedures. Some universities run summer and winter schools for matriculants and offer career counselling services. Unfortunately, these initiatives are costly and limited in range, and solutions to the problems of access and equity do not lie solely at the door of the university (Gelderbloem 1996:61).

There are major controversies and paradoxes concerning debates on the issue of access and equity in the South African context. The first relates to the claim that universities should help address the imbalances caused by Apartheid by admitting more students from disadvantaged backgrounds. This usually requires a variety of academic support programmes that cannot be sustained without large capital funds, which are unlikely to be provided by the state. A second controversy concerns the issue of relevance. Universities are required to be relevant in what they teach and research. If greater emphasis is placed on science and technology, it is inevitable that it will be at the cost of human sciences, where most of the disadvantaged students are currently located.

A third controversy lies in the debates around access and selection. Universities are expected to be institutions of excellence. If selection does not take place, it is unlikely that standards of excellence will either be maintained or improved. If the studies conducted at the University of the Western Cape (UWC) (Kreel & Low 1995) prove to be true of other universities, then candidates with marginal results should be excluded from entering universities.

Admissions for equity at an HBU

The quest for redress and equity at South African HBUs has understandably focused on open admissions or limited restrictions on access to disadvantaged students without necessarily addressing educational outcomes and equality of life chances after graduation. The main reason for this was because university admissions to HWUs were so heavily skewed in favour of the white minority, and that the policy of admissions on academic merit was excluding many black students who were challenging for university places from a position of huge inequality as a result of Apartheid and Bantu education.

In 1982, UWC, having liberated itself from the ethnic separatist ideology upon which it was established, defined its mission. It committed itself to 'the development of Third World communities' in South Africa (UWC Mission Statement 1982). It was clear that access to universities in general in South Africa was clearly unequal in terms of race, class and gender. The situation was even more complex as many applicants for admission to UWC were marginal achievers in the matriculation examination, a category for whom prediction of academic success was proven statistically to be unreliable. In spite of the obvious attraction of the liberal, meritocratic argument on admissions, the university decided to adopt a more 'open' admissions policy (Herman 1995).

The consistent policy and practice regarding admissions during the 1980s was one of accepting all who met the minimum statutory requirements for admissions, except in certain programmes of study in which space or resource limitations made selection a necessity (Van den Berg & Gerwel 1990). Before 1988 the university was able to take all students who applied and met the statutory matriculation requirements. However, as the fastest growing university at the time, it had to reassess its admissions policies. In 1990 there were more qualifying applicants than places and targets had to be set for first-time intakes. It was decided to admit 80 per cent of the target figure of first year students for each degree or diploma on the basis of random computer selection from the total number of applicants who met the statutory matriculation requirements. The remaining 20 per cent were selected on the basis of a number of criteria the university felt were academically, ethically and politically defensible (*ibid.*). The criteria were:

- Matriculation pass level – no applicants with high pass marks (usually As and Bs, that is, aggregate marks above 70 per cent) were excluded.
- Gender – equality of admissions of males and females would be the goal.
- Population group classification – an attempt was made to make the university's intake reflect the composition of the population at large.
- Geographical origin – UWC had always to some extent been a national university and an attempt was made to ensure that students from beyond the Western Cape made up a meaningful proportion of the intake.
- Rural candidates – the goal was a rural – urban balance in intakes.
- Social class – the intake made due allowance for opportunities for working-class students using gross family income and parents' highest education qualifications as criteria (Badsha 1992).

According to Gelderbloem (1996) some of the positive outcomes of this initiative and the university's open admissions policy are:

- It has contributed to sustaining the growth at UWC. Student enrolment increased from 6 000 in 1986 to 12 000 in 1989 and even with the need to limit growth from 1990, the figures had further increased to almost 15 000 by 1995.

- In terms of the *Universities Extension Act* of 1959, universities could admit students from only the population group for which they were established to cater. This resulted in a coloured dominance in UWC's student composition until the government repealed the Act. The number of African students has grown from 400 in 1986, to 1989 in 1989, and it increased to 6 617 in 1994, with Africans then constituting 50 per cent of the first year enrolment.

- The intake of female students has risen from 2 681 in 1986 to 5 165 in 1989, and 7 274 in 1994 (Official statistics released by UWC). Females now constitute 51 per cent of the first year enrolment.

- It is estimated that about 30 per cent of students who graduate would normally not have been admitted to HWUs (Gelderbloem 1996:65).

However, such a policy raises serious concerns regarding the chances marginally qualified matriculants have to successfully complete their studies in the absence of any other criteria than meeting the minimum entrance requirements; the costs in respect of high failure rates and dropouts; the inability of many of the students to pay for their tuition; and the fact that most of these students qualify to enrol for courses only in the arts, social sciences and education. Seventy per cent of African students enrolled at South African universities are enrolled in these disciplines. Another offshoot of this policy is the fact that because much of the university's energy and resources are directed towards undergraduate studies, research inevitably suffers. Gerwel admitted that UWC's admission policy had taxed the institution heavily and acknowledged that admitting people from these categories (D and E aggregates) 'is in itself no virtue, unless one creates circumstances conducive to success for a significant proportion of them. This means thorough and ongoing revision of the teaching programme' (Gerwel 1991). The University is currently revising its admissions policy and has already decided to give preference to all candidates with A, B and C aggregate scores in the matriculation examination. Applicants with marginal results (E aggregate) will be excluded from certain courses (Gelderbloem 1996:66).

Dilemmas facing universities striving for increased access and equity

In an earlier paper on selection and equity in higher education in South Africa (Herman 1995), a number of dilemmas confronting HBUs as they seek redress and equity are discussed.

One of the dilemmas is increased class differentiation among post-secondary educational institutions that is experienced in many industrialised countries. Institutions which absorb the bulk of the students from lower social class origins invariably get relegated to a lower status. There are already clear signs that higher achieving students of both the middle and working class prefer enrolment at HWUs in South Africa in lucrative professional fields.

Another dilemma facing universities is the dilution of instructional and other resources. Enrolments at HBUs have increased at a much more rapid rate than the increase in qualified staff and facilities. The enrolment of students at UWC increased more than threefold between 1980 and 1991, while financial subsidy and other resources increased at a slower rate. Class sizes have increased dramatically and there are concerns about the quality of teaching and research. Levin asserts that the most élite paths of study and most élite institutions in the developed world have been less affected by the dilution of resources than institutions that have been enrolling mostly students from working class and lower middle class backgrounds (Levin 1982).

Towards the end of the 1980s a number of universities instituted programmes to address the needs of disadvantaged students. As they were liberalising their admission policies to include more black students, English-medium HWUs introduced academic support programmes for low achievers and second language English speakers. The University of Cape Town, for example, introduced an academic support programme and an Alternative Admissions Research Project for new students (CINTSA 1992). The University of the Witwatersrand also developed academic support programmes and a College of Science for marginal achievers in the natural sciences. The University of Natal initiated a development selection procedure with a Teach-Test-Teach programme for disadvantaged new students (*ibid.*). The Academic Development Centre at the University of the Western Cape adopted an infusion model of academic development, which is different from the adjunct model of academic support in that it places greater emphasis on the integration of support structures and strategies into the mainstream curricula. It contributes towards quality teaching and learning through supporting staff and student development, institutional change and transformation (Walker & Badsha 1993).

Universities have to look very seriously at the possible fusion between the issues of access, equity and quality as the number of students who have to participate in academic development programmes increases. Jakes Gerwel, former Vice-Chancellor of UWC, saw in 1991 that the two major challenges facing South African universities were, firstly, admitting larger numbers of students from the 'disadvantaged majority' and, secondly, to offer education of quality (Gerwel 1991). It is significant how little was said about educational quality in, for example, policy research such as that of the National Education Policy Investigation (NEPI 1993a). Kenneth King (1993), in a discussion of entitlement and achievement in South African universities, contends that the past with its unequal provision and highly uneven achievement can be seen to imply that there is a need to suspend judgement about present quality. He argues that there may be a strong thread in the academic development and support programmes that indicate that it is the lecturer, the curriculum and the university that need to change, not the student. The sheer scale and costs of these academic support and development programmes, and the extra time allowed for black students to make up for their past deficits, may support the view that the programmes are predicated on assumptions of the individual student being responsible for his/her success, but this is something for which the university must take major responsibility. There is reason to doubt whether these programmes, which at present are mostly privately funded, will be able to achieve their lofty goals.

Another key problem facing HBUs, and indeed many other educational institutions in South Africa, is the so-called breakdown of the culture of learning and teaching. This is a legacy of the period of student struggles of the 1970s and 1980s in which students confronted the Apartheid state and rejected separate, unequal education. The success of protest action gave students a voice and a feeling of power but has also led to disarray in education. Morrow, in a paper on entitlement and achievement, says that somewhere near the heart of the breakdown in the culture of learning stands 'the loss amongst both teachers and learners, of a sense of the *significance* of systematic learning, of what its point or purpose might be, and how it contributes to human flourishing' (Morrow 1994:33). He continues, 'Explanations for the breakdown in a culture of learning in terms of political oppression obviously have some substance. However, they can all too easily be woven into popular political rhetoric in such a way as to provide a gloss of respectability to what, on closer investigation, turn out to be a little more than evasion of responsibility. This is an aspect of the "victim syndrome"' (*ibid.* pp. 33 – 4). He describes a culture of entitlement which is putting increasingly severe pressure on many orthodox policies and practices in formal institutions of learning, such as

47

many students demanding access to these institutions. Entry requirements come to be seen as merely an aspect of the legacy of the exclusionary policies of the past, and lack of institutional resources or capacity as simply a more subtle form of exclusion (Herman 1995).

Since the establishment of a democratic system of governance in South Africa after the 1994 elections, there has been increased tension, strife, academic boycotts and calls for the radical transformation of universities. Contrary to expectations, it is not only the HWUs but also HBUs who had led the struggle by academia for liberation, that have been major targets for dissenting black students calling for increased access and free university education. Students have opposed what they call 'academic and financial exclusion' of disadvantaged students who fail their examinations or cannot afford to pay fees. Academic programmes have been seriously disrupted to the extent that local and international commentators (Holiday 1996; Johnson 1995; *The Argus* 1995) have described South African campuses as being in crisis, chaos or a state of collapse. Writing in *The Times* of 9 January 1995, R. W. Johnson says:

> Indeed, so great is the crisis facing universities that it may be impossible to prevent the complete collapse of several institutions, and a large-scale drop in standards and morale in many others...all universities have suffered badly from repeated government funding cuts in the last decade, so that most are now 40% or more underfunded. At the same time, the system has expanded to accommodate vastly greater numbers of black students...Yet ahead lies the likelihood of a continuing financial squeeze, for the African National Congress (the governing Party) has made it clear that it will give top priority to primary education...The HBUs, despite attempts to market themselves as both the most discriminated against and also the most progressive universities, are in the worst plight. A decade and more of continuous student rebellion has left them awash in a culture of permanent and populist extremism. At the same time 'open entry' has led to large intakes and a calamitous collapse in standards, to the point where many students are barely literate in the language of instruction.

Although these descriptions are somewhat overstated, there can be no doubt that the transformation of access and equity policies at South African universities will have to take these dilemmas into account. It is not in the national interest, nor in the interest of the historically disadvantaged, to allow the academic ethos and stability of universities to be eroded to the point where their basic functions are in question.

4

The state of schooling in South Africa and the introduction of Curriculum 2005

DIRK MEERKOTTER

The new outcomes-based curriculum, officially referred to as Curriculum 2005, is described as follows by the Minister of Education, Professor S M E Bengu:

> Essentially, the new curriculum will effect a shift from one which has been content-based to one which is based on outcomes. This aims at equipping all learners with the knowledge, competencies and orientations needed for success after they leave school or have completed their training. Its guiding vision is that of a thinking, competent future citizen (Department of Education 1997b:1).

This chapter provides an account of the state of schooling in South Africa and, then, turns attention to three issues:

1. The introduction of a new curriculum for South African schools and the educational and economic costs thereof.
2. The 'overselling' of Curriculum 2005 and the question of whether what is being sold as a 'paradigm shift' is indeed more than empty rhetoric.
3. The question of whether Curriculum 2005 will not, in fact, widen the gap between the haves and the have-nots in our country.

Curriculum reform in an unstable educational context

Curriculum reforms initiated by South Africa's democratically elected government have resulted in the launching, during 1997, of Curriculum 2005. This curriculum venture has been put forward by the Department of Education as a radical move away from the school curricula of the Apartheid dispensation. Politicians and their government officials are presenting outcomes-based education (OBE) in the classroom as the solution to the country's educational problems, which are a result of the discriminatory policies and practices of the pre-1994 period in our history.

It is common knowledge that the 1976 school riots that started in Soweto gave momentum to the liberation struggle of the disenfranchised majority in South Africa and it is also well documented that the protest action against the enforcement of Afrikaans as a medium of instruction in schools of the Department of Bantu Education was, to say the least, not the only reason for mass action amongst blacks in the country. Low wages, savage political oppression by a minority government, the uprootment and removal of millions of black people to meet the greed of whites for economic prosperity and land, as well as the pass laws and influx control, certainly provided a climate for unrest, which soon developed into an organised social, economic and armed struggle to overthrow the Apartheid regime (Meerkotter 1993:10; see also Cross & Chisholm 1990:61). However, the spark that set light to the powder keg was indeed the crisis in Sowetan black schools, which erupted on 16 June 1976, an ordinary sunny winter day on the Transvaal highveld (see Christie 1986:238). There is no doubt that the symbolic and political significance of 16 June is immense, but one should ask if the participation of school students in the struggle contributed as much to teaching and learning as it has done to change in the political arena. Perhaps the direct mass political action of students (and teachers) during the times of school boycotts and other disruptions created more educational havoc than it contributed to political liberation. Although we do not deny that the student struggle was important in forcing the previous regime into retreat and negotiations.

At this stage, in the late 1990s, more than a generation has passed without the majority of students knowing what school learning actually involves, and what makes the situation even worse is that school students are at present being taught by thousands of teachers who have had very little experience of what systematic and uninterrupted learning and teaching in schools are about. This is because many of the teachers in the formerly disenfranchised communities attended, as students, schools which were often disrupted, due to political instability.

As the struggle continued, so did the culture of non-learning and teaching in the schools of the marginalised, oppressed and poor in South Africa – with tragic implications for the now doubly and triply *disadvantaged*.[1] Vandalism, the low morale of teachers and dwindling educational resources further compound the negative learning and teaching climate in many of our schools. Although the reasons for this are complex, one could safely say that, firstly, the long, difficult years of struggle for liberation against a very powerful white minority regime often resulted in feelings of despair and hopelessness. Secondly, schools were, correctly, viewed by students and teachers as instruments of ideological oppression. A prominent 'Back to School Campaign' organised by the National Education Co-ordinating Committee (NECC)[2] to restore a culture of learning and teaching in schools in the early nineties, and a period of hope for a better education system after the unbanning of the African National Congress (ANC) and the release of Nelson Mandela in 1990 contributed to a change of mood from desperation to hope. During the period between 1990 and 1995 several examples of an improvement in school learning could be cited, but much of the positive energy released by the 1994 election and the will to reconstruct and develop South Africa dissipated as many workers continued to lose their jobs and school-leavers found it increasingly difficult to find work. Kallaway (1997:37) writes that 'there is no getting away from the fact that all the publicity and all the fanfare around the Reconstruction and Development Programme (RDP) in 1994–5 has gone rather silent in 1996'. According to Nzimande (1997:foreword), 'this government is…committed to the Reconstruction and Development Programme (RDP), a programme whose implementation stands to benefit the working class and its allies'. Overall, many would agree that not much has materialised with regard to the pre-election promises of the ANC in respect of the transformation of education. In an article in the *Sowetan* of 19 February 1998, Johnson (1998) asks the following questions: 'With unemployment increasing what options do the youth have? If they fail, they are unlikely to be employed. If they pass, where do they go?'

Although the advantaged (largely white) community in South Africa are also affected by economic pressure at present, they remain a population group with an enormous amount of wealth (*Die Burger*, 7 March 1998). In addition, most former white schools were little affected by the more than twenty years of struggle and strife, which in a certain sense means that they are now doubly and triply *advantaged* in the new South Africa – a new South Africa that, in essence, inherited the educational and other problems of the past.

Over the past few years newspaper, television and radio reports have vividly, and on an almost daily basis, supported the view that the culture of teaching and learning has been destroyed in many of our schools. Sadly, and overwhelmingly, this has been so, mainly in the schools of the disadvantaged and marginalised black majority. Blackman Ngoro (1998), a staff reporter at the *Cape Argus*, writes as follows on 24 February 1998:

An education official in the Mitchell's Plain office area said: 'We can't be proud that coloured schools, Muslim schools and white schools are getting better results while we remain at the bottom of the heap.' Some schools in Guguletu, Langa, Crossroads, Nyanga and Khayelitsha had a pass rate of only 18%. 'People should be made accountable for the low pass rate', said the official. 'Take Fezeka in Guguletu for example. In 1996, it registered a pass rate of 70% and, all of a sudden, that rate fell because of violence and vandalism.'[3]

The present South African government follows an economic policy that is largely based on free market principles, which include tight control over government spending. This policy of fiscal prudence has had a vicious effect on service areas like health and education in a province such as the Western Cape. This is mainly because the policies of the previous government resulted in a situation where especially whites, and to a lesser extent coloureds and Indians,[4] were in a more privileged position than the black majority. The majority population group in the Western Cape is coloured and, of the remainder, a substantial proportion is white. This is why, historically, education in the Western Cape was more favourably funded than in all the other provinces (with the exception of the Northern Cape), which have black majorities. This resulted, for example, in the Western Cape enjoying more favourable teacher:student ratios than seven other provinces in the country.

With equity as one of its goals, the present government decided that the teacher:student ratio for the entire country must be 1:35 for secondary and 1:40 for primary schools by 1999. This meant that the more privileged provinces (Gauteng and the Western Cape) would no longer be given the funding they required from the Department of Education to maintain their favourable teacher:pupil ratios. Provincial education departments decided to reduce teacher numbers in an effort to solve what became a funding crisis. Permanent teachers in the more privileged provinces like Gauteng and, especially, the Western Cape were given the option of accepting financially attractive retrenchment packages and leaving the public service (and, in many cases, effectively the profession), or being placed on a redeployment list if the school where they taught had more than the prescribed number of teachers. At the end of 1996 the Western Cape reduced its numbers by some 6 000 teachers (see *Sunday Times*, 11 January 1998) with another 8 000 to be shed by the end of 1998 (see *Cape Times*, 3 December 1997; 10 December 1997; 16 December 1997). To understand the scale of the reduction in the number of teaching posts consider that in 1997 there were 32 770 teachers employed by the Western Cape Education Department (this translates into a more than 36 per cent reduction in teacher numbers over three years). In addition, 3 000 temporary teachers lost their jobs by the end of January 1998 (*Cape Times*, 13 January 1998).

The well-resourced former white, but also coloured, schools, were hard hit by the measures mentioned above as many qualified and experienced teachers opted for the retrenchment package deal. At the same time, black schools in the country's disadvantaged communities did not benefit from the redeployment list, which proved to be inefficient in practice.

While all the schools were affected by the loss of teachers, especially temporary teachers, coloured and black schools suffered the most. Schools in the wealthier middle class (mostly white and a few coloured) areas are in a better position to appoint temporary teachers and pay for them from school funds (see Botha 1998:10).

In essence the Western Cape has lost thousands of qualified teachers and the other provinces have not gained from the exercise. To implement a new curriculum in a country where a previously well-resourced provincial education department finds itself in a serious staffing and financial crisis and where the other provinces have large numbers of underqualified teachers could only mean further demoralisation and waste (see *Die Burger*, 7 February 1998).

The poor matriculation results at the end of 1997 further confirm the declining situation in education. Only 47,1 per cent of matriculants in the country passed, and of the successful candidates the majority came from the former white, coloured and Indian schools. The percentage pass rates for all the provinces dropped significantly from 54,7 per cent in 1996 to 47,1 per cent in 1997. In 1994 South Africa had a 58 per cent pass rate for matriculants (see *Sunday Times*, 11 January 1998). Recent additional financial and social constraints are likely to impact negatively on the 1998 matriculation results.

Much of the blame has to be put at the doorstep of the previous Apartheid regime, but it would be misleading not to look at the negative effects of the struggle for liberation as well. In spite of the decisive role that students played in the struggle for democracy, perhaps their focus on the political side of life and their perception of schools as an ideological instrument used by the enemy distracted them too much from actual school learning. Even so we can find examples of schools where it is as if the political energy harnessed by democratic organisations in the four- or five-year period running up to the election in 1994 and well into 1995 had a positive effect on learning. Some of the many reasons for this might have been a sense of destination, the discipline exercised in political organisations, the values that underpinned the organisations or all of these combined. After 1995, however, very little of this was left. The excitement of the struggle was replaced by the reality of poverty and hopelessness. Without a tradition of school learning and without the prospects of a job after leaving school, formal education had, for many, become meaningless. The organised political activity during the struggle could not be replaced by organised school activity. The culture of teaching and learning was absent for so long that the energy of many young people had already been channelled in less noble directions.

At this point I would like to look at a specific black township school on the Cape Flats in the Western Cape – a school that might well match those in Soweto, or other parts of the country. The particular school is (or was) a well-resourced secondary school which opened in 1988. From an 18 per cent pass rate for matriculants in the early 1990s it moved to a pass rate of above 60 per cent in the year before the democratic election in 1994. The principal was a committed educator and many of the teachers and students were politically aware and belonged to political organisations in the education sector. They were building a school for the new South Africa.

Since 1994 this pass rate has worsened and dropped to an all time low when only 30 out of some 175 matriculants passed in 1996, with fewer than ten students attaining matriculation exemption, which is the minimum requirement for registration at a university. At the same school the pass rate in 1997 was worse than in 1996. The average pass rate was more or less the same, but in 1997 only one student obtained a matriculation exemption. Part of the reason for this is, in my opinion, a loss of direction and the disappearance of disciplined participation in some of the political structures which have disbanded or simply stopped functioning since the 1994 elections. At the particular school students started mobilising around issues that were previously seen as irrelevant in the South African context and not in line with the struggle against racism, classism, élitism and sexism.

In 1996, for example, matriculation candidates vandalised the school and took teachers hostage because the parents and teachers were not prepared to give them R6000 for a matriculation farewell at an expensive hotel in the city. This was at a school where parents could hardly afford R50 in annual school fees. The students resorted to violence and in the end the Western Cape Education Department had to provide a twenty-four hour security guard at very high costs to protect the school's property, the teachers and students. The situation at the school was aggravated by theft, students and teachers arriving late and leaving early, and a lack of support from an Education Department that had to cope with similar problems at other schools.

In an article carried by *Drum*, one of the largest popular magazines, with a mainly black readership throughout South Africa, the particular incident of violence was reported under the heading 'Trashing their own school' (Weideman 1996:20–4). One of the captions to a photograph read: 'Nothing escaped their fury when Matric pupils…went on the rampage, smashing bookshelves, shattering windows and scattering papers all over the teachers' staffroom. They clearly enjoyed the orgy of violence … and the smiles on their faces said it all' (*ibid.* p. 21).[5]

It is common knowledge that the same type of disruptions also occur in other schools in the country, most of which provide education to the formerly disenfranchised majority. Is it not sad then that a particular student community that fought against all forms of élitism before the 1994 elections, in 1996 used their emancipatory pre-election energy to vandalise a school in a poor community because they could not get R6000 from school funds for a matric farewell? The political vision that students and their political organisations had for a democratic society was indeed very different from events such as this – events which many of them would have referred to as 'petty bourgeois' three or four years before. The violence around the farewell function could be ascribed to reasons which were mentioned above:

- The high expectations they had of a new and just democratic dispensation had not materialised and the reality of poverty had remained.
- Frustration about the difficult circumstances in which they continued to live while little had changed for their white counterparts with their lavish functions and farewells might have encouraged them to act in the way that they did.
- Since the publishing of the 1997 dismal matric results – the worst in the country's history – numerous newspaper reports attributed the blame not only to Apartheid education, but also to the mismanagement of human and financial resources at the national and provincial levels under the new dispensation.
- The media also pointed to a lack of discipline and commitment on the part of teachers and students to work towards a culture of teaching and learning to the best of their ability.

The disparity between former white, coloured and Indian schools on the one hand and black schools on the other has become more glaring than ever. In spite of this, a few examples of excellent schools in some of the disadvantaged communities do exist. One ex-Department of Education and Training school (Luhlaza Senior Secondary, a black school in an extremely poor community on the Cape Flats) achieved a matric pass rate of 86 per cent in 1997 (*Die Burger*, 10 January 1998). This is 10 per cent higher than the average for the province, which was a comparatively impressive 76 per cent. As far as facilities, resources and qualified teachers are concerned, this school in Khayelitsha compares with the school mentioned above. I have, however, no doubt that at Luhlaza teacher commitment, and student and parent involvement, must have contributed greatly to a climate of orderliness and accountable school management, which are so essential for meaningful learning to take place.

However, Luhlaza is an exception to the rule. The *Cape Argus* of 24 January 1998 reports that, during the registration period at the beginning of the 1998 school year, several schools were held up by armed youths, teachers were detained and enormous amounts of money in the form of school fees, paid by mostly poor parents, was stolen at gunpoint in some of the black townships on the Cape Flats. In response to this situation teachers at some schools threatened to come to school early in the morning to report and then go home because of the threat of violence so close to them.

The violence and vandalism linked to a matric farewell at a particular school can thus be seen as a reflection of what is happening at other schools on the Cape Flats and elsewhere and is symptomatic of the frightening state education finds itself in throughout the country, particularly in the schools of the poorest of the poor. However, Luhlaza Senior Secondary is a symbol of hope, and although such examples are few, they demonstrate that more should and could be done than blame everything on Apartheid and our sad past.

From the above, it is clear that the country will have to take drastic measures to solve its problems in education. However, with the financial crisis in education, and competing priorities in spheres such as housing, health and crime, it is difficult to know what should be addressed first in the education sector. In addition to problems mentioned above, years of bad teaching (or no teaching), little order and discipline in schools and a lack of examples of what school learning actually involves have had a negative impact on education.

As an answer to the problems in education, the national Department of Education has introduced a new curriculum – Curriculum 2005. It is not difficult to understand why the new government would want to introduce something that is totally different from the curricula used by the Apartheid regime, but we must ask if a new curriculum can improve what is happening in our schools, especially in view of the examples given above. This is the central question of the chapter and will be elaborated on below.

The answer to the question is, in my mind, 'certainly not'. Some of the reasons for my scepticism are that the country does not have the financial and other resources to train teachers to put a new curriculum in place. Most of the former white schools, because of their long history of educational stability and supportive middle class parent communities, would find themselves in a situation where the transition to a new curriculum would be reasonably easy to cope with, but for the majority of, mostly black, poorer schools, the new curriculum could be an extra burden. Whether the envisaged outcomes-based curriculum, which will cost billions to implement, is a suitable curriculum for South Africa or not will be discussed below.

Why then are the national and provincial departments of education pushing ahead in spite of fundamental criticisms from educationists, economists, philosophers and parents? The answer to this question should be sought on the political terrain. The new ANC government has, I would argue, a preoccupation with what is often referred to as 'Bantu education', 'Apartheid education' and/or 'Christian National education'. Many also regard 1976 as a very significant year politically speaking, with many voters romanticising around the specific place of the Soweto uprising in the struggle for freedom.

Indeed, 16 June 1976 is one of the most important days in the history of South Africa, but the interference by political parties and politicians in education at present with regard to the introduction of the new curriculum is a cause for concern. To put it bluntly, education is being used to catch votes in the 1999 elections. My objection here is not aimed against the ANC government only. In the Western Cape, the only province controlled by the former Apartheid government's National Party (NP), the Education Department has worked as hard as any, and at times against all odds, to get the new curriculum implemented. There can be said to be two reasons for this. First, for the 1999 elections, the NP dominated Western Cape Education Department would be able to claim that they were better organised in implementing the new curriculum, and this could be presented as grounds for returning the NP to office in the province. Second, the new curriculum is in line with the mechanistic and quasi-psychological educational and social views prevalent before 1994. The new outcomes-based Curriculum 2005 is retrogressive and in a certain sense even more technicist and mechanistic than the previous curricula. With its skills-based and technological focus the new curriculum might sound very modern and be in line with current macro-economic plans for Third World countries, but the important question is whether it will meet the needs of the marginalised and poor in South Africa.

I have discussed the intellectual and material state of disrepair in which education largely finds itself at present, and implied that a school improvement project is a more important priority than the hasty introduction of a new curriculum. Because of the unstable situation in the schools, teachers are largely unprepared for and largely uncommitted to the kind of change proposed. An editorial page of the *Sunday Times* (22 February 1998) underscores this view with regard to the introduction of Curriculum 2005:

> There were signs last year that the introduction of the new curriculum was heading for problems. KwaZulu-Natal Premier Ben Ngubane, for one, warned that he believed it would be virtually impossible to make the switch, given the inadequate training of teachers in the province.
>
> But the government pressed ahead.

When Grade 1s across the country arrived at school in January, the least one might have expected was that their teachers would be prepared and that they would have the new textbooks.

But, as we report on our front page today, scores of Grade 1s across the country are still without textbooks.

Many schools have not even received booklets printed by the central government for use by teachers and pupils until the textbooks become available.

The editorial continues by saying, as I have above, that:

Schools which are the best equipped and have produced the best results, primarily the traditionally white schools, are set to come out on top again. Their teachers are trained and they have stationery and textbooks.

There is a perception that billions of rands will be wasted and that the major problem areas in our schools will remain unchanged or might even get worse. South Africa might have, yet again, betrayed millions of school children.

Curriculum implementation in South Africa today is very different from the introduction of a new curriculum in some First World countries where similar outcomes-based curricula are being introduced but where the financial resources exist, where teachers and students are used to planning ahead and where a stable schooling system functions with a long history of continuous in-service education for teachers. There are, however, also other reasons why we should look carefully at the introduction of a curriculum such as Curriculum 2005. In the next section I turn to some of these reasons.

A critical look at some key concepts underpinning Curriculum 2005

In a very simplistic way the promoters of the new initiative contrast the 'old' curriculum with the so-called 'new' curriculum in easy-to-read booklets and pamphlets with cartoon-like characters and other pictures. One of the booklets, issued by the national Department of Education (1997b:6–7) highlights the following 'differences' between the 'old' and the 'new' paradigms and is a very vivid example of the merely rhetorical nature of the 'adventure'.

It is not difficult for the thinking and experienced teacher to see the inconsistencies in the table below, and it is, for example, not true to say that the 'old' curriculum did not make provision for the active involvement of students in the classroom situation. What the learner should become and what they should understand is certainly not something new. An emphasis on critical thinking, reasoning skills, reflection and action has not been unknown in learning and teaching in South Africa. While it might be that the rote learning

Table 4.1 Comparing curriculums

Old curriculum	Curriculum 2005 (new)
Passive learners	Active learners
Exam-driven	Learners are assessed on an ongoing basis
Rote learning	Critical thinking, reasoning, reflection and action
Syllabus is content-based and broken down into subjects	An integration of knowledge; learning of relevant and connected to real-life situations
Textbook/worksheet-bound and teacher-centered	Learner-centered; teacher as facilitator; teacher constantly uses group work and teamwork to consolidate the new approach
Sees syllabus as rigid and non-negotiable	Learning programmes seen as guides that allow teachers to be innovative and creative in designing programmes
Teachers responsible for learning; motivation dependent on the personality of the teacher	Learners take responsibility for their learning; pupils motivated by constant feedback and affirmation of their worth
Emphasis on what the teacher hopes to achieve	Emphasis on outcomes – what the learner becomes and understands
Content placed into rigid time-frames	Flexible time-frames allow learners to work at their own pace
Curriculum development process not open to public comment	Comment and input from the wider community is encouraged

Source: Jolly (1969:38).

of isolated facts has taken place, possibly in the majority of our schools, it need not be ascribed to the curriculum alone. Learning a particular piece of content need not be in a rote learning mode, where the main purpose is to regurgitate isolated facts, often in an unconnected way, during an examination session. Thirty years ago Ausubel (1968) wrote about the importance of meaningful verbal learning – where the structure, underlying problems and questions of a particular section in, let's say a Mathematics curriculum, are understood and appreciated.

The way in which the 'new' curriculum is sold in official documents and the frequent references to a 'paradigm shift' also deserve sharp critical comment. 'Paradigm shifts' occur *gradually* as more and more practitioners, in our case teachers and other educators and educationists, come to see their practice in a different light. One could even say that a new 'paradigm' grows out of a previous 'paradigm' and that it builds on previous practices and understandings. A mere *uncritical* rejection of a previous or existing paradigm is not a paradigm shift but a step into chaos.

Here I would like to refer in general terms to Thomas Kuhn's *The Structure of Scientific Revolutions*, written in 1970, and subsequent debates on 'paradigms' and 'paradigm shifts'. Kuhn speaks of 'pre-paradigmatic' modes of investigation (and I would like to add 'action'), which are eclectic and, thus, do not contribute to a coherently growing body of knowledge. Some theorists have suggested that the social sciences (including education) are 'pre-paradigmatic' and that this is the reason why they do not develop well-grounded knowledge. Whether one agrees with this notion or not, it does seem clear that the chaotic schooling system in South Africa is at its best 'pre-paradigmatic'. There is thus a very sound reason for avoiding ill-conceived changes that have to be hastily introduced in a system that is already very unstable. Again, this situation is very different for countries such as Scotland, New Zealand, the Netherlands or Canada, which have regular systems running and from which they could then move in a new direction.

'Paradigms' are, furthermore, not merely intellectual frameworks – they involve coherent systems of beliefs, values, practices, institutions and norms. For a 'paradigm shift' to occur, change over a period of time is needed in all the different spheres mentioned above. To talk about a 'paradigm shift' with the introduction of a new policy (such as Curriculum 2005) is an empty way of asserting that there is radical change when in fact there may be very little.

Another problematic area is the way in which the 'new' curriculum is marketed. The so-called 'old' curriculum and the 'new' curriculum are compared in an 'either-or' fashion: one is 'teacher-centred', the other 'learner-centred'; one is 'content-based, the other 'skills-based', etc.

Of the many aspects to be considered with regard to the 'new' curriculum, I would briefly like to focus on three:

1. curriculum content,
2. learner-centredness, and
3. the mechanistic 'psychologisation' of school learning.

On the issue of content and the negative way official documents speak of the 'old' content-based curricula, I agree that existing (old) curricula focused too heavily on the rote learning of huge numbers of isolated facts, which are often forgotten shortly after tests or exams. However, this problem has more to do with the ways in which we teach and learn than with the content itself. The majority of teachers have probably not made enough of a didactic analysis of content in terms of the questions to which it is a response, and the ways in which it makes some sense of the diffuse reality in which they live. Furthermore, the fact that teachers and researchers often focus on specific learning areas is due to the complex reality that no single person can know everything. However, school teachers and students have to seek the interrelatedness of different areas of focus and study. If teachers were educated to look at things such as coherence and structure around them, it might be easier for them to teach students to acquire the skills that lead to a better understanding of the world. My fear is that if we move away from discipline-based or subject-based curricula, we would not only lose the structure and values inherent in what exists already, but also the skills which could be developed through the authentic engagement in specific practices.

What is happening at the moment is that content analysis and the meaningful engagement with curriculum content by students are not addressed. Instead, curriculum content itself becomes the target of those who look for problem areas in existing curricula.

This brings me to the second issue. It is conceptually confusing to say that we are moving away from a teacher-centred curriculum to a learner-centred curriculum. In an educational situation there have to be those who explain their understanding of certain things – and here I use explanation in a wide sense (not necessarily referring to someone lecturing to others) – and those who have to learn to understand the world in which they live under the guidance of somebody who has a better or more appropriate understanding of the questions which we are confronted with in the world. Teachers and students have different roles to play in the teaching and learning situation. At times these roles may change where the teacher learns from students – where students become explainers or teachers.

With regard to the responsibilities of the teacher concerning student learning, I have to object strongly to the view that the teacher is no longer responsible for the students' learning. It is, after all, the teacher's job to motivate students in such a way that they want to engage with what is presented to them. The better the teacher is able to identify the question or questions that led to practices which moved a person (or more persons) enough to find out, the more likely it will be that students will engage energetically and, yes, critically and rationally with what is put in front of them. It speaks for itself that students also have a responsibility towards their learning, but it would be more appropriate to speak of co-responsibility in a teaching and learning situation.

Another point about the key role of the teacher is that because of the powerful position that they find themselves in, teachers can either impact negatively on education in a country like South Africa, or contribute greatly to the improvement of educational practices in schools. This is where the intervention has to be made in the first place. It is naïve to think that a 'new' curriculum will, like a magic wand, turn the educational ship around. Teachers as professionals will have to take more responsibility for those things that should happen in schools. In many of our schools these things are quite simple, for example, getting to school on time, going to classes when the bell rings and accepting responsibility for what should happen in school class-rooms. A responsible adult committed to the educational well-being of learn-ers is actually at the core of all meaningful teaching and learning in schools.

The third issue which I would like to address, briefly, has to do with the instrumentalist and mechanistic link between education and economic growth. At the root of this link lies the idea of human capital theory and the way in which individuals and government could best make use of education to promote economic growth. This is, in my view, also a reason for the conserva-tive approach of OBE and the focus on skills which might serve economic growth optimally.

It is with regard to this point that the work of (educational) psychologists like Bloom, Krahtwohl and Gagne of a few decades ago becomes important (see Department of Education 1997e:22). At the rhetorical level the national Department of Education in its booklet (1997b:16) speaks of *critical cross-field outcomes*, which could be described as some form of *transformational outcomes*, but are very vague and difficult to measure with competency or mastery learning-based criteria. The so-called critical outcomes are, from an educational point of view, extremely important, for example, the ability to 'identify and solve problems by using creative and critical thinking' (Depart-ment of Education 1997b:16), or to 'show awareness of the importance of effective learning strategies, responsible citizenship, cultural sensitivity, education and career opportunities and entrepreneurial abilities' (*ibid.*). In the Department of Education's *Curriculum 2005* (1997b) document little men-tion is made of the critical outcomes and how these might be achieved; instead, a regression to the psychological taxonomies of yesterday surfaces in a signifi-cant way: 'For clarification then: An outcome must conform to the following structure; active verb(s) + object + any conditions which set the boundaries of the activity. This will assist in describing what a person should be able to do' (*ibid.* p. 21).

This merely reinforces the present causal and mechanistic ways in which learning and teaching are understood. A more progressive approach would be to educate teachers to become better in the didactic analysis of content, rather than to dismiss the 'old' curricula as content-driven. Why should one buy into a non-transformative OBE approach when it has already been proven repeatedly that psychological taxonomies are inappropriately superimposed onto the structures and questions of disciplinary content? In Curriculum 2005 one finds the rhetoric of a transformational OBE initiative but the reality of an instrumentalist and behaviourist criterion-referenced approach.

Conclusion

First, in spite of all the political talk about a paradigm shift and a move away from the 'old' to the 'new', Curriculum 2005 runs the risk of further entrenching mechanistic and inappropriate quasi-psychological conceptions of school learning and teaching. Second, the proposed new venture in education is not affordable. The country simply does not have the financial and other resources to change direction as proposed. Third, I think it is unwise to assume that an entire teaching and learning population in schools could, by the introduction of something like a new curriculum, overcome all its deeply rooted social and educational problems.

South Africa is moving too hastily, and partly for party political reasons, into 'something new', and partly because it is different from the previous regime. There is no doubt that education in South Africa should move away from its past, but it will move into more chaos if it does not take into consideration the roots of its birth, even if this does involve its colonial past.

The most pernicious effect of the implementation of Curriculum 2005 is likely to be that the previously white schools will implement it in a more effective way than other schools because of better infrastructures and stronger parental support. At these historically advantaged schools, extra classes for those who struggle with English, Science and Mathematics are likely to continue alongside programmes in art, ballet, athletics, rugby, cricket and leadership. Teachers and students in the schools which were least affected by the disruptions experienced by the majority will be assisted in coping with additional curriculum demands – with or without financial assistance from the provincial authorities. They will still turn out heart surgeons, engineers, lawyers, accountants and architects, as they have in the past. However, for the poor and disadvantaged who suffered in the past, Curriculum 2005 will certainly not change their situation in a way that will enable them to begin to play their rightful part in our country.

Bearing in mind the state of physical and intellectual disrepair in the majority of our schools, Curriculum 2005 remains a pipedream, perhaps even if we had huge improvements in the administrative and financial infrastructures in our education system. For most teachers a phrase such as: 'Learners make and negotiate meaning and understanding' (*Sunday Times*, 22 February 1998) remains empty rhetoric. The same newspaper states in its editorial, that: 'South Africa has already betrayed too many of its children. We cannot afford to lose another generation'.[6]

Endnotes

1. By 'doubly and triply disadvantaged and doubly and triply advantaged' I refer to the way in which blacks were disadvantaged by, first, being disenfranchised, second, through the segregated and unequal education system and, third, by the political unrest before 1994 and the continuing instability in the schools of the black majority after 1994. During the same period, whites had political and economic power, as well as properly resourced, functioning schools untouched by the problems faced by students in black schools. In addition, the former white schools still find themselves in a situation where they have sufficient financial resources, well-qualified teachers and the infrastructure to implement the new curriculum.

2. The National Education Crisis Committee (subsequently it became the National Education Co-ordinating Committee) was one of the more than 600 organisations affiliated to the United Democratic Front (UDF), which formed an extra-parliamentary body in opposition to the Apartheid government. The UDF was founded in 1983 and collapsed into the African National Congress (ANC) structures shortly after the unbanning of the organisation and the release of Mandela (Van den Berg & Meerkotter 1994:305–6; also see Levin 1991).

3. Ngoro is referring to the matriculation pass rate, which we elaborate on later in the chapter.

4. In this chapter I use the previous regime's racial categories because the inequalities in South Africa are still, largely, a result of the Apartheid government's discriminatory policies, so glaringly tied to race. Furthermore, I believe that at this stage in our history the wrongs of the past would not be adequately addressed if we were simply to glance over the differences and discrepancies.

5. Name of particular school omitted for ethical, educational and professional reasons.

6. This chapter has drawn on press comments in many instances. This underlines the absence of good quality empirical data on South African schools. Fortunately a series of research studies on the present cultures of teaching and learning, has begun.

SECTION TWO

Integrating education
and training

Introduction

The *White Paper on Education and Training* (WPET) of 1995 heralded a fundamental transformation in the system of education and training in South Africa. Since then, lifelong learning has become a central tenet of education policy, around which is built a new National Qualifications Framework (NQF) under the umbrella of the South African Qualifications Authority (SAQA). Within these structures are processes and procedures for modularised and accredited areas of learning, which are defined through competencies in prescribed learning outcomes.

The approach, outcomes-based education (OBE), is deemed appropriate for the integration of education and training needs in South Africa. The WPET proposed that through these mechanisms, demands for equity and redress and for access to quality education for all could be met. At the same time, OBE within a NQF would be able to respond to industrial and commercial demands for growth and development by preparing the 'right kind' of workers for the country's future human resource needs.

In making these demands, employers and education policy-makers define knowledge as areas of competence usually vocationally driven. Thus there is no such thing as 'absolute' or 'real' knowledge but rather skills and competencies, only some of which have a basis in classical 'forms' of knowledge, areas of learning which owe their origins to epistemological and coherentist foundations. However, in addressing knowledge and learning in more vocationally orientated ways, the South African policy community is no different from many others involved in such praxis. Indeed, a global educational discourse is emerging which impacts heavily on practice, be that practice in South Africa, Malaysia, Australia, America or Europe (for further elaboration of this approach, see Ritzer 1998).

In this global context one can see qualifications and curricular innovations being shaped significantly by the ideology of the market. They may take particular forms in the South African context, shaped as education has been by the historical legacy of Apartheid education, and by the contradictory demands for equity and redress on the one hand, and economic growth and development on the other. Yet current South African education policy is very much part of these interwoven and global discourses involving the rationales for and developments in particular forms, structures, processes and procedures of education and training. Indeed, South African policy-makers have been heavily influenced by Australian and Scottish models of learning-through-competence and emergent qualifications structures to assess these competencies.

One might question the efficacy of such developments within the current South African climate of social and educational transformation. Indeed, this is the aim of the chapters in this section. They will interrogate these discourses, most notably the developments, structural and procedural, which integrate education with training. The chapters seek to delineate, examine, analyse and reflect upon current discourses in the education policy community by focusing on the conceptual bases of policy and their roots in these national and global discourses. They explore the nature of policy-making processes, and the pedagogical implications of policy. In so doing, they all raise critical questions about the nature and potential of policies for the integration of education and training in South Africa.

Gari Donn commences by exploring the emergence of qualifications frameworks in three countries: New Zealand, Scotland and South Africa. She argues that these frameworks, seen by policy-makers as 'solutions' to economic and educational problems, are firmly located within global economic and political contexts, within an international policy climate characterised by 'market rules of engagement'. By discussing the relevance of and rationales for qualifications frameworks in Scotland and New Zealand (with their post-Fordist flexible markets, orientated to profit accumulation through new contracts between employers and labour), her work raises critical questions about the NQF and SAQA. Given their macroeconomic and political underpinnings, she asks whether such constructs can be (or should be) of value to a South Africa undergoing transformation.

Donn identifies elements of exceptionalism in South Africa, most significantly, the central role played by the trade union movement in formulating ANC education and training policy. This has led to debate about the role and nature of the NQF, encouraging conceptions of a framework to promote equity and redress alongside one to respond to the market-driven needs of employers.

Zelda Groener interrogates the role played by the trade union movement in shaping the nature of the NQF, exploring the political roots of debate in the early 1990s. The chapter focuses on the political rationales underpinning early policy proposals for the integration of education and training in a process co-ordinated by the National Training Board. Groener casts the debate in terms of dispute around 'socialist' and 'capitalist' models. Drawing on in-depth interviews with key representatives, she demonstrates that while formally the Congress of South African Trade Unions (COSATU) expressed a commitment to socialism, a variety of political positions may be discerned, ranging from socialism to capitalism. Groener highlights the dominance of capitalist discourse amongst other members party to the negotiations, particularly business, and the extent to which this constrained COSATU representatives. She thus identifies contradictions within COSATU's own position, which led to the weakening of 'socialist discourse'. Read in conjunction with Donn, this chapter provides insight into the balance of forces and policy values shaping the form and nature of the NQF. Such debate – questioning whether the NQF can address demands for equity and redress, with their roots in the socialist commitments outlined by Groener, whilst the global imperatives outlined by Donn increasingly exert their influence – continues to resonate through contemporary policy processes, as the following papers demonstrate.

Glenda Kruss draws attention to the policy process by examining policy-making models which act to shape the nature and form of the new system of education, OBE. Curriculum 2005 is taken as a case-study of the ways in which teachers have been encouraged to see themselves as stakeholders in an open, transparent and participatory policy process. However, she argues that it may be in contra-distinction to the reality of the process, characterised by traditional rationalist practices. The tendency has been for teachers' participation to take place at the point of implementation of blueprints developed by experts, in consultation with stakeholders' representatives, with the assumption that an automatic consensus process will ensue. Kruss questions whether such consensus can be taken for granted, especially as the implication of education policy may come to have very different results and impacts on different stakeholder groups. As Kruss notes, the role of teachers is particularly important for the implementation of Curriculum 2005, not only, but importantly, in the classroom. Her chapter highlights the difficulties and demands of implementing policy, of changing curriculum and pedagogy in the practice of individual teachers, particularly in an under-resourced context. Kruss concludes with a call for active teacher engagement and strong organisation to construct a new educational politics that allows real space for engagement with curriculum and pedagogy.

Simon McGrath echoes many of these concerns as he considers the challenges of moving from education and training policy to practice. He notes that the very recent emergence of critical dispute within the official ANC/COSATU policy position may well indicate the need for policy to be informed more by practice than by the research community's continuous, perhaps pedestrian, reflections. McGrath's concern is whether the new qualifications system will lead to the empowerment of learners – a concern shared by Donn and Kruss – and whether there is a need, especially in the light of future policy initiatives, to develop a critical edge to current and ongoing research on the NQF. The chapter highlights key issues that must be addressed to ensure that South Africa moves towards the best possible system it can achieve, given the political and economic imperatives towards implementation. McGrath concludes by noting that current interrogation of proposals for the integration of education and training is related to the policy cycle and the difficulty of moving from principles of policy to detailed programmes of action.

Mignonne Breier, like McGrath, focuses attention on concerns about the empowerment of learners. In her case, she conducted a detailed study of one central principle of the NQF, the recognition of prior learning, RPL. By drawing on social practices of learning theory, Breier argues that current conceptualisations of RPL could become problematic in that they imply potential equivalence between informal and formal learning which may not be achievable in practice, or might not even be desirable. These place strenuous and contradictory demands on the assessment process. Breier also raises critical questions about the conceptualisation of the transfer of learning in terms of decontextualised, generic skills or knowledge. She highlights central dilemmas for the developers of the NQF which are not easily resolved, and which require a deeper, more nuanced commitment to the principle of empowerment of learners.

In essence, the chapters in this section are of their time. They form part of the critical debate and disputes around the form in which the principles of the NQF become translated into educational practice. Whether South African policy-makers work through these disputes and develop a framework to overcome central policy contradictions still remains to be seen. As a collection, the chapters aim to contribute to delineating the problems and provide insight into potential solutions.

Glenda Kruss

5

International policy-making: global discourses and the National Qualifications Framework

GARI DONN

Across a range of fields the 1990s have seen a major concern with notions of globalisation and the impact that globalisation pressures might be exerting or come to exert on national and local experiences (Stewart 1995). This has been particularly marked in the spheres of trade, technology and industry policy where global pressures are held to be operating to transform national competitive positions. At their epicentre is the creation of a global economy that has led to an intensification of economic competition between firms, regions and nation states (Mitchie & Smith 1995). The globalisation of economic activity has called into question the future role of the nation state and how it can secure economic growth and shared prosperity (Brown & Lauder 1997). Similar pressures and ensuing discourses are currently developing in education, especially in the global interface of training with education policy.

It is argued (Mathews 1989) that the increasingly globalised economy makes the challenge of developing and sustaining a competitive economy both more pressing and less straightforward. Central to the changed circumstances is an education system that reflects both quantitative and qualitative shifts in the emergence of new technologies.

The rapid obsolescence of technologies and the growing scale of information available for analysis and manipulation mean that the transformation of data rather than concrete materials becomes central to competitive positions (Reich 1991). Thus, it is suggested, the most successful economies of the twenty-first century will be in countries that have transformed themselves into learning societies, with a cultural and institutional stress on the new priority given to information. The role of education in that process is crucial for successful transference from a twentieth-century manufacturing economy into a political and economic power of the twenty-first century.

Indeed, the latter quarter of the twentieth century has seen the development of an international policy-making climate which is characterised by 'market rules of engagement' (between employer and trade unions) whereby workers trade their skills, knowledge and entrepreneurial acumen in a global market place (Brown & Lauder 1997). Enterprise that can deliver a living wage to workers now depends on the quality as much as the price of goods and services, and the value of education in the production of quality has become integral to the labour market. Not only is education integral to the skilling of personnel for the labour market, but it has become part of that market through legislation which supports competition between schools, colleges and universities, the extension of parental choice and the development of 'variety' in institutional structures and funding, in curriculum and in assessment (Ball 1993).

Such commodification of education can be seen in a number of Anglophone countries notably, Scotland and New Zealand. In such countries, it has been argued, education has become market-orientated and commodified, leaving as (perhaps ancient) history the view of education as a social good – a force for equity and social justice, enhancing equality of opportunity and a means of empowering those individuals and social groups having few social, economic or political skills, or little 'cultural capital' (Bourdieu 1973; Richardson 1986).

The result of current policies which advocate education as a private good, one to be purchased in the market and in the quantity required by consumers, has been to marginalise groups and organisations which had previously been involved in the process of redistribution – those groups working from the principles of the importance of accountability, transparency and civic responsibility in educational decision-making. In the wake of these principles are the driving demands of the post-Fordist market (see Chapter 8 of this volume), the striving for niche markets and the absence of criteria other than financial success or failure, through which one can judge the efficacy of a particular policy initiative.

Considering the internationalising context of education policy, it is interesting to note recent developments in post-compulsory education in a number of Anglophone countries (Young 1992). Education and training opportunities become pivotal to visions of a 'just, yet competitive' society. At the forefront of such visions is the concept of lifelong learning for all, a commitment to investment in the 'employability' of present and future workers, and a new social contract between the individual and the state.

71

To develop such visions, a number of countries have introduced qualifications frameworks through which lifelong learning can be accredited and articulated, through which skills and competencies can be learnt and updated, and through which social justice and equity are said to prosper. New Zealand and Scotland are two such countries, South Africa is a third.

In the new economic paradigm – illustrated by greater production flexibility, new computer-led technology, flattened management hierarchies, more participatory working environments, a more educated labour force and by added value through innovation – the role of innovatory education and training qualification structures is central (Donn 1996). In South Africa these qualifications structures are especially important – as approximately 900 000 students will soon be leaving school each year with the equivalent of matriculation certificates. Whether they progress to further education, higher education or employment, it is important for there to be permeability between their employment practice and their qualifications.

Given the macroeconomic and political background of the introduction of qualifications frameworks, this paper will seek to address questions about the relevance of and rationales for qualifications frameworks. From the wider perspective of the internationalisation of education policy, it will outline the manner in which similar educational reforms are being introduced in New Zealand, Scotland and, most recently, in South Africa.

Attention will be drawn to the intense relationship between educational goals and the agendas of the labour market in post-Fordist capitalism. As McGrath (1996a) and others have argued, the task of education is to provide skilled labour for a society moving from a low skills economy (LSE) to one of high skills (HSE), flexible and consonant with a diverse economy. Flexibility and transferability of skills both within and between occupational areas and the ensuing role of human resource development (HRD) therefore become vitally important. The acquisition of skills through education and training, which is embedded in National Qualifications Frameworks (NQFs), requires examination. These frameworks are considered to represent the most efficacious groupings of areas of competence (Jessup 1991) so that transferability and flexibility flourish and become the mainstay of innovative employment practices.

In addressing these issues, it will be the central aim of the paper to question the utility and validity of a South African NQF. If, as it is argued, the rationales for qualifications frameworks are located in post-Fordist, flexible labour markets, markets orientated towards profit accumulation through a new 'contract' between employers and labour – one where learning, skills and competencies take centre stage – one must ask whether a construct such as the NQF can be valuable for education or for employment in a South Africa undergoing transformation.

72

Qualifications frameworks

The emergence of a qualification authority may be seen as indicative of a changed focus – from formal knowledge to a stress on skills ahead of knowledge, and on 'soft' skills such as problem-solving and communication in preference to 'hard' skills such as those in carpentry or electronics. All this occurs at times of economic and political crisis and change, a fact that forms the basis of a theoretical understanding of the rationales for the emergence, nature, structure and provisions of NQFs.

One might contextualise the introduction of qualifications authorities and frameworks as occurring at times of intense economic and political pressure, or as O'Connor (1973) would argue, at times of fiscal crises of the state. As Offe (1985) states, the capitalist state has two simultaneous and often contradictory roles: to support the process of capital accumulation (for example, by providing transport systems and business subsidies) and to legitimise this role by maintaining electoral support, by endeavouring to enhance the value of labour (for example, through education and training policies) and to ameliorate the social costs of private accumulation (for example, through welfare policies and environmental protection policies).

At times, the legitimacy of a state – whose underlying rationale, as seen by Habermas (1976), Offe (1985) and others, is the accumulation of profit for a small minority at the expense of the majority's labour – comes into question. At such times, traditional commonsense beliefs – such as those in the Protestant work ethic – need to be supported, perhaps, through the establishment of structures and processes that are, in Habermasian terms, highly 'scientific, technical and rational'. Habermas (1976) urges us to see the ways in which social institutions, such as those in educational systems, are constructed through highly scientific terms and rationalised by technical experts and hence how political problems become converted into manageable technical ones, with technical solutions.

For educators, this is particularly worrying. Whilst critical and reflective practice may be seen as inherent to the education project, qualifications frameworks instil highly developed bureaucratic practices. As such, they tend to exclude from discourses those who are not conversant with (or competent in) the reasoning of, logic for and language surrounding that construct. The central role of experts in a self-serving qualifications discourse may be said to counteract human emancipation (Habermas 1991). For Habermas, such emancipation, as a form of practical democracy, is located in the comprehensibility of everyday communication and interaction. He argues that meanings are inter-subjective and based on an 'ideal speech situation' where utterances are 'true, correct, comprehensible and sincere'. The justice of an institution or validity of behaviour, therefore, is evidenced in 'an ideal speech situation' where it is presupposed that any person entering into that particular sphere of discourse does so on an equal basis and would come to the same conclusions. If, through the specificity and peculiarity of language used, the possibility of entering into the qualifications discourse is barred, there is an argument that its role as an empowering, even transforming, construct has to be questioned.

In South Africa, at a time of social and political transformation, these are crucial concerns. It will be important to discuss just how emancipatory is a construct which, although designed to support lifelong learning and the unification of academic and vocational curricula, may in fact disenfranchise sections of the population it is meant to help. In New Zealand these are also current and key concerns. Indeed, educational innovations and structural changes have made New Zealand a fascinating country for the study of macro- and micro-educational policy (Lingard *et al.* 1993).

The New Zealand Qualifications Authority

In New Zealand during the 1980s and 1990s there have been highly-charged controversies surrounding the abandonment of welfarist economics, the acceptance of programmes funded by the International Monetary Fund (IMF) and the World Bank, and the introduction of an articulated structure through which education feeds into employment, the labour market and the economy at a macro-policy level.

From the 1950s to the 1980s, the New Zealand government played a steadily increasing role in the management of education as a social good. However, by 1988 the Picot Task Force Report identified 'failings' in the education system – over-centralisation in decision-making, complexity in the administration of education, lack of information and choice, lack of effective management practices, and feelings of powerlessness on the part of 'consumers', parents and employers. In response, a more market-orientated approach to education was developed (Picot *et al.* 1988). The role of education as a force for social justice and equity was diminishing.

During the 1980s and early 1990s, the commitment by the United Kingdom to the markets of the European Community, the removal of international trade barriers and the emergence of the global economy all impacted upon education and resulted in legislation (see Lange 1988; New Zealand Ministry of Education 1989; 993; 1997) which developed market approaches to schooling through parental choice, encouraged competition between schools and focused on ethnic minority access through changes to admissions policies – generally known as 'dezoning'.

In this context, governments of New Zealand have recognised that future success and prosperity depend on a high skill/high wage economy. This high skill/high wage 'magnet' economy is based on the view that the more technologically advanced a society becomes, the greater is the demand for technical, scientific and professional workers who require extensive periods of formal education and training. Also there is a need to maintain and update the skills of those in skilled and semi-skilled jobs.

The establishment, in 1990, of the New Zealand Qualifications Authority (NZQA) was a response to these visions and demands. The government saw, and still sees, the NZQA and its NQF as a 'vital part of an education system which will serve employers' and students' needs into the 21st century' (New Zealand Ministry of Education 1997). Relationships between education and the market and these with employment, education and training have been defined as essentially about human resources. In particular, questions about certification and the general qualifications discourses appear as extraneous to political controversies. In this depoliticised arena, debates focus on the role and importance of certain types of permeabilities between education and training. The socio-economic and political context in which they occur has become marginalised.

This is apparent in various policy documents. A policy paper relating to schools qualifications for 16–19 year olds, for example (New Zealand Ministry of Education 1998), outlines the human resource needs society requires from schooling. Earlier documents (New Zealand Ministry of Education 1993; 1997) point to the types of skills and competencies which schools boards and college authorities must take into account when developing policies. However, the primary aims of education and training go beyond the human resource needs of the state. Also important are personal development, the intertwining of education and training of the citizen, socialisation as well as enhancing employability, and the capacity to create self-employment (European Commission 1997).

Like many other countries, therefore, and with the support of the World Bank and the monitoring of the Organisation for Economic Co-operation and Development (OECD), New Zealand has forefronted the importance of human resource development as a strategy for improving competitiveness in the global economy. Reports by the OECD and other agencies have highlighted New Zealand's relatively poor performance – low participation rates in education and training, especially amongst 16–19 year olds, a poorly qualified workforce (with 25 per cent of the population leaving school without formal qualifications) and a low commitment in industry to ongoing and systematic training. This was the result of a society in the 1970s and early 1980s with a high standard of living, protected internal and external markets and a very low level of unemployment, having little incentive for education and training beyond the initial and secondary school. Further, normative assessment systems, which seemed automatically to fail a large proportion of young people (Lingard *et al.* 1993), gave little encouragement to view further education and training as attainable or even as relevant.[1]

As the government stated,

> if New Zealand is to prosper, we must be internationally competitive. We must produce goods and services which not only measure up against imports, but which achieve their share of world markets. With limited economic power and physical resources, we must look to the skills and knowledge of our people to feed innovation and improvements in productivity. In a world marked by rapid technological change, intellectual skills will increasingly command a premium over manual ones (New Zealand Ministry of Education 1997).

In 1991 the NZQA was established in an attempt to co-ordinate the integration of academic, intellectual and manual, vocational, skills. The NZQA took responsibility for what had previously been a number of independent examination and certification agencies with responsibilities for different sectors of post-compulsory education and training. The remit of the NQZA was to ensure that all qualifications – the objective recognition of learning having taken place – have a purpose and a relationship to each other. Further, it was intended to ensure that there was a flexible system for gaining qualifications with recognition of competence already achieved. In addition, a system of standards was established with quality in provision and outcome for the learner, to ensure post-school educational and vocational qualifications, to maintain international comparability and to administer national examinations in the school and post-school sectors.

> As skills and knowledge grow in importance, so does the way we recognise that learning has taken place, skills have been acquired and a standard achieved. Qualifications provide such recognition. When students and employers invest in education, it is important that their choice of qualification is made on the basis of sound information. They need to be clear about what skills and knowledge the qualification recognises, about the quality inherent in the qualification and how one qualification compares with another (New Zealand Ministry of Education 1997).

To address the problems of dovetailing different qualifications systems, the NZQA is currently, after eight years, developing the NQF. It includes in its coverage the 'portability' (transferability) of all learning from senior secondary school, through trades, technician and professional levels as well as higher education. It is intended to facilitate the transfer of credits from one qualifications provider to another, so that credits towards a desired qualification may be accumulated easily.

Although the NZQA and its NQF were popular politically, universities only joined the proposed Framework in 1994. Even in 1998, accreditation of universities is the responsibility of the New Zealand Vice-Chancellors' Committee. The Committee had argued that the necessary preparatory work prior to joining could 'not be avoided, or rushed', before universities participated with colleges and other institutions in a NQF. In this way, universities have maintained an independence from the structural, curricular and procedural constraints of the NZQA, and in so doing they have placed the efficacy and relevance of the NQF of New Zealand under considerable pressure.

By being allowed to maintain their own curricula, the autonomy of universities may have been protected *pro tem*. However, it is anticipated that, in time, different curricula will be built into the structure of the NQF, so that more universalised standards come to serve as the basis for articulation within and between the parts of the NQF and curriculum development in higher education. A demand for a single co-ordinated system (from school, through formal education to higher education) with one national standards-setting body is part of current policy discussions. Whether it becomes part of policy formation depends on the role played by the university sector.

Currently, the NQF comprises five elements: a coherent framework of eight levels encompassing all post-compulsory education (but excluding the university sector) and training plus a unit standards approach with each unit containing a number of learning outcomes and performance criteria. The unit standards have a credit rating to provide currency and facilitate credit accumulation towards new national qualifications. The NQF also comprises assessment methods that ensure performance against the standards contained in each unit and a system that enables assessment to occur outside formal education or training environments through the recognition of prior learning. Finally, it consists of a framework which has a common quality management system which applies to all learning situations to guarantee the acceptability of assessment across diverse sectors.

> Qualifications policy is part of a package which ensures that education and training are of high quality. The package includes policies for ensuring the quality of education providers; how those providers are established, managed and funded; and specific programmes such as those for developing industry training and for training people with low or no qualifications (New Zealand Ministry of Education 1997).

The Green Paper on the NQF (New Zealand Ministry of Education 1997) – the first policy review of the NQF since its inception in 1991 – notes that qualifications consist of tailored packages of units normally determined by professional and industry groups. These groups ensure the quality, credibility, portability and structural soundness of that qualification package. Traditional barriers which limited the delivery of courses leading to particular national qualifications to specific sector providers have been removed. For example, polytechnics and private training establishments can now offer degrees, which were previously the domain of universities only. The pathways for all learners in the upper secondary school and beyond are the same. The emphasis is no longer on courses but on flexible programmes to meet individual learning needs and learning styles. Standards are open to assessment through provider provision, on the job or workplace assessment and recognition of prior learning.

Fundamental to the NQF, therefore, is the commitment to removing any distinction between 'educational credentials' and work-based qualifications. The NQF does not contain a unique secondary school qualification. The unit standards available to school children can build towards national certificates and national diplomas.[2]

As in any education system there is concern for quality assurance. This has been addressed through interlocking mechanisms: through the clear definition of learning outcomes and the unit standards approach; through registration of private training establishments to ensure management and financial viability; through accreditation of all providers, including workplace providers, who wish to assess against standards, to ensure fair, valid and consistent assessment; through moderation, to ensure national consistency or assessment; and through audit to ensure quality assurance processes are in place and are working (Hood 1995).

The foregoing has outlined how, in New Zealand, the qualifications framework has become central to a specialist discourse. It requires of its participants, practitioners and detractors alike, highly rational, scientific and technically advanced articulations. It has become symbolic of an education and training system in a society undergoing political and economic change. Whilst such unified, co-ordinated systems are not without merit, undoubtedly, their rationales have in fact little to do with emancipation and liberation – the end goals, some would argue (Carr & Kemmis 1986; Ewart 1991), of education. Rather, their resonances are to the political and economic crises which existed in New Zealand in the 1980s and gave rise to a need to restructure welfare generally and education (Lauder et al. 1994) in particular. Such analysis is, of course, not unique to New Zealand. Scotland's qualification structures may also be understood through similar socio-political discourses.

The Scottish Qualifications Authority

The development of NQF systems in Britain – England and Wales and Scotland – can be analysed through Habermasian constructs. During the early 1970s, the four-fold increase in oil prices gave rise to fiscal constraints in all areas of the economy. Concerns were raised about the extra cost imposed on industry by the burgeoning apprenticeship schemes. Captains of industry argued that the cost of training labour ought to be part of the state's education bill (Hargreaves 1993). Thus waged labour ought to be trained outside the industrial or commercial enterprise. Mr Callaghan, the Prime Minister in 1976 and, later, Mrs Thatcher, Prime Minister after 1979, proclaimed the importance of a vocational element in schooling. Mrs Thatcher introduced a technical and vocational initiative in the secondary school and the programme has led to many others. That philosophy formed the basis of the co-ordination and, where possible, unification of education and training. Post-1979 education's resonances were with work, vocation and employment.

The development of NQFs in England and Wales and the Scottish Qualification Authority (SQA) with modular approaches to teaching, learning and assessment are, like the NZQA, good examples of the way a society turns to highly technical structures in times of socio-political or economic crises. In Scotland, with a population of 5 million – similar to the population of New Zealand – most people (60 per cent) live in just 20 per cent of the land area, around the 'central belt' between Glasgow, to the west, and Edinburgh, to the east. In the past, heavy industry, ship-building and coal-mining were the main sources of employment; but in recent years, especially in the late 1970s and 1980s, foreign investment has been encouraged and technology-based industries have been developed. In addition, employment in the Scottish oil industry and jobs in tourism have flourished. Whisky, agriculture and forestry enterprises also provide substantial sources of employment. Yet Scotland has had, and continues to have – in relation to the rest of Britain – comparatively high rates of unemployment. However, its school children have tended to remain at school comparatively longer than pupils elsewhere in Britain (McPherson & Raab 1989).

It is in this economic and social context that debates have focused upon the importance of developing a relevant system for education and training. Since 1985 the national training system had been under the auspices of the Scottish Vocational Education Council (SCOTVEC), a body created some years after recommendations in policy guidelines on post-compulsory education for 16–18 year olds had been published by the Scottish Office (Scottish Education Department 1979). During the period 1979–85 there was intense discussion about the structure and nature of the educational and training needs of 16–18 year olds and young adults, which resulted in changes to the Scottish Certificate of Education (SCE) (Standard Grade, taken at 16, and Higher Grade taken at 17 and 18). In some schools SCE subjects were replaced by modules of the new (Scottish) National Certificate, administered by SCOTVEC.

In light of the momentum for change, the separation of the vocational from the academic curriculum and qualifications was becoming 'irrelevant'. This view was particularly visible in demands made by many schools for 'relevance' in curriculum and assessment reform. Employment opportunities proliferated in information technology-related work and skills acquisition. Transferability of such skills was demanded both by employers and by politicians.

Educational institutions, therefore, were required to produce students with appropriate skills. In this way the focus of education changed from formal academic qualifications (which were not attained by over 40 per cent of the school-leaving population) to a more vocationally-orientated structure.

In 1997, the demands for 'relevance' led to the merger of SCOTVEC with the Scottish Examinations Board (SEB), previously the Board validating Standard and Higher Grades syllabi, to form the Scottish Qualifications Authority (SQA). Thus the merger of these two bodies is indicative of the political and educational debate which has taken place during the last decade.

Recently, the Dearing Committee (in England) and Garrick Committee (in Scotland) reviewed qualifications for 16–19 year olds and emphasised, once again, the importance of communication and numeracy for progression through the education and training system. The Skills Audit, for the Department for Education and Employment (DfEE) in England and Wales and the Cabinet Office, contained a chapter devoted to the basic skills of literacy, oracy and numeracy plus others, including the ability to speak a foreign language (Department for Education and Employment 1996). Whilst there is some agreement that the attainment of key skills is the responsibility primarily of the education system as opposed to employers, there is also an awareness that the formal examinations system is failing many children. In England and Wales, in the summer 1996 examinations, 9 per cent of the age group were not entered for Mathematics and 9 per cent were not entered for English.

In light of these concerns and the stated need for improved economic performance, skills, competencies and qualifications, and the articulations between and within these, become increasingly important (Hart & Shipman 1991). Further, as an individual's labour market prospects appear to be harmed by low levels of numeracy and literacy, it has become important to support the development and integration of skills and competencies (especially in literacy and numeracy) within a highly developed and clearly articulated framework (Furlong & Raffe 1989).

To a great extent, Scotland's education and training system is seen as a success story. Its approach is said to have minimised the more technicist approaches to modularised learning that are inherent in the system of National Certificates in England and Wales. Perhaps this is due to the more dualist approach taken by SCOTVEC, and now by SQA, whereby students achieve qualifications through study and through work, on a day-a-week or block release basis. Raffe (1991) detects a need for this dual approach to the definition of quality because, he argues, the further education service has multiple customers. Some customers, such as the Local Enterprise Councils, employers and higher education providers recruiting from full-time courses, will be interested in outputs in terms of qualifications achieved, while others, such as employers sending their trainees and employees to college or students themselves, may be more interested in progressing levels of achievement – 'value addedness'.

The development of quality in the Scottish system has therefore progressed through many initiatives and has focused on definitions of 'quality standards' consonant with the needs of industry, agencies of Scottish enterprise, SCOT-VEC and SQA itself and the Scottish Office. Internationally owned firms are an important part of the Scottish economy and together with indigenous firms, have increasingly committed themselves to developing and delivering 'quality services and products'. Colleges and, more recently, some secondary schools have therefore developed a service industry approach to complement their traditional public sector background. In so doing they have moved from their highly acclaimed academic traditions (McPherson & Raab 1989) towards a competence-based education.

There is a fear, however, that competency-based approaches with specific learning outcomes could lead to a deterioration of the education system as a whole. For example, there is concern that much of the value of learning might be lost if explicit outcomes are required. Commentators have valued student-centred approaches to learning and knowledge delineation and are concerned that these may be lost in the drive towards competency and outcomes-based education (OBE). What of critical reflection (Carr & Kemmis 1986), the basis of so much political, social and economic progress?

In light of the foregoing, it is argued that there is a need to focus discussion and, eventually, educational policy-making on more appropriate ways of using the strengths and opportunities of both competence-orientated, OBE approaches and the more open-ended, reflective and, generally, academic approaches to learning. This discussion is germane in the international arena, but it is particularly relevant to current educational developments and to the socio-political transformation in South Africa.

Current situation in South Africa

Education and training systems are the backbone of any learning society, and President Mandela has defined South Africa as such a society. In South Africa current policies for education and training view co-ordination and integration as an answer to pressures brought on by globalisation (see Chapter 8 of this volume). Indeed, renewed concerns with education can be seen in the plethora of official and unofficial commissions in South Africa. The Report of the National Commission of Higher Education (NCHE) and the ensuing Green and White Papers (1995) on higher education, along with government policy documents for education (Education Act 1996), further and adult basic education and training (Department of Education 1997f) have all supported the development of a NQF with its integrated approach to education and training, under the umbrella of a South African Qualifications Authority (SAQA).[3]

The SAQA has both developmental and implementational functions. In terms of the former, it oversees the development of the NQF, formulates criteria for registration of standards-setting bodies and qualification bodies and accredits monitoring bodies. The South African NQF is intended to provide opportunities for access to further and higher education, accreditation and recognition for prior learning, flexibility in gaining and accumulating credits to achieve qualifications, as well as enabling the development of possibilities for horizontal and vertical mobility and for linkages between institutions.

However, a critique of the system, even as it develops, has focused upon issues of insufficient access, insufficient support for horizontal and vertical mobility in the system, difficulty of movement between one sector and another, little articulation between institutions, no qualifications structure to give meaning to qualifications and a lack of recognition for prior learning.

In terms of implementation, the role of SAQA is to oversee each provider developing its own curriculum – so that not every institution will have identical curricula. This has been seen as crucially important for the autonomy of universities, a sector where historically black universities (HBUs) have welcomed the NQF but previously white universities have emphasised its 'voluntary' nature. Policy-makers and implementers alike have noted, as in New Zealand, that it would be 'inappropriate to rush the process'.

Conclusion: globalising qualifications frameworks?

The relevance for South Africa of the New Zealand experience in developing a NQF is profound. So too is the situation in Scotland. It has been seen that an integrated approach to education and training has been adopted in New Zealand and Scotland and is now being developed in South Africa. The global nature of these concerns means that policy initiatives in New Zealand and Scotland shed light on the rationales for and origins of SAQA and the emerging education and training policy in South Africa.

The South African qualifications system has resonances with the systems in Scotland and New Zealand. Indeed, there are historical antecedents to these resonances. All three educational systems have been influenced by the educational work of the Church of Scotland. Both the Cape Education Department and the New Zealand Education Department were established by Church of Scotland ministers (Clarkson 1994). Education policy-makers in both Wellington and Cape Town refer to Rev. Murray as a founder of their administration. Further, in the first state-commissioned South African discussion document on the NQF, approximately 70 per cent of references were to the NZQA (by then 3 years old) and 20 per cent to SCOTVEC – the remaining 10 per cent referred to the English National Council for Vocational Qualifications (NCVQ) (Phillips 1993).

However, South Africa has many elements of exceptionalism. In particular the central role of the trade union movement in the African National Congress's (ANC's) policy formulations, allied to the huge negative impact of Apartheid education and training on today's adults, has driven current debates concerning the role for the NQF. This is especially important in the context of demands for equity and redress in education and training policy. However, in South Africa as elsewhere, how are demands for education and training policies to respond to the market-driven needs of employers and of capital?

In addition, the specificity of South Africa is seen most profoundly in relations between central government and the nine provinces. The national government has responsibility for higher education, whereas the provinces have responsibility for general education, including colleges and the formal education sector. The national–provincial tension provides a framework for understanding the sectoral division between higher education and formal-education/school-based education and the various networks of influence over policy-making (Donn 1995). Whereas central government's policies may well be influenced by demands for equity and redress, those originating at a provincial level have different agendas, not least being those derived from the contentious political arenas of the National Party in the Western Cape and Inkatha Freedom Party in KwaZulu-Natal. It remains a key concern to examine how policy-makers in the nine provinces define their educational agendas, for the form and content of the policies they generate in relation to the NQF will be addressed by that definition.

Although the situation is different, centre–local (or provincial) tensions occur also in Scotland, where education policy-making has become more centrally located. In recent years, there have been pressures through policy initiatives from both the national centre (Westminster) and the Scottish Office Education and Industry Department (SOEID) which have promulgated alternative (and conflicting) visions of education. The Scottish Qualifications Authority emerged from a Westminster-defined conception of 'the problem' (paucity in educational provision for communication and literacy and a general lack of transferability in skills) and its 'solutions' (opportunities for access to formal education and higher education; accreditation and recognition for prior learning; flexibility in skill acquisition and qualifications – the NQF).

In Scotland and South Africa, and in New Zealand, there has been a thorough critique of the existing educational system. In all three countries, for different socio-political and economic reasons, the critique focused upon issues of insufficient access to formal and higher education; insufficient support for horizontal and vertical mobility within the system; difficulty of movement between one sector and another; little articulation between institutions; weak qualifications structures failing to give meaning to qualifications and a lack of recognition for prior learning. Qualifications frameworks are intended to remedy these problems.

In contrast to the German and Dutch systems,[4] the Scottish, New Zealand and South African qualifications systems are being formulated within a marketised, commodification-based vision of competency and training. They appear to confirm worries that highly specialist, discourse-driven and expert-led innovations do little to empower, liberate or emancipate populations. Indeed, such innovations may well disenfranchise populations from the policy and planning contexts whilst demanding of the same populations attendance and support through their participation and practice.

Given that situation, one might ask how far the New Zealand and Scottish experiences can inform and help to evaluate the efficacy of the South African qualifications system? Does a NQF provide a potential answer to the perceived economic-political and educational needs and challenges? Or are such frameworks merely an indication of a society undergoing crisis? It would be worrying, indeed, if, at the time South Africa adopts an NQF, that should be the case.

Endnotes

1. However, the situation has improved considerably. The retention of students to Form 7 (the final year of schooling) has improved from 15 per cent in 1980 to more than 50 per cent in 1995. By 1996 only 16 per cent of pupils left school without formal qualifications and a relatively high percentage of the population (30 per cent) now (1998) attains tertiary education.

2. Indeed, a few national certificates could be completed at school. In response to significant concerns about the absence from the NQF of national school examinations, the NZQA proposed that school certificates, university bursaries and scholarships should provide credit towards the new Qualifications in Educational Achievement – which in October 1996 was registered as an NQF qualification.

   A new national certificate recognises significant achievement across a range of learning areas, including communication and numeracy skills, and is expected to become a major qualification in secondary schools. Further, the Board of the NZQA resolved that national school examinations should yield NQF credit towards the National Certificate in Educational Achievement, thereby allowing school children to decide whether they want to be assessed through examinations, internal assessment or a combination of assessment methods, and allowing these children to work towards achieving one or more of the national certificates, other qualifications assessed against unit standards, and qualifications gained through external examinations.

3. The construction of qualifications and rules for the combination of credits is currently being developed by SAQA. But all education and training qualifications will be registered by SAQA at the appropriate level on the NQF.

4. Although the focus for this paper has been on Anglophone countries, one should not underestimate the relevance of other countries' qualifications systems to an understanding of those in South Africa. In Germany and Holland qualifications authorities and qualifications systems are being developed in an attempt to maintain and sustain long-term economic growth whilst making explicit commitments to widespread access for all.

6

Political roots of the debate about the integration of education and training

ZELDA GROENER

The notion of the integration of education and training has become a cornerstone of policy in South Africa, yet debate continues about the nature, form and implications of this policy commitment. Critical questions central to understanding this debate are the following: Where has the notion of integration originated? Why was this notion considered important? What was the political rationale undergirding this notion? What did its proponents hope to achieve by integrating education and training? This chapter will address such questions, by analysing the political roots of the debate about the integration of education and training in South Africa.

A research investigation was conducted into the struggles around the notion of integration during the early 1990s, tracing the early genealogy of the debates (Groener 1997).[1] This chapter aims to illuminate a central contradiction which lies embedded in the early debates about the political rationale undergirding the notion of integrating education and training. The key political contradiction is that the integration of education and training was regarded as a means through which capitalism could be preserved and, at the same time, as a means through which socialism could be advanced.

The focus of research was on identifying the positions articulated by participants in the National Training Strategy Initiative (NTSI) during the period 1993–1994 when the NTSI conducted an investigation into a National Training Strategy (Groener 1997:226–302). Interviews with these participants revealed differing and conflicting perceptions of the political and economic rationale underlying the notion of the integration of education and training. These differences and conflicts were apparent not only among the representatives of participating stakeholders, but also among the representatives from the Congress of South African Trade Unions (COSATU) who were participating in the NTSI. They reflect the broader transitional struggles in South Africa and in the global economy. This chapter analyses the debate between those who promoted capitalism and those who promoted socialism in conceptualising the policy of integrating education and training.

Integrated education and training: Contest and consensus

Research into the conflicts surrounding COSATU's adult education and training policy proposals, particularly in relation to the notion of 'integrated education and training', was instructive in uncovering the history of current policy debate. The study revealed that the socialist underpinnings of COSATU's proposals became a major site of struggle. In particular, the socialist rationale underlying the notion of integrated education and training provoked intense conflict. There is clear evidence that COSATU's policy proposals, in general, were explicitly linked to their commitment to socialism. COSATU's policy proposals expressed this formal commitment in the following way: 'Our objectives in education and training should remain in line with our political vision (of the attainment of socialism) and we should ensure that skills acquired through education and training empower the working class to participate actively in shaping industrial, economic, social and political processes' (COSATU 1993:15).

Reflecting their socialist commitment, the empowerment of the working class and the restructuring of the economy provided the rationale for COSATU's conceptualisation of their policy proposals for integration. It can be inferred that integrated education and training was seen as a means through which the working class could be empowered.

The National Training Board (NTB) reported that COSATU cited Cuba as a model which linked adult basic education (ABE) to training: 'countries where ABE was linked to training e.g. Cuba; curricula frameworks; financing and costing; planning for large-scale programmes' (National Training Board 1994:5).

A COSATU representative elaborated the socialist rationale for integrated education and training in the following way:

> I think we would argue that it's a framework which, if implemented in the way in which its been argued, would assist and strengthen the hand of the working class tremendously in relation to (1) both access to education and training and high

levels of skill, (2) sort of eating away at the deskilling of a whole range of professions, (3) it would make provision for bringing into the labour market a whole range of [those] excluded from it, (4) it would make provision for giving credit for training and (5) by and large it would be able to, we would argue, improve the lot of the average worker tremendously, but (6) would also enable the next generation of workers coming to the education system to have much better opportunities to access a whole range of broader professions but also to be able to bridge and straddle those divisions between the head and the hand, mental and physical labour and so on. It virtually could be argued as taking forward the socialist cause, I suppose (Interview, 31 October 1994).

Among the members of the COSATU delegation to the NTSI, however, differences emerged around the ideological underpinnings for integrated education and training. Another COSATU representative gave a contrasting position, suggesting that the notion of integrated education and training was not explicitly socialist. He represented a more limited position which was promoted to obtain consensus from other parties in the NTSI:

It never became explicit. Clearly we were coming from very different agendas to the table. I mean the framework we were working on isn't necessarily restricted to a socialist one. The examples of what we were attempting…could very often [be pulled] from the Australian experience or New Zealand or Germany or a whole range of other national situations that people could identify with…the other examples we looked at were all examples of this kind of approach which was structured after either Germany was coming out of World War II, Australia developing its economy up to collapsing in the 60s etc. They were all national situations in which it was necessary to find a new way of structuring education and training systems. And we were arguing that this was South Africa's equivalent period and therefore one could look at those situations and pull out the major lessons. I think initially a lot of reticence had to do with the perception that we were propagating was some disguised communist plot…Partly because of the work that [the international comparator's group] were able to do, we were able to persuade people in the end that the framework we were talking about isn't one that is necessarily narrowly linked to a socialist economy. That in fact many of the more successful capitalist economies were built and developed on the basis of such an integrated system, but it did have to do at the very least with a social accord between government and labour and about the way in which you [proceeded under] the tripartite accord of government, capital and labour. I think that's the way in which we were able to bring people along.…and in the end it worked (Interview, 31 October 1994).

Here it becomes clear that Cuba's education and training system was not the only one which was cited by COSATU representatives as a potential model for South Africa. The New Zealand and Australian systems of integrated education and training were also held up as potential models. The direct influence of experience in these countries can be traced to participants in the National Union of Metalworkers of South Africa (NUMSA) Vocational Training Project and the COSATU Participatory Research Project (PRP), who learned about integrated systems of education and training when they studied training systems in different countries around the world. Among the countries visited were New Zealand, Australia and Germany.

Further probing of the origins and the ways in which COSATU adopted the notion of integrated education and training led another COSATU representative to reflect on the arbitrary nature of key influences on policy:

NUMSA starts in 1989 to say 'we've got to look at training'. So they get together the NUMSA Vocational Training Project, they get funding for it and they get together twenty-four shop stewards, all NUMSA. Adrienne is one of them, they go off. Adrienne happens to go to Australia. That is how it happened for me. I mean, that's the version that you know. She comes back. She's one of the few people who can write a report. So she writes the report.[unclear] Some people I know went to other places and came back but never filed a report. So Australia is in and the Australian Labour Movement. Various people favour it and that's how Alastair and Chris eventually get here. The issue – COSATU sets up a Participatory Research Programme because they understand that, this is my version of it, that if they are going to open up this issue they need capacity. So its about capacity-building (Interview, 16 December 1994).

Based on this evidence, it became apparent that some COSATU representatives promoted the notion of integrated education and training by citing the model of capitalist societies where institutionalised systems of integrated education and training are found. It appears, however, that they referred to these examples as a means of convincing other participants in the NTSI of the value of integrated education and training. As the COSATU representative said, if examples of Cuba or the Soviet Union were cited, 'people just go blank'. At the same time, this informant argued that some COSATU representatives constructed the notion of integrated education and training on the model of capitalist societies such as Australia and New Zealand. It appears that the fundamental differences between COSATU's rationale for integrated education and training, which was based on the Cuban socialist model, and the rationale based on the models of other capitalist countries, such as Australia, were never adequately problematised by the COSATU representatives. Hence, there is little clarity about which models or aspects of models of education and training drawn from different countries were ultimately adopted in their proposals.

That representatives drew on the models of both socialist and capitalist societies, however, which appears to have led to somewhat ambiguous and contradictory positions. A range of political positions underpinning policy may be discerned among the COSATU representatives as follows. First, there were COSATU representatives whose model of an integrated system of education and training was premised on the Cuban socialist experience. Second, there were those COSATU representatives who maintained the socialist commitment, but, as a strategy to win over other stakeholders, quoted examples of capitalist societies where education and training were integrated. Third, there were COSATU representatives who actually drew on the experiences of those capitalist countries to construct a socialist notion of integrated education and training. Fourth, there were COSATU representatives who based the notion of an integrated system of education and training solely on the experiences of capitalist countries.

While there were differences between the COSATU representatives concerning the political rationale underpinning the notion of integrated education and training, the perceived socialist stance of COSATU was opposed by members of the business sector who participated in the NTSI. A member of the business sector proposed the notion of an integrated *approach to* education and training as opposed to the notion of an integrated *system of* education and training:

> Well, you have to be very careful. If you look at the documents, from our point of view, we've never said the integration of education and training. We've said an integrated approach to education and training. And the difference is that, again, on this assumption, business will become a quasi-school sector, providing education. That's not necessarily true at all. The integrated approach and the qualifications framework and the articulation of standards at levels to which we can all relate our education and training so that they have an equivalent value in terms of a national certificate is the vehicle that we see as the one which can provide for integration, for an integrated approach. It seems to us that other people understand it to mean general education in your training programmes at work. Now that's a fiction, it's a nonsense (Interview, 9 November 1994).

While strong opposition to COSATU's position was expressed by the business sector, this informant also observed a convergence of interests between the trade unions and the business sector. This convergence, the informant argues, undermines the dichotomy between capitalism and socialism in a shared commitment to productivity:

> I think that the union's ends, COSATU's ends certainly, are useful means for business. And let me elaborate that for a minute. A person like Adrienne Bird,

massively influential, has been able, to a large degree, to lead people from business to accept that broad banding, skills formation, job enrichment are all very worthwhile ends for business but that they're in fact, means, useful means. Flatter hierarchy is another one; flatten the hierarchy. Those are means to business's ends. So skill formation and ready access to a broad education base and a strong skills base is a means to business's ends, which is a multi-skilled work-force. The broad banding, the flatter hierarchy is one means – greater participation is one means towards a new workplace culture which is accepting and encouraging of innovations – the kind of innovations that we have to have in order to respond and implement new technologies and new ways of organising work. We don't have the multi-skilled work-force. If we don't have the work-force participating in decision-making around those kinds of objectives, we don't develop that innovative capacity. O.K. Without innovative capacity we're not productive enough to compete. So, its the means-end argument. But the means-end is production-focused. So the ideological argument between socialism and capitalism is, to a large degree, dead in the water. We're post that analysis, I think (Interview, 9 November 1994).

Socialism or capitalism?

The interviews reflect the intense conflict around the political rationale underlying the notion of integrating education and training. At the heart of these conflicts lies the struggle between the values and principles of capitalism and socialism. As the evidence demonstrates, some COSATU representatives admitted that they explicitly declined to wage an open struggle for socialism within the NTSI, yet others placed socialism on the agenda in a low-key way. One representative we have already noted highlighted the dominance of capitalist discourse, and the constraints it placed on the explicit promotion of socialism: 'I think initially a lot had to do with the perceptions that what we were propagating was some disguised communist plot in some sense' (Interview, 31 October 1994).

In this light, another COSATU representative described how, in a surreptitious way, she tried to make socialist gains in the NTSI:

I think that for a short while, right at the beginning, we tried to see whether we could get some kind of way where we could win. It became clear that we weren't going to win because at that time there was even no RDP. There was just COSATU's position on growth through redistribution. And then at the same time socialistic economies were collapsing like skittles all over the world. So the ideological battle – we were on unfavourable terrain. We've captured some of the terrain now with the RDP. But as you can see this terrain shifts and it gets redefined. So I think that that wasn't the main focus of the NTB anyway. It was meant to be a reference work because if you agree on the economic model or development model, all sorts of other things become clearer (Interview, 31 October 1994).

Another COSATU representative revealed the tension between promoting a general political vision and translating it into specific educational proposals:

I don't think you'll find the word written anywhere, and in a sense we didn't see that placing that on the agenda as part of the reason why we were participating in particular. We saw the task as a lot more restricted till we were informed by a different framework, but the nature of the economy that is to be developed, is essentially a political issue which needs to be fought out between political parties and between labour and capital etc. and we didn't really see the participation in this working group as a battleground for that. Clearly we were talking about a specific issue around which people would come to the table with very different positions, informed by their particular vision of a future society. Now clearly, the COSATU delegates were informed by COSATU's vision which is a move towards expanding as much as possible with the socialist elements in the broad national political economy, but there never was a debate about [it] ... (Interview 31 October 1994).

Another COSATU official reflected the extent to which policy positions subtly shift and are remoulded through debate at key points of the process:

We came out with our own ideas. Like most people always argue to say whether you have a blueprint of socialism or what socialism actually is. I think that within the National Training Board when we came out with some of these ideas ... we thought them through and we went there to fight in order to defend them. Some of them were actually saying that ... we are sitting with a communist plot or a socialist plot but they couldn't come out with [it], they couldn't come out clearly. And whether it is a socialist approach which [we] endorsed is something else.

You must also understand the status of the report as well because in terms of the National Training Strategy process, the report normally was to come out and to be tabled for comments by various stakeholders. After the comment, it would be tabled to the Minister and then the Minister would use the report to effect changes to the Education and Manpower Act [which] will be tabled in Parliament and become law. But because of the processes which emerged and the implication of some of the proposals, especially the integration of education and training, one strong recommendation which came out was that the report [not go through] the formal process. We had a fear that it might be thrown out at some stage, and already sabotage had emerged because if you look at the report written by the Chairperson of the National Training Board to the then Minister, Minister Wesse, where we had put emphasis on education and training he went out and wrote a report that talked about vocational education and training [unclear], something completely different from what we had. We felt that maybe because these ideas are far-reaching, the report should be a discussion document which gets tabled at the National Education and Training Forum (NETF) because we felt that this serves as a [more satisfactory forum for] discussion ... around the integration of education and training. The NETF is a forum where we thought maybe these ideas will be further explored and developed although we thought that the document, at an initial stage, will be tabled at the training sub-committee of the NETF and then the plenary of the NETF. [An] other reason was that maybe the NETF, the manner in which it was structured, will give an opportunity for these ideas to be further debated because there we have the universities and technikons which never participated or gave any input into some of the discussions although they've raised quite a lot of substantial interest (Interview, 4 November 1994).

This informant reflects the difficulty of explicitly promoting a socialist blueprint, given the dominance of capitalist discourse. COSATU representatives were cautious and apprehensive about explicitly promoting socialist ideologies and values, so, on the one hand, he does not deny that he engaged in the struggle for socialism, yet he does not admit it either, arguing that they 'came out with their own ideas'. It is unclear whether, and the extent to which, these ideas, to which he was referring, were socialist. The informant regarded the NETF, rather than the NTSI, as the appropriate forum where more explicit political struggles were waged.

Instead the aim was to achieve more limited gains in terms of promoting socialist ideals in the NTSI report. An illustration of such struggles against the dominance of a traditional free market model was conveyed by another COSATU representative:

We succeeded in holding back a free market position from dominating because a free market development model would have resulted in all sorts of other positions on education and training. The old NTS is located within a free market, within a free market development model, which is why it sees training as the responsibility of the employer and sees the unemployed as a sideline activity. So we succeeded in holding that back. I think that is often overlooked, it is not understood that we had to fight a battle (Interview, 31 October 1994).

Moreover, despite the position of those COSATU representatives who, in the face of much adversity, explicitly saw themselves as conducting a struggle for socialism, there were other stakeholders who denied that such a struggle had ensued within the NTSI forum. One business representative reflected the dominant discourse – hostility to socialist values in a new context:

I think the debate is alive and well and residing in the ranks of COSATU as well as a number of people who are now in the formal sector. They have a vision for a socialist society. I think that if the Nationalists did not dispute the short-sightedness of that kind of notion, then we're all blind. We will perpetuate the mistakes until eternity. But it seems as though the new government, at least until this stage, has understood what kinds of imperatives exist in a modernising economy which is intent on growing (Interview, 9 November 1994).

Grand compromise?

The contradictions evident in the COSATU policy for integrating education and training reflect their ambivalent position in a context of globalisation.

> COSATU doesn't know what its own socialist position is at the moment. I think, no, its a fair question but its almost one that cannot be answered. I think that COSATU is being pulled, like the rest of the world. They understand crucially about global markets, global economics, global competitiveness. They understand that technology is going to create a core of highly skilled, mostly temporary workers. And that is their constituency. So they're saying that these people are going to lose their jobs unless they can be upskilled (Interview, 15 December 1994).

By the end of the NTSI process, therefore, a fundamental contradiction emerged in the notion of the integration of education and training, understood in terms of its contribution to advancing socialism or to serving the needs of the global capitalist economy.

> So from COSATU's point of view the end [the consequence of education and training] could be that people participate fully in the democracy, that they can build a socialist society. For business, it could be to strengthen capitalism (Interview, 9 November 1994).

What has become evident from these in-depth interviews is that this contradiction was found not only between COSATU and other role players, such as business, but within the ranks of COSATU itself. Contradictions in COSATU's objectives for integrating education and training created the aperture for the dominance of capitalist discourse.

Conclusion

This chapter has highlighted conflicting positions between different stakeholders, within a single group, and identified similarities between apparently opposing stakeholders in different groups, in the early debate around the integration of education and training. While dispute occurred around the notion of integration *per se*, around the approach to integration and around underlying principles, a great deal of consensus was apparent in the deliberations of the NTSI forum.

Exploring the political roots of the debate around the integration of education and training therefore reveals that there is little inherently socialist in the principles underpinning the notion, despite COSATU's formal position. The collapse of authoritarian socialist societies, the shift towards a liberal democracy in South Africa, the dominance of the free market model and the growing demands of the global economy set the stage for COSATU to compromise the fundamental political values underlying their initial proposals. At the same time, the chapter exposes some contradictions which lie embedded in the political roots of the debate. The implications for contemporary debate and the broad thrust of the new qualifications framework are that there may be little difference between the South African version and the models drawn so uncritically from capitalist societies.

Given current trends, it is likely that global economic needs will continue to shape education and training in South Africa, but at the same time, the struggle for equity continues in the political arena. The contradictions between these political and economic needs set the stage for continuing struggles around the notion of integrated education and training.

Endnote

1. This investigation was a central component of my doctoral research, conducted during the period 1993–4.

7

Teachers, Curriculum 2005 and the education policy-making process

GLENDA KRUSS

When the Minister of Education, Sibusiso Bengu, announced the framework and philosophy for a new curriculum for the South African education system in April 1997, many teachers and educators were unprepared and rather vague about the new outcomes-based curriculum they were due to implement in four standards (or grades) by January 1998. Many educators had little knowledge or understanding of how the new curriculum would be underpinned by the National Qualifications Framework (NQF), which had been adopted as the central mechanism for integrating education and training through specifying learning in terms of nationally and internationally accepted outcomes.

A central tenet of emergent education policy in the period of transition is that the integration of education and training is desirable and, indeed, necessary to further the dual goals of economic growth and development, and of equity and redress. The education policy framework promoted in the *White Paper on Education and Training* (WPET) of 1995 is based on a vision that all individuals must 'have access to and succeed in lifelong education and training of good quality' (Department of Education 1995a), to meet the social and economic challenges facing South Africa. The WPET proposes to address the demand for equity by promoting access for all to education of quality, and proposes to meet the country's human resource development needs by promoting a new form of high quality education and training. This is to be achieved through initiating a system of qualifications which encourages further or ongoing education and training, and through changing the status and nature of learning away from its academic orientation to prepare learners more directly for the world of work (Christie 1997; De Clercq 1997).

With the NQF proposals having emerged from the 'training' lobby, much of the policy debate after 1994 centred on the vocational dimensions of the NQF and implications for non-formal education, adult basic education and training (ABET) and literacy (McGrath 1997b). However, the pace of development of the NQF has intensified since mid-1996, with the elaboration of the WPET's framework and principles in the form of the new outcomes-based education (OBE) curriculum for the formal schooling system.

A great deal of concern has been expressed by teachers and educators at the rapid pace at which this new curriculum policy has been developed, and the ambitious proposed time line for curriculum and materials development and implementation through the programme of Curriculum 2005 (Govender *et al.* 1997; Jansen 1997). Such concerns and widespread ignorance exist amongst those scheduled to implement the new curriculum policy, despite the Department of Education's widely professed commitment to a 'fully participatory process of curriculum development and trialing in which the teaching profession, teacher educators, subject advisors and other learning practitioners play a leading role along with academic subject specialists and researchers' (Department of Education 1997c; 1997e).

What is the nature of the education policy development process around Curriculum 2005 and what is the role of teachers in the policy-making process? Through a critical analysis of the model of policy-making currently in use in the new Department of Education, this paper raises questions about who is participating in the process and how policy-making is occurring in practice. What are the implications for teachers specifically, and for curriculum change in general? These questions form the focus of this chapter.

Conceptualising the education policy-making process

Conceptualising education policy and the policy process has become a field of academic enquiry in its own right (Ball 1990; Ball 1994; Prunty 1985; McNay & Ozga 1985). In South Africa, a vigorous academic and political debate around the nature of education policy began from 1990 (Badat 1991; Kallaway 1997). For the purposes of this paper, a distinction will be drawn between two common conceptual models of the education policy process.

The first is known as a 'rationalist' model of policy-making. It assumes that policy-making is essentially a rational process, which operates through classic steps, from formulation through to implementation. The educational problem is seen as one which requires technical solutions. Policies are seen as blueprints which exist prior to action, and which are implemented on the external world through a controlled process. The process is assumed to be a consensual one.

The second, 'political', model of policy-making typically begins from the assumption that policy is 'the authoritative allocation of values', and, hence, that policy-making is essentially a political activity (Prunty 1985). In this model, understanding power relations, conflict and contestation is crucial to understanding the nature of policy. Policy analysts who adopt a 'political' model are critical of the notion that implementation is a matter of automatically following a fixed policy text and putting legislation 'into practice' (Bowe & Ball 1992).

Ranson's work illustrates this 'political' or 'values' approach. He proposes that policies 'have a distinctive and formal purpose for organisations and governments: to codify and publicise the values which are to inform future practice and thus encapsulate prescriptions for reform' (Ranson 1995:440). Hence, policy is essentially contested, intrinsically political and necessarily a temporal process, involving issues of task and people. Ranson raises two apparently simple questions for investigation – how is policy to be formulated and carried into practice, and who is to be involved in the process?

Researchers and policy-makers have questioned the assumptions and analytical validity of the 'rationalist' model. Gordon et al. (1993:8) note that 'the power and survival ability of the "rational system" model is surprising, given that its assumptions have been undermined by empirical studies of the policy process, and that its predictive record is uneven'. They explain this durability with reference to its status as a normative model, and to the fact that it is often supported by policy-makers themselves.

The distinction between a 'rationalist' and a 'political' model of the policy-making process is a very broad one, which masks debate within each model amongst those who claim to offer superior explanatory frameworks. Bearing in mind that the distinction provides a very broad tool of analysis, it is useful for the purposes of this paper. The distinction between these two conceptual models will be used to interrogate the policy-making process for the new outcomes-based curriculum.

State and education policy-making

Since 1994, the government has attempted to forge a new hegemonic project which will ensure the conditions for capital accumulation and increase legitimacy through the incorporation of popular aspirations. The new hegemonic project is embodied in a contradictory policy which attempts to interweave social democratic values and rights with market-orientated values and rights.

Coming to political power after the elections on a wave of popular power, the government, led by the African National Congress (ANC), has increasingly shifted rightward, with the adoption of neo-liberal economic policies in the form of the Growth, Employment and Redistribution strategy (GEAR), as opposed to the redistributive policies of the Reconstruction and Development Programme (RDP) (Kallaway 1997). The ongoing tension between these two political imperatives is important in understanding educational politics. New forms of state governance have emerged and limited, gradual reforms have been initiated to address glaring inequalities in provision.

The ANC-led education ministry was faced with the legacy of an education system that was 'not working'. It was responsible for formulating education policy in the context of a declining economy, an under-skilled labour force, high unemployment rates and gross inequality based on race, gender and urban–rural divides. The global economic and social order, with the dominance of international capital and a neo-liberal ideology of the market promoting privatisation, deregulation and fiscal discipline, has exerted a strong pressure on policy. All contributed to a growing consensus among influential policy actors that economic development requires a generally well-educated population equipped with the competencies and skills required by the economy as well as the qualities of flexibility and the capacity to learn. In this context, there developed the commitment to a National Qualifications Framework (NQF) and a curriculum grounded in a philosophy of outcomes.

Education policy continues to be driven by political imperatives (Morphet 1997; Greenstein 1996). Education remains one of the key spheres for the state to meet the social and political demand for reconstruction, redistribution and equity, in a way that is highly visible.

In this conjuncture, education becomes a key site for meeting popular aspirations for redress and equity and, at the same time, for meeting the reformist economic agenda of capital. Consequently, education will continue to be a site of hegemonic contestation. Such structural conditions limit and constrain the form and nature of new education policy, and the policy-making process.

The education policy-making model of the ANC-led government

A defining feature of the education policy formulation process post-1994 is the constitutional division of powers and responsibility between the centre and the regional provinces. The national ministry is responsible for establishing a national policy framework of 'norms and standards' for education in general, and has direct control over education at universities and technikons. The nine provinces have power to legislate on and manage all aspects of basic schooling and education (including teacher education), subject to this national policy framework. The national Department of Education has argued that its role is to 'establish norms and standards with respect to curriculum frameworks, standards, exams and certification in terms of the National Education Policy Act 1996' (Department of Education 1997e).

The relationship between the centre and the provinces has been legislatively framed in these very general terms, leaving the precise nature open to a great deal of interpretation and variation. The political, economic and educational context and dynamics of each province differ, and will shape the way emergent national policy is mediated (Kruss 1996; Samoff 1996). The process of developing a new curriculum is one of the first instances where the division of powers and responsibilities between the centre and the provinces, between the ministries and the departments is being worked out in practice.

Prior to coming to power in 1994, the ANC prepared a key education policy proposal document in which, amongst other things, it established its vision of the policy process and the management of change.

> In democratic systems of government, policies must be arrived at through open social and political processes which involve all major stakeholders and interest groups and which citizens feel free to influence, for example, through the media. Implementation has to be steered by the public service or statutory bodies, but can only succeed if the affected organs of civil society feel that they are partners with a stake in the outcome (ANC 1994).

Two key principles have been promoted in education policy-making – that processes of policy-making should be open and transparent, and that there should be participation by stakeholders and role-players as representatives of civil society. This was enshrined in the WPET, in which the Ministry of Education invited 'the goodwill and active participation of all parents, teachers and other educators, students, community leaders, religious bodies, NGOs, academic institutions, workers, business, the media and development agencies, in bringing about the transformation we all seek' (Department of Education 1995:20).

In relation to curriculum development specifically, the WPET reiterated the commitment to a participatory and transparent process. It promised that proposals and critique would be 'requested from any persons or bodies with interests in the learning process and learning outcomes' (*ibid.* p. 27). The paragraph of the WPET reflecting this commitment has been widely and frequently quoted in documents publicising Curriculum 2005, becoming a mantra of policy intent (*ibid.* chapters 5 and 16).

Thus, the explicit model of the policy-making process proposed by the new state may be characterised as a 'political' one, which, in calling for participation and transparency, would recognise the political and contestatory nature of the process.

Bureaucrats versus stakeholders and role-players

To what extent has this 'political' model driven the curriculum policy-making process in practice, in line with the vision outlined above? The process was initiated centrally by the Ministry of Education, as the political authority, in July 1996. It was driven by a Curriculum Management Committee (CMC), consisting of representatives of the national and provincial education departments – the bureaucratic authority of the state. In line with ANC policy, the process was initiated as a participatory, open and transparent one. Policy documents and statements explicitly posed a contrast to past curriculum processes, which were claimed to have been dominated by technical experts and to have occurred outside of the public domain in a manner that was too 'secretive' (Department of Education 1997e).

The new policy discourse of 'major stakeholders and interest groups' was invoked, representing an attempt on the part of the new state to ensure legitimacy for new policy by involving civil society. Groups in civil society – teacher unions and professional associations, organised business and labour, educational bodies, NGOs and organised learners – were all defined as stakeholders in the curriculum development process. The policy-making model at work assumes that stakeholder representatives have the responsibility of keeping their membership informed and articulating their concerns.

A review of the process reveals that stakeholders were represented in the curriculum development process at key points. However, the nature of the relationship between stakeholders and education bureaucrats leads one to question whether there was not another, more implicit, model of policy-making operating alongside the explicit commitment to stakeholder participation.

The exigencies of government and the new macro policy framework of GEAR have promoted values of fiscal restraint and efficiency, which have influenced and constrained the new education bureaucrats. This has been reinforced by the enduring nature of bureaucratic power and practices. The educational officials and technocrats inherited from the Apartheid system are also concerned with control and efficiency of the system. Thus, a powerful grouping of what Greenstein (1996) calls new–old bureaucrats has emerged, who share institutional interests, regardless of their political affiliation. As Gordon *et al.* (1993:91) argue, government departments have 'deep structures of policy – the implicit collection of beliefs about the aims and intention of the departments and about the relevant actors who influence or benefit from the policy'. The curriculum policy process is increasingly driven by these new–old state bureaucrats and technical experts, who tend to work with an implicit 'rationalist' model of policy-making.

This becomes evident when we examine the process of developing an OBE curriculum. The first substantial step was in July 1996 with the establishment of eight Learning Area Committees (LACs). The LACs consisted of stakeholder representatives, together with representatives of both national and provincial departments of education. Their task was to take the critical outcomes developed by the South African Qualifications Authority (SAQA) and develop for each learning area, a detailed rationale, area outcomes and specific outcomes, which would drive the new curriculum. In addition, five co-ordinating committees were established to represent each of the five phases of the new system – Foundation, Intermediate, Senior, Further Education and Training (FET) and Adult Basic Education and Training (ABET).[1] A process of workshops, working groups and consultation was initiated across the country to develop the new curriculum.

The list of stakeholders invited to participate initially in LACs was broad and the education authorities made efforts to be inclusive and to ensure participation by organisations of civil society. Actual participation was not very broad, and nor did it run very deeply. Sieborger (1997:2) notes that stakeholder representation in the LACs operated at three hierarchical levels: the new–old bureaucrats from the national and provincial education departments were primary stakeholders, teacher organisations were secondary stakeholders, and non-governmental organisations (NGOs), professional associations, colleges, universities and technikons formed a third category, with fewer representatives.

Difficulties were experienced in identifying stakeholders and ensuring their presence at meetings. Stakeholders are not a monolithic group, but have conflicting interests, and differential ability to participate. Only a few stakeholders were sufficiently organised to participate consistently in the process. For instance, teacher organisations do not operate in the same way as the new–old bureaucrats responsible for curriculum development. Teachers' involvement in curriculum policy development is secondary to their main responsibility in the classroom. They have dispersed constituencies, and may not meet regularly to consult and inform members. Many representatives have in effect tended to participate as individuals, with little accountability to their organisations. Teacher organisations themselves may have different political interests, and may argue for conflicting positions or have differing resources and capacity to participate. Moreover, many teachers are not members of the teacher organisations represented as stakeholders.

The extent and depth of stakeholder participation, particularly of teachers, was thus problematic. Sieborger (*ibid.*) points to the 'progressive diminution of broad representivity as time went on'. By early 1997, the national centre took firm control of the process, which became increasingly state-driven. Rigid time lines for policy formulation and implementation were issued and declared to be non-negotiable. Many have argued that this time-frame is driven by national political interests, by a concern to have visible educational change prior to the 1999 elections (Govender *et al.* 1997). The politicised notion of time available for the policy process has profound implications for curriculum development.

Curriculum policy formulation was taken out of the hands of the stakeholder LACs in early 1997, when the Minister appointed a Technical Committee on Standards and Frameworks for Learning Programmes – a committee of experts ostensibly appointed to 'crystallise' the work done by the LACs.[2] One cannot quibble with the argument that a small group was required to integrate and make coherent work which had been undertaken by a large number of committees. However, the task is not simply technical, but has significant educational and political dimensions. International consultants from Canada and Scotland were brought in to support the Technical Committee's work, and their contribution had substantial impact on the form and nature of the emergent policy of OBE. After objections from participants in the LACs, stakeholder participation was maintained in the form of a Reference Group to the Technical Committee, consisting of the sixteen LAC executives and five Phase representatives. This Technical Committee finalised outcomes, assessment criteria and range statements for each Learning Area and submitted a final document to Curriculum Committees, reconstituted from LAC and Phase representatives (Department of Education 1997h).

Thus, the core framework of the new OBE curriculum was formulated. The report of the Technical Committee became the central curriculum policy 'blueprint'. It was submitted for formal approval to the CMC, for public comment, and then for adoption by state structures in the form of the Heads of Education Departments Committee (HEDCOM) and the Committee of Education Ministers (CEM) prior to ministerial approval. A high-profile launch of Curriculum 2005, replete with the release of 2005 balloons from the steps of Parliament, took place. Minister Bengu declared national policy, explaining that: 'As from next year, on a phased-in basis, the learners of this land will begin to enjoy the benefits of a system of lifelong learning which has become the norm amongst the leading nations of the world, namely outcomes-based education. This is the culmination of months of planning and consultation at all levels ranging from grassroots to international experts in education' (Bengu 1997:2).

At this point, once the curriculum blueprint had been developed by the education departments and experts, with limited participation of stakeholders, promotional material and guides for teachers were released to schools in an effort to inform and educate teachers (Department of Education 1997b; 1997c).

Increasingly, an implicit 'rationalist' model of policy-making as a technical solution to education problems was operating alongside the explicit commitment to stakeholder participation. The public commitment to participation had rapidly given way to issues of efficiency and the power of the new–old bureaucrats. The degree of stakeholder participation is questionable, and tended to be defined as consultative and advisory. The fact that crucial curriculum decisions – over what would count as knowledge, what would count as valid transmission, and what would count as valid realisations of knowledge (Prunty 1985) – were interpreted as a technical issue is significant. The educational problem of designing a new curriculum was in effect seen as a technical one, which required technical solutions and the involvement of technical experts. Greenstein (1998:11) has argued that there has been a shift in education policy-making from 'an explicitly political and ostensibly stakeholder driven process, to one driven by state bureaucrats and experts, who are no less political but whose authority is backed up by a technical, professional and expert aura'. The process of developing an outcomes-based curriculum is an illustration of this trend.

Formulation and implementation – the relationship between centre and province

In line with the implicit model of policy-making as classic steps in a rational process, what began to emerge was a firm conceptual and sequential division between the steps of curriculum formulation and curriculum implementation, and the agencies responsible for each. Curriculum policy formulation was under national control. Once the process was complete, the Minister declared national policy, and then implementation was to be the preserve and responsibility of the provinces, and under their guidance, teachers. Departmental documents at the national level expressed the view that implementation would be a relatively smooth and straightforward process. There does not seem to be any anticipation of conflict and contestation in putting the curriculum framework 'into practice'.

Thus, the centre attempted to control the direction of curriculum policy, arguing that the provinces had scope to interpret and implement national frameworks. However, contestation occurred over relative powers and control of the process at each step. For instance, there were ideological differences over the uniformity of the curriculum – would there be a single national curriculum, or would each province develop its own regionally specific learning programmes? Some provinces, notably the Western Cape, the only National Party dominated province, argued that they had the competence to develop the curriculum and wanted to proceed independently. Other provinces argued that they did not have sufficient capacity; the majority seemed willing for the national team to drive the process. Constant changes were made to plans following provincial protests, leading some observers to claim that the entire process had been managed in an *ad hoc* manner (Interview with LAC participant, 1997).[3]

A second instance of these dynamics is the proposal that once national curriculum guidelines for each learning area had been developed and approved, responsibility for the next phase would shift to provincial education departments. They would develop draft learning programmes, learning support material and professional development programmes to operationalise the national curriculum guidelines. However, the Provincial Review Report has raised critical questions about the capacity and ability of provincial education departments to effect change and deliver quality education (Department of Public Service and Administration 1997). When a number of provinces argued that their officials lacked the capacity and resources to develop specific learning programmes, the centre took over the task and co-ordinated the process (Govender *et al.* 1997).[4]

The process of developing a new curriculum was thus characterised by constant tension between the national and provincial education authorities, which spilled over any neat division between steps in the policy process. It is apparent that a gap was developing between those who formulate and drive policy, and those who implement it. The power and involvement of the centre over policy formulation has constantly shifted downwards, redefining the point at which provincial and local participation in curriculum development would come into effect. This impacts on the provincial departments' ability to effect curriculum change. Describing the challenges for the implementation of Curriculum 2005, a Western Cape Education Department (WCED) curriculum advisory services document identified national–provincial relations as a key issue, alongside financial, political and capacity conditions. 'The way the integrity and credibility of provincial department officials are being put on the line: teachers and other stakeholders are demanding a greater role and are protesting against a perceived top-down process. Yet provincial departments are being forced into this by the headlong national process. Provincial departments are feeling the brunt of stakeholders' concerns' (Western Cape Education Department 1997).

Greenstein (1997b) points out that such a disjunction between power and accountability is structural, and likely to be an ongoing source of tension. The provinces have the responsibility of implementing policy that has been formulated largely under central control, with no allocation of extra resources to ensure effective implementation. Given that many provinces have tightly stretched education budgets, the financial resources for curriculum innovation and support in the provinces is a major concern and a cause of conflict. Nevertheless, the 'rationalist' assumption is that policy as formulated will automatically be implemented, without sufficient regard to the financial and organisational capacity of provinces to deliver. To what extent then, has the policy-making process taken into account those ultimately responsible for translating curriculum policy into educational activity – the teachers?

Teacher participation

If there is an explicitly 'political' model of policy-making operating in tension with an increasingly dominant implicit 'rationalist' model, what are the implications for teachers?

The rationalist model assumes consensus between all participants in the policy process, which leads to a notion of stakeholders working together in an uncomplicated way towards a common goal. However, the history of conflict between some teacher organisations and state departments has not laid a good basis for participation and working together. As one departmental official in the WCED explained, 'you are supposed to form an interest group with another stakeholder. Yet, we come from such different backgrounds that we haven't yet established a proper working relationship, we don't understand one another yet... If we must now nominate one person to participate in one particular activity, am I going to trust you, that you will represent us?' (Interview with senior official, Curriculum Advisory Services WCED, 1997).

Teachers have also begun to mistrust organisations such as the South African Democratic Teachers' Union (SADTU), which entered into agreements with the state on their behalf through the Education Labour Relations Council, in the form of teacher redeployment policy. Some teacher organisations have tended to focus on economic-corporate interests of their members, and not sufficiently on organising members around pedagogical and curriculum concerns. The difficulties of stakeholder representation were discussed above. Thus, the curriculum policy development process has been characterised by contestation and by difficulties in achieving consensus between stakeholders, and between stakeholders and the state. The absence of a strong organised civil society, particularly teacher organisations, facilitates the dominance of the implicit rationalist model, and the centralising thrust of education policy-making.

The conceptual gap between formulation and implementation as separate steps in a rational process impacts on the legitimacy and ownership of the new curriculum for the key agents of implementation, the teachers and educators. The previous section showed that the Education Department is increasingly firmly in control of curriculum policy formulation, in a way that is separated from the provinces, and from teachers and education. The points in the process and the kind of work teachers and their organisations have been involved in are an issue. Teachers and teacher organisations were under-represented at key phases of the curriculum policy-making process. For example, the Western Cape was the only province which included representatives of teacher organisations in their delegations to develop draft learning programmes. A key example is the National Pilot for Grade 1, which was implemented by each province simultaneously for six weeks from August 1997.[5] Tight national control over monitoring, evaluation and assessment of the process occurred (Interview with subject advisor, WCED, 1997).[6] Teacher organisations like SADTU participated as part of the national monitoring team. The pilot was used to develop a national training programme for all Grade 1 to 3 teachers in October, to prepare and equip teachers to introduce the new curriculum in January 1998.

Significantly, however, it was the first point at which individual teachers were brought systematically into the process on a mass scale. Final outcomes and a curriculum blueprint had been decided prior to the piloting process, so educators' views and experiences were not to be incorporated at the level of curriculum policy formulation, but rather at the level of implementation. For many teachers it was the first time they were introduced to complex curriculum and pedagogical principles, which require a considerable conceptual and practical shift. It would appear that teachers are being informed about changes, rather than having been involved in a process to produce them. Nor are teachers being equipped to produce the learning materials required by the logic of OBE. Moreover, there has been a basic lack of dissemination of information about the curriculum development process itself. To address the paucity of information, the national department has initiated publicity strategies, including informational booklets, supplements in newspapers and a toll-free help line. Whether these reach those teachers in isolated and under-resourced schools is an open question, never mind the interpretations such teachers will bring to bear on the information.

In general, teachers have received the curriculum 'blueprint' as a *fait accompli*, and are simply required to participate in a pilot, or go for 'training'. Their interests, expertise and concerns have not been incorporated into the form and content of OBE in any significant way, despite the official commitment to a participatory policy-making process.

The 'rationalist' model which has come to dominate not only assumes that there will be consensus between the new–old bureaucrats and teacher organisations in developing policy, but that consensus from all teachers will be forthcoming with regard to the curriculum plans. Table 7.1 reflects the schedule for training of educators, using the cascade model proposed nationally, by the WCED, which has approximately 1780 schools.

Table 7.1
Schedule of training, WCED 1997

Pilot schools	Training	31 July to 2 August
Pilot schools	Trialing	11 August to 19 September
Provincial training (Grade 1)	Training	6 October: 61 circuit clusters, 70 venues, approximately 140 working days required, 140 trainers
Provincial training (trainers)	Trainers	27 August: training of trainer teams for orientation of Grades 2 to 6
Orientation (Grades 2 to 6)	Orientation	8–16 September: 61 clusters, 1 representative of each grade per school, responsible for capacity building of rest of teachers in school

The schedule reflects the enormous financial, physical and human resource demands required to train teachers in the new curriculum. It raises serious doubts about the quality of training offered to teachers and, as a consequence, about the ability of teachers to actualise the promised 'paradigm shift' in curriculum and pedagogy. It reflects the 'rationalist' model operating, which has assumed that policy implementation will be automatic, and that teachers simply require some training to be able to become practitioners of Curriculum 2005. In the way it has gone about making policy, the Education Department has not developed adequate plans for actively and systematically winning the consent of teachers for new policy.

The problem, as Carneson (1996:110) phrases it, is that 'many policy-makers expect teachers to respond predictably to their initiatives, even though we know surprisingly little about the ways in which teachers actually come to change their everyday patterns of practice'. The resistance of teachers to change at a classroom level and the difficulties of implementing new curricula and pedagogical styles are well researched (Fullan 1993; Davidoff & De Jong 1997). Cohen (1991) has argued that a teacher's prior instruction in and experience with a discipline is as powerful in shaping the organisation and pedagogy of the classroom as any curricular framework. His research reveals how difficult it will be for teachers to learn and to incorporate new patterns of practice in their daily activity, even when they are committed to and attempt to follow new curriculum policy directives enthusiastically. The difficulty is more acute in conditions where teachers receive minimal training in complex new curricular principles and frameworks.

The constraints and challenges of curriculum and pedagogical innovation in the context of black schools which are under-resourced and in which the quality of teaching and learning is impoverished raises further questions about the assumptions of the 'rationalist' model. Training as a technical process, offered on a uniform schedule to all teachers across the provinces, is not able to take specific contexts into account.

The disjunction between curriculum policy formulation and implementation which arises from contradictory policy commitments and contradictory models of the policy process is a serious constraint but, at the same time, offers some possibilities for teacher participation in Curriculum 2005. These will be briefly explored in the concluding section.

Conclusion

This chapter has aimed to facilitate understanding of the curriculum policy-making process, in the hope that it can identify spaces where teachers can push for greater participation. In analysing how curriculum policy-making is occurring in practice, the distinction between a 'political' and a 'rationalist' model of the policy-making process has been useful. The new education authority has proposed, in line with a 'political' model, that teachers as stakeholders would participate in an open and transparent policy-making process, particularly around curriculum. It has been argued that this commitment is in tension with policy practices conceived of in a 'rationalist' way. The tendency has been that teachers' participation in curriculum policy development takes place at the point of implementation of 'blueprints' developed by experts, in consultation with stakeholders' representatives. Implementation of the curriculum blueprint by teachers is seen largely as a technical issue, with an assumption that the process will proceed as planned automatically and mechanically, and that there will be consensus to these plans. The nature of policy contestation between centre and province, between civil society stakeholders and the state, and between different stakeholder groupings has been largely ignored. The impact of the way in which policy was made on the form and nature of the new OBE curriculum is thus considerable.

The disjunction between the Department of Education's professed commitments and teachers' concerns described at the beginning of this paper is now explicable. The question remains for teachers: What is my relationship as a teacher to the curriculum policy-making process?

A strong argument has been made that the process is not simply a technical one, but is inherently political. A political intervention is thus required for teachers to become involved in the process of curriculum development and to actively organise broad consent to a policy imperative, but to contest the development of curriculum policy in the light of teachers' interests and experiences.

The tension between 'political' and 'rationalist' models means that space does remain for teachers and their organisations to promote the notion of stakeholders and to strive for the involvement of civil society in the development of curriculum, down to classroom level. However, teachers can allow the process to continue in the 'rationalist' mode, in which case they are likely to be called in for (inadequate) training, and then left to take responsibility (and blame) for effecting complex curriculum change.

On the other hand, teachers can challenge the process, for instance by demanding that the pace of change be slowed, or that teachers should participate in developing provincial implementation strategies, or that the quality of training should equip teachers for their task, etc. Teachers can articulate what understandings (of NQF, OBE, curriculum design) they realistically need before they can begin to participate actively in curriculum and materials development. They are well placed to identify the resources schools in specific contexts may need, before they can participate in curriculum change. Teachers will need to engage actively and build working relationships with provincial education authorities, given the devolution of responsibility from the centre to the provinces for implementation of Curriculum 2005.

Most crucially, if teacher stakeholder representatives are not to become mere 'rubber stamps' for decisions made elsewhere, active teacher organisations are required. Strong teacher organisations are needed at school, district, provincial and national levels, and with a focus which equips members to engage with the complexities of OBE. The challenge for teachers and their organisations is to construct new educational politics that allows real space for engagement with curriculum and pedagogy.

Endnotes

1. Representatives were drawn from provincial departments and educational experts from each phase.
2. Of the fourteen members of the Technical Committee, five are from the provincial departments of education and one from the national department.
3. For instance, the initial plan was to introduce Curriculum 2005 in four standards (or grades), and after a number of revisions, it was decided to introduce it only in Grade 1 in 1998.
4. Much of the work was done by provincial departmental representatives.
5. Senior departmental staff from each province were sent for national training, to act as facilitators within their province. They then trained teachers of Grade 1, and co-ordinated a number of schools, supporting teachers and conducting classroom visits.
6. Monitoring of the trialing process took place through visits by a national team to selected schools and classrooms, to assess the manner in which programmes were being implemented, and the extent to which teachers understood the workings of the programme and the philosophy of OBE.

8

Questioning education and training in South Africa: the challenge of moving from policy to practice

SIMON MCGRATH

At the level of discourse during the development of the new South African education and training system there has been a remarkable lack of critical contestation of the official ANC/COSATU position which began to emerge from the beginning of the 1990s. Until recently, it was almost impossible to find critical commentary in print. This has much to do with the political realities of the period since 1990. The unbanning of the African National Congress (ANC) and the beginning of a period of negotiations required those inside the organisation and its allies to develop a new orthodoxy and then defend it. This applied to education and training as much as it did to other areas of policy. Before the overthrow of the Apartheid regime, critical academics were attuned to the same demands of intellectual discipline and orthodoxy that prevailed in political circles.

After the 1994 elections, concentration on the challenges ahead, the euphoria of victory and the desire to give the new government the benefit of the doubt all helped to further suspend critical judgements of the new systems being developed. It is only recently, as attention begins to turn towards the next election, the next century and the next millennium, that critical voices have begun to come to the fore, as this volume makes apparent.

The growth of criticism of the new education and training system is also related closely to the nature of the policy cycle. Getting the stakeholders to agree on the broad principles outlined in a document such as the National

Training Strategy Initiative (NTSI) (National Training Board 1994) was relatively easy. Getting the far wider group of interested parties to agree and act upon detailed proposals and programmes emanating from these principles was always likely to be a far more contested activity.

Another reason why the new policies were initially insulated from serious criticism was their apparent merits. Whilst a large proportion of South Africans could very easily see faults in the proposals of Eiselen (Department of Native Affairs 1951), De Lange (HSRC 1981b) or the Education Renewal Strategy (Department of Education 1992), the NTSI (National Training Board 1994), the National Qualifications Framework (Department of Education 1996a) and Curriculum 2005 (Department of Education 1997d) sound far more attractive (and plausible) with their commitments to redress, equity and internationally recognisable quality.

However, even in the earliest of the ANC/COSATU documents it was possible to discern inconsistencies in these commitments (McGrath 1996). It was possible to imagine ways in which policy might actually develop that would undermine rather than enshrine some, if not all, of these founding principles (McGrath 1996; 1997b). It was possible to fear for the capacity of the new South African state to implement what were huge ambitions (McGrath 1997d).

It is possibilities such as these with which this chapter will concern itself. At the heart of these is the question of whether, as claimed, the new system will lead inevitably to empowerment of learners. In asking questions of the process of developing a new South African education and training system, this chapter will highlight some of the key issues that must be addressed by researchers of educational policy to ensure that South Africa moves towards the best system it can achieve for the start of the twenty-first century and beyond. Elsewhere in this volume there is a great deal of detailed description of Curriculum 2005, the National Qualifications Framework (NQF) and international experience, for example from New Zealand. The concern here will be to attempt to bring together the substantive and methodological aspects of researching the new South African education and training system.

From vision to practice

Much of the proselytising done for the NQF/Curriculum 2005 process over the last few years has centred around its empowering nature. It is claimed to do away with the failings of the Apartheid/racial Fordist system, which both systematically discriminated on racial and gender grounds and focused on the preparation of drones for heavy industry. Instead, it is argued that the NQF is grounded in the principles of non-sexism and non-racism and focused on learning experiences designed to develop individuals who are adept in both the practical and the theoretical domains.

Certainly, the introduction of the NQF can be expected to have some positive effects on the struggle to overcome racism and sexism in education and training. However, it must be noted that the anti-racist, anti-sexist principles of NEPI (the National Education Policy Investigation) have fallen away from centre stage in more recent documentation (McGrath 1996). Moreover, the NQF is concretised in terms of neither pedagogy nor content. It is these factors, and the broader socio-economic context, that will be the determinants of the inclusiveness of the NQF in practice.

The claim that the new system will produce a more integrated kind of learning and hence empower individuals to take better control of their lives is also not necessarily true. There is considerable debate internationally about whether the type of competencies and outcomes that come to be developed in practice are in fact typically a reinforcement of the compartmentalisation and fragmentation of learning (Hyland 1994; O'Connor 1994).

The work of the Education Training and Development Practitioners project (1997) is illustrative of the need to replace rhetoric with detail in the NQF debate. The project has come up with two possible versions of how an NQF could be structured. One of the models suggested may be termed the pragmatic option. Given the perceived urgency of developing the NQF, it is argued that the process of developing unit standards should begin immediately in order to produce a large bank of modules in the shortest possible time. The other model takes the more principled stand of calling for the overall qualifications and career pathways to be kept as the central focus from which holistic courses should be constructed. This second approach also contains a powerful notion of reflective competence. This seeks to take learning and practice in South Africa far away from narrow behaviourism and Taylorism, privileging instead the type of reflective, autonomous professionalism identified as true expertise by authors such as Benner (1985).

These two models each have their strengths and weaknesses, but they help to illustrate the point that the real debate on the NQF must be at the level of detail. The former model seems to be that favoured both by the project's German sponsors and by the South African Qualifications Authority (SAQA), yet it is subject to much of the progressive critique that has surrounded reforms in the United Kingdom and elsewhere (Smithers 1993; Hyland 1994; Young 1995). The latter model found support, although implicit, in the Department of Labour's Green Paper (Department of Labour 1997) which used its notion of competence in the preface.

It is only in the process of implementation that it will become clear whether either of these visions is realised, in whole or in part. Whilst the international experience is instructive, it does not determine what will happen in South Africa. Though the policy commitments will serve to shape practice, individuals, interests and structures will also be vital actors in that shaping.

Much of the empowering benefits claimed for the NQF are embedded in the workerist origins of the ANC's version of the notion, described in detail by Groener in Chapter 6 of this volume. Empowerment is largely that of the worker who is given the kind of training that is broad enough for her/him to be able to take a more proactive role in the workplace, as part of a broader system of co-determinism. It is also a vision of the career path so that all training has the ultimate goal of individual advancement. These are legitimate and intrinsically laudable aims. However, they are in danger of contributing to a narrow notion of the NQF, and of learning, which empowers some whilst disempowering others. The Department of Labour (1997) has sought to expand the scope of the NQF beyond organised labour to agriculture and the informal sector. However, at its heart there are strong elements of an instrumental and, hence, economic vision of what learning is about.

The notion of certification is particularly relevant to debates about the NQF and empowerment. Internationally, it is claimed that one of the principal benefits of a modularised competency-based approach is that it increases certification. Giving certificates to those ignored in the previous system, it is suggested, doubly empowers them. First, there is the positive psychological effect of giving certificates to those previously labelled failures. Second, giving someone, who had no qualification previously, a work-related certificate should make her/him more employable. These positive effects should not be underestimated. Nonetheless, there are also potential disempowering effects in the focus on certification.

More than two decades ago, Dore (1976) wrote about the effect of the 'Diploma Disease'. In a situation where education and training opportunities far outstrip employment opportunities in the formal economy (as is very clearly the case in South Africa), the power of the certificate is likely to become overwhelming. Whilst an outcomes approach is alleged to overcome the stultifying effects of the norm-referenced, examination-based learning of which Dore was so critical, Dore's critique should be read as one which points to the negative effects of external economic effects on learning. Such a critique is about far more than the effects of a particular form of examination. The following quote from Dore (1997:xxvii) can resonate with outcomes-based education (OBE) as strongly as with its predecessors: 'those who have been subjected to a ritualistic examination-oriented learning as children and adolescents are likely to turn into ritualistic, performance-evaluation oriented workers, incapable of the sort of entrepreneurial initiative-taking which developing countries need'.

The case simply has not been proven that learning outcomes make such a fear outdated. Rather, we might expect that the expansion of the number of examination events in a learning system within a broader context of acute labour surplus could be a way of exacerbating the backwash effect of the assessment process.

Does the emphasis on outcomes necessarily empower individuals to a greater extent than was the case with knowledge-based education? This depends to a large extent on what OBE means in practice. The rhetoric of Curriculum 2005 raises the possibility of a shift to a constructivist model of curriculum development in which pupils and teachers become subjects in their own development of really useful knowledge and skills. This, however, is only a possibility. International experience with competency-based approaches raises the alternative vision of a behaviourist practice in which the focus is on appropriate knowledge, skills and attitudes (O'Connor 1994), determined by those in authority (usually economic), which instrumentalises learning and objectifies learners (and teachers).

The politically-driven rush to implementation in South Africa, which has seen the authority of learners, teachers and even the provinces subsumed to that of centrally-defined experts, is a stark reminder of the dangers of taking the rhetoric of the new government, like any other, at face value. There is a need, therefore, to explore how new South African practices are emerging as the learning outcomes approach enters the school system and as its sister movement of competencies expands through the training system.

However, critique will not be enough. Internationally, there is a growing discourse of user-orientated research (Gibbons 1997). Students, parents, teachers and state officials do not want to know simply that the system is succeeding or failing. Rather, they expect academics to be able to suggest ways of improving practice or, if the practice is irredeemable, of radically reconceptualising the learning process. If the research view of the learning outcomes approach is not to be dismissed as irrelevant, it will need to be grounded in a concern with both principles and practicalities.

It is probably not a viable moment to have a debate about the principles on which the NQF and Curriculum 2005 are built. Equally, it is too early to dismiss the ANC's economic strategy and the linkages between this and education and training policy. The political and economic imperatives towards implementation are simply too strong at this juncture. Therefore, it is imperative that research should begin to focus on implementation, whilst maintaining a concern with the feedback loop to future policy development.

In spite of the many reservations that can be raised regarding South African policy, it is clear that the policies developed so far are amongst the most ambitious in the world, and this ambition is not to be decried. However, there are serious potential problems, a few of which can be articulated at this point. Already, the decision to drive the first phase of the school curriculum reform from Pretoria has been criticised. This decision was, to a large extent, because of fears about capacity to engage in curriculum development both in schools and provinces. Although a national programme of seminars designed to inform teachers about Curriculum 2005 has taken place, there is still considerable room for a comprehensive programme of in-service support to school, district and provincial curriculum development capacity. If the new curriculum is to live up to the highest principles and ambitions of the 'new South Africa', then radical methodological and attitudinal shifts will need to take place that empower parents, students and teachers to become authentic subjects of the reform process.

Thus the process of curricular reform in schools (but also in colleges, technikons and universities) is inseparable from other key educational debates. Governance, community involvement and the culture of learning and teaching are all intertwined with a radical, empowering vision of Curriculum 2005. The building of viable institutional cultures and capacities is a necessary condition for the realisation of such a vision. It is important to consider not just curriculum development but also the emergence of new pedagogies. Curriculum 2005's commitment to problem-solving, critical thinking and discovery learning is reinforced by the growing discourse of competitiveness through worker-based innovation.

However, it is fallacious to argue that curriculum reform necessarily leads to complementary reforms of pedagogy. Personal experience as a teacher in a rural secondary school in Zimbabwe reminds me that a shift to a more skills-orientated curriculum and examination can lead to the teaching of stock phrases and specimen answers which allow students to fabricate evidence of having learned skills. Pedagogical practices can ossify into new orthodoxies after a major curricular reform or they can continue largely along old paths that serve to subvert the critical dimensions of the reforms. These may be at least as plausible outcomes as the intended transformation. Any such subversion may be deliberate and ideologically based. However, it is more likely to be the result of lack of teaching and learning resources, of inadequate salaries and motivation or of insufficient training and support.

Conclusion

The messages of this short paper are simple, but also complex. First, there is little point in focusing on a critique of the philosophical or ideological underpinning of the NQF and Curriculum 2005 at present. Second, it is naïve to expect that the reality of these reforms will closely resemble the statements of policy documents or the pronouncements of their supporters.

These point to a more complex and challenging reality in which the task of academics is to engage with both practitioners and policy-makers in a two-pronged strategy. On the one hand, it is essential to promote the development of a form of education and training system which is owned by the people of South Africa and which reflects their needs and aspirations. On the other, it is necessary to begin critiquing the emergent system and generating detailed alternatives both within and, if necessary outside, the current paradigm.

Whether in trying to make the new system work or in proposing another, the challenge will be to go beyond policy theorising. The theory and process of implementation must be central to a new education policy research agenda. This will require educationalists to consider not only curriculum and pedagogy, certification and assessment, but also to link these to governance, institutional cultures and capacities, and funding regimes.

In so doing they will need to reshape and revive the proud South African tradition of a political economy of education. It is vital that a detailed rereading be attempted of education and training's role in the context of a new ideological order characterised by post-Apartheid, post-Fordism and post-modernism. The attempts in this book, and in another recent collection (Kallaway *et al.* 1997), to deal with South Africa's particular blend of local and global pressures and opportunities constitute an important first step, but much is still to be done.

9

Faint hope or false promise? The recognition of the prior learning (RPL) principle of the National Qualifications Framework (NQF)

MIGNONNE BREIER

Jonah is a 12-year-old who has never been to school but who has become aware of the value of learning. He has some street learning. How will he benefit from the National Qualifications Framework? When Jonah returns to school he will be assessed against the standards and his prior learning will be determined and used to place him at an appropriate level (HSRC 1995:24).

Grace is 25 years old and is unemployed. She has had odd piece-work jobs, but would like to study so as to develop a career. How will she benefit from the National Qualifications Framework? ... her prior experience and learning can be assessed against the requirements of the individual unit standards.[1] She can then embark on a learning programme which leads in a direct way to a career of her choice rather than first having to complete a matric (HSRC 1995:25).

These quotations, from a Human Sciences Research Council (HSRC) publication, illustrate some of the expectations which have come to surround the proposed National Qualifications Framework (NQF).

The NQF, which is designed to promote an integrated approach to education and training, among other things aims to facilitate access to formal education, to ease articulation between different domains of education and to ensure progression through various learning pathways. One of its thirteen main principles is that through assessment, education and training should give credit to learning which has been acquired through formal, non-formal and informal learning and/or experience.[2] This principle, commonly known as 'recognition of prior learning' or RPL, is also the NQF's main tool for the achievement of educational redress, the means whereby people who were denied educational opportunities during the Apartheid years will now gain access to formal education at levels appropriate for their age and experience.

The *White Paper on Education and Training* (Department of Education 1995:15) sees RPL as one of the bases of an integrated approach to education and training and suggests that it will also 'open doors of opportunity for people whose academic or career paths have been needlessly blocked because their prior knowledge (acquired informally or by work experience) has not been assessed and certified, or because their qualifications have not been recognised for admission to further learning, or employment purposes'.

This chapter[3] considers theoretical challenges to the RPL principle of the NQF. It concludes that current conceptualisations of RPL could be problematic in that they imply potential equivalence between informal and formal learning, which might not be achievable in practice, or might not even be desirable. They make demands of the assessment process which are not only strenuous but also contradictory and they conceptualise learning transfer in terms of generic outcomes, at a time when the concept of decontextualised skills or knowledge is receiving extensive critique.

Theoretical challenges to the NQF

The social practice theories of learning of Lave and Rogoff (Lave 1988; Lave & Wenger 1991; & Rogoff 1990) suggest that learning and knowledge are inextricably bound up with context. They cannot be considered in isolation from the everyday practices in which they are embedded and are generally characterised by 'guided' or 'legitimate peripheral' participation within communities of experts. These theories raise immediate doubts about whether one can expect equivalence between 'street' or 'workplace' learning and that which occurs in formal sites of learning, as suggested by the examples quoted above.

Lave *et al.* (1984:93) describe the arithmetic involved in supermarket grocery shopping, for example, as a process of gap closing in which the activity is dialectically constituted in relation to the setting. In other words, 'setting and activity mutually create and change each other, in the process "problems" are generated and resolved'. These characteristics emerged from an analysis of arena, setting and activity and would not have become obvious had the template instead been the school ideology concerning linear algorithms for problem solving.

Commenting on this research, Ensor (1997:8) concluded: 'For Lave there can be no equivalence between street and school practices because school mathematics and grocery shopping (or forms of work practice) are distinct activities, regulated according to different goals'.

The theories of Gee (1990) and Bernstein (1994) (from the perspectives of socio-linguistics and educational sociology respectively) suggest that different learning processes lead to different forms of knowledge. Again this has implications for a framework that aims to be 'blind as to where learning took place' (HSRC 1995:15).

Gee (1990:146) distinguishes between 'meta-knowledge' or content which is taught overtly (what Gee calls 'learning') and the 'ways of being'[4] associated with a subject which is the result of unconscious exposure to meaningful role models in real-life situations (Gee calls this 'acquisition'). This distinction makes one question what aspect of knowledge should be the focus of RPL procedures. It suggests that while meta-knowledge or content can be similar across contexts, mastery of the discourses associated with a subject, or in the words of Gee (1990:143), 'the ways of using language, of thinking, feeling, believing, valuing and of acting that can be used to identify oneself as a member of a socially meaningful group', can only be achieved through a form of apprenticeship experience, which must be context-specific. Lave would argue that the knowledge acquired through overt instruction is equally context specific.

Bernstein (1994), building on Durkeim's distinction between sacred and profane forms of knowledge, draws a distinction between everyday, oral[5] or commonsense forms of knowledge (called 'horizontal discourses') and the forms of knowledge associated with the disciplines we teach (called 'vertical discourses'). He argues that horizontal discourses are segmentally structured and acquisition is equally segmented and context-specific, usually tacit, involving demonstration or exemplar modelling. For instance, learning to live in London, to use an example of Bernstein's, involves the acquisition of separate, context-specific discourses and skills – how to use the video shop, the supermarket, the tube, etc. – with most of these discourses and skills acquired tacitly by following the example of others. Vertical discourses, on the other hand, are 'constructed, evaluated, distributed to different groups and individuals, structured in time and space by principles of recontextualisation' (*ibid.* p. 4). (In this way, we have Standard 6 Science for 13-year-olds, Standard 7 Science for 14-year-olds and a very different, almost unrelated form of Science for 'real scientists'.)

Gee's (1990) distinction between 'acquisition' and 'learning' could be seen to add a further dimension to Bernstein's theory, allowing for elements of the profane within the sacred. So, for example, becoming a scientist or philosopher requires not only mastery of the content and meta-knowledge associated with the subject (vertical discourses), but mastery also of the ways of using language, of thinking, feeling, etc. associated with being a scientist or philosopher, and the 'ways of doing', of performing experiments, conducting seminars, structuring arguments, etc. These elements can only be achieved through a form of academic apprenticeship or 'exposure to meaningful models', in much the same way that horizontal discourses are acquired.

At the same time, it is possible that there are elements of the sacred in the profane, as Muller (1995:19) found when he examined the account of an illiterate farm worker which was part of the Social Uses of Literacy (SoUL) Research Project (Gibson 1996). This worker had never been to school and could not read or write but made complicated wagons from plans which he developed in his head. He demonstrated, in Muller's terms, 'elements of a primitive (in the sense of under-elaborated) faculty of verticality' which took the form of a 'germinal horizontal knowledge structure, admittedly with a highly simple grammar'(1995:19).

A practical question for the designers of the NQF

In general, the theories of Bernstein and Gee add weight to the concerns raised by Lave and Rogoff. Together they lead one to pose the following major question for the designers of the NQF: 'If knowledge and skills are linked as closely to context and mode of learning as these theories suggest, how can competence acquired in one context be equated with (or recognised or accredited as) competence acquired in another?'

To illustrate the above dilemma, let me take an example from the SoUL project. During ethnographic research at a Cape factory, Sait (Breier et al. 1996; Breier & Sait 1996) observed workers whose job it was to mould garden pots out of material containing asbestos. They also worked daily with the concept of 'percentage'. They used the term confidently and fluently to refer to the extent to which they were able to reach production targets, for example, but their understandings of the term seemed far removed from its mathematical origins. It was clear at times that any other word could have been substituted in its place. It was the numbers that went with the concept that mattered, the way in which the numbers increased with higher production and greater pay and the mental images of quantities of products which they seemed to evoke, linking them to particular work experiences.

Now how would RPL assessors credit these hard-working people for this aspect of their work-based knowledge? To what extent could their working knowledge of percentages be compared with the algorithms and parts of 100 that are taught in schools?

Ensor (1997:2) argues that by attempting to establish equivalence between knowledge and practices in school, work and domestic settings, the NQF attempts to render equivalent what many would regard as sociologically and epistemologically distinct: 'by imposing the template of schooling on work place knowledge and decontextualising practices from their sites of use, there could well be a distortion of what happens on the factory floor.... Mathematics could come to serve as a critical filter, not to move workers on but to hierarchise them and hold them back'.

Michelson (1995; 1996) suggests that accreditation of informal knowledge against formal standards can serve to devalue the informal. She argues that RPL operates within a deficit view of other-than-formal learning: 'Applicants are evaluated only within pre-determined norms for what kinds of knowledge are acceptable ... These norms represent Eurocentric organizations of knowledge and work, as well as first world access to resources' (1996:5). The implication is that only a massive revision of standards will do justice to the strengths of informal knowledge.

A key dilemma for RPL assessors lies with the notion of 'competence', a central concept of the NQF as it has been developed by the HSRC and the Department of Education Ministerial Committee. Their definitions of the term include the notions of outcomes, performance, continuity and capability. Capability is seen as the 'basic enabling component of *performance* which involves generic abilities acting in relation to defined *content* areas, contexts and value frameworks'(HSRC 1995:1).[6] In this way the NQF goes beyond a behaviourist emphasis on visible performance only and requires attention to knowledge, skills and values which underlie performance.

The HSRC metaphor that was developed to explain this concept of performance illustrates the dilemma for RPL. In this metaphor, the visible part of performance is depicted as the tip of an iceberg and said to include 'the *manipulation of "tools" and manual dexterity* within a *communicative or interactive context* which includes *gesture*', as an indicator of value orientation (HSRC 1995:43). The invisible part of performance (the submerged part of the iceberg) is said to consist of information or content, 'interpreted within a *particular value orientation*, through employing *particular mental* abilities such as problem-posing, problem-solving and judgement or decision-making abilities'(*ibid.*).

The dilemma for RPL is as follows: to what extent can one compare two icebergs by looking at their tips? To what extent should one consider the full extent of knowledge, skills and values that underlie visible performance when conducting an RPL assessment? If underlying capacities are important (and the HSRC and Ministerial Committee interpretations of the NQF suggest they are), then how does one design a form of assessment that enables one to judge the full extent of an iceberg (capability) by its tip (performance)? In

123

particular, how does one do this in a way that ensures the NQF remains blind to 'old school ties', that is, to the site where learning takes place?

To illustrate just one aspect of the dilemma, let me take another example from the SoUL research. Researchers in the minibus taxi industry found that adults with no formal education were functioning relatively successfully as taxi drivers, performing the same tasks as formally-educated drivers (Breier *et al.* 1996; Breier & Sait 1996). They even passed the same tests, although the illiterate driver would be given an oral test and the literate driver a written one. At one level they demonstrated similar skills; at another there was a vast difference between the full capabilities and capacities of the one type of driver and the other. In certain contexts, such as reading directions or unfamiliar traffic signs, this would inevitably become obvious and relevant. This is not to say that illiterate people made unsafe drivers. In fact, quite the contrary had been proved in research by the HSRC (Maree 1993). What it means is that in only some contexts they would find themselves at a relative disadvantage. Formal sites of learning would be among these contexts.

As currently conceptualised, it seems that the NQF is dependent on ambitious (and contradictory) expectations of the assessment process. The process is required to take account of capabilities and potential as well as performance, and yet find equivalence between the outcomes of vastly differing learning experiences.

The question thus arises: on what theory of learning is the NQF based? It seems to be associated with what Lave (1988:8) has identified as the theory of learning contained within the 'functionalist position'. This is the idea that 'children can be taught general cognitive skills (eg reading, writing, mathematics, logic, critical thinking) *if* these skills are disembedded from the routine contexts of their use. Extraction of knowledge from the particulars of experience, of activity from its context, is the condition of making knowledge available for *general* application in all situations'.

In this way, unit standards (the building blocks of the NQF) are required to indicate both specific contextualised knowledge and skills, called 'specific outcomes', and generic knowledge and skills, called 'critical cross-field outcomes', to use the latest NQF terminology (SAQA 1997:13). Examples of critical cross-field outcomes include: 'Work effectively with others as a member of a team, group, organisation or community' or 'Communicate effectively using visual, mathematical and language skills in the modes of oral or written persuasion' (*ibid.* p.15).

Through the notion of unit standards RPL is linked to both specific and critical outcomes, in that adults who wish to have their prior learning accredited must demonstrate that they have mastered the outcomes specified in appropriate unit standards (Department of Education 1996a:15). Both forms of outcomes present dilemmas for informally educated adults. Unless a concerted effort is made to incorporate the types of knowledge and forms of literacy (or lack of literacy) associated with informal learning processes in unit standards, informally educated adults will have difficulty in passing formal tests (Michelson 1995; 1996).

It might be argued that critical outcomes have something in common with a formally orientated unit standard, but here one faces the common critique of generic outcomes – they are meaningless unless related to a specific context, and once related to a specific context, they lose their transferability (Marginson 1993). So, for example, a trade union shop steward and a university law student both need oral communication skills. At the level of specific outcomes, their skills are very different. There are particular literacies associated with the law school context which must be avoided on the shop floor where one is required to speak off the cuff. The content of the communication differs, as do the values, attitudes and conventions – in other words, the ideologies and discourses associated with it. To say that the one form of communication skill could be usefully 'recognised' in the other context is to deny the complexities and specific demands of both contexts and activities.

At the level of 'critical cross-field outcomes' the two speakers would have something in common – 'oral communication skills' – but to what extent is it useful to consider these in isolation from the specific procedures and contexts of the whole activities in which they are embedded? Ensor (1997:8) has suggested that generic outcomes 'distort or 'misdescribe' what occurs in any specific setting'.

Lave (1988:187) offers a theory of 'continuity of situationally specific activity across occasions and contexts' which could lead to new and useful ways to conceptualise use of prior knowledge in new contexts. She suggests that such continuity

> … is a matter of social reproduction, and thus of dialectical relations between the constitutive order and the experienced world. Continuity may be thought of as an active production of the reproduction of settings, activities and selves. It is achieved partly through change and improvisation, partly subjectively and partly through reproduction of the constitutive order. That is, continuity of activity over occasions and settings depends on consistently flexible variability in the structuring of activity.

Lave's theory seems to suggest another way in which learning transfer (and indeed the recognition of prior learning and the NQF itself) might be conceptualised. In these terms, it is not the generic skills that are important in the new site, but the specific skills. They are adapted to the new context in a dialectical process in which the 'prior learning' impacts on the new environment, while simultaneously the (now changed) environment impacts on the old skills, the (now changed) old skills impact … and so on.

Conclusion

This chapter has argued that one of the most important principles of the NQF – the RPL principle – is flawed conceptually in two important ways. Firstly, it does not take account of the growing body of research and theory which emphasises that formal and informal forms of knowledge are structured differently and associated with different learning processes. Attempts to find equivalence between formal and informal learning could serve to devalue and misdescribe the knowledge of the very constituency which the NQF would most like to advance, working to the ultimate disadvantage of this group. They could lead to informally educated people having unrealistic expectations of success in formal learning contexts, and they are based on over-ambitious and contradictory expectations of the assessment process. Secondly, there are suggestions that it is misguided and unhelpful to see the transfer of learning in terms of decontextualised (generic) skills and knowledge.

New conceptualisations of RPL, which take account of social practice theories of learning, need to be researched and developed.

Endnotes

1. Unit standards are the 'building blocks' of the NQF. The Department of Education Ministerial Committee defined them as nationally agreed and internationally comparable statements of specific outcomes and their associated performance/assessment criteria, together with administrative and other necessary information (Department of Education 1996:15). More recently, the definition was expanded to include 'critical cross-field outcomes', that is, generic skills and knowledge (SAQA 1997:14). Unit standards are one of the most contentious aspects of the proposed NQF, particularly at higher education and secondary school level, because of the way in which they break down knowledge and skills into discrete units. Developing unit standards is also a very time-consuming and expensive operation.
2. Formal learning involves credited courses at universities, technikons, schools, etc. Non-formal learning is associated with non-credited courses such as on-the-job training and trade union worker education. Informal learning is about learning from life or work experience. In defining these terms I draw on the definitions offered by Harris et al. (1994) and Wain (1987:51) quoted in Garrick (1996).

3. This chapter draws on an earlier paper by the author, entitled 'Whose learning? Whose knowledge? Recognition of prior learning and the National Qualifications Framework', which was presented to the Kenton Conference, Wilgespruit, in October 1996, as well as an early draft of her doctoral thesis proposal, which carried the same title as this paper and was presented at a seminar in the Faculty of Education, University of the Western Cape, in May 1997.

4. This term comes from Geertz (1983:155) and is also used by Chiseri-Strater (1991: 141).

5. It should be noted that the 'great divide' theory that marks some societies as 'oral' and others as 'literate' has been debunked by recent research and theory (see Street 1993; Barton 1994; Prinsloo & Breier 1996). However, I accept Bernstein's earlier notion of an 'oral-based' society, provided that the way in which written texts permeate such societies is also recognised.

6. The italics which appear in this and subsequent quotations from this section of the HSRC document are in the original text. In other words, this is their emphasis.

SECTION THREE

Transforming professional
teacher education

Introduction

A total restructuring of the segregated South African education system became one of the most important objectives of the democratic South African government which was elected in 1994. The problems in a very unequal system are many and complex. These range from financial constraints to violence and vandalism, from irrelevant curricula to a lack of infrastructure to implement a new curriculum for schools, and from a demoralised teacher corps to students who do not see the importance of obtaining a matriculation qualification if such a qualification does not guarantee employment.

Such conditions impact negatively on both pre- and in-service programmes aiming to improve teaching practices in schools. However, the situation is not hopeless and many committed teacher educators are still working around the clock to improve the situation in South African schools through rigorous pre- and in-service programmes, which are aimed not only at the improvement of the practices of teaching in a technical sense, but are also geared to raising the morale of teachers in schools.

This section comprises three chapters addressing different dimensions of the task of transforming professional teacher education. In Chapter 10 Brian Gray reflects on his practice regarding curriculum implementation in science education in KwaZulu-Natal, and points out that the key issue when implementing curriculum reform is the gap between curriculum intent and curriculum in practice. One of the conclusions drawn is that the changes envisaged by the new Curriculum 2005 are fundamental and will be difficult for even the most experienced teachers to implement, not to mention the vast majority who teach in difficult circumstances, often with minimal facilities and support, and appropriate training. Some of the doubts expressed by Gray are shared by

Meerkotter in Chapter 4 of this volume. Gray's chapter focuses on a bottom-up approach to curriculum implementation and in-service education.

The second chapter in this section, Chapter 11, was jointly written by colleagues from Edinburgh University and the University of the Western Cape. The authors examine the extent to which new paradigms have influenced and informed policies for supporting learners with special educational needs. In doing so they consider the situations in South Africa and Britain in comparative perspective – the former is in the process of transformation; the latter is a developed system, undergoing reform.

This section concludes with a gem by Edith Jantjes. Professor Jantjes has been part of the educational scene in the Western Cape for four decades and has played a major role in influencing school children, aspirant teachers and others in her many educational community initiatives. She was also amongst the first coloured women to obtain a doctor's degree. Chapter 12 is a personal account of Jantjes' life and work as an educator and it puts much of the book's work in a very particular South African context.

This section provides the reader with some glimpses of the central issues facing teacher education in South Africa, while comparing what is happening in South Africa to some events in Britain.

Dirk Meerkotter

10

Implementing curriculum change and development in the school: lessons from experience in South Africa

BRIAN GRAY

A major curriculum reform initiative, under the guise of Curriculum 2005, is currently under way in South Africa. However, developing new curricula is the easy part of the task; implementing it in a way that narrows the gap between curriculum intent and curriculum practice is what matters and is far more difficult. Alongside this, policy-makers see Curriculum 2005 acting as the springboard for teachers to become curriculum developers, responsible for developing their own learning programmes. Desirable as this may be, it needs to be seen in the context of past history and the current state of education in the country. The paranoid urge to control by the Apartheid authorities has seriously undermined the professionalism of teachers and discouraged initiative or engagement in curriculum development. Syllabi, developed by faceless committees, tightly determined what was to be taught, with the final external matriculation exam being the final arbiter of success or failure of the learning task. The top-down approach to introducing what little curriculum change there has been was limiting and stultifying. Curriculum development, in the true sense of the term has, by and large, never been practised in South Africa. For example, the current school science syllabus, but for a few minor revisions, has remained largely unchanged for over thirty years. Despite the drive for transformation in education and equity in schools since the establishment of democratic government in 1994 we find schools and teachers somewhat demoralised and many without a great deal of professional commitment.

Fullan (1982), drawing largely from experiences of curriculum reform in 'developed' countries, asserts that effecting meaningful educational change is a very complex and difficult business and many well thought-out curriculum programmes have failed to achieve their intentions. Such failures can largely be attributed to the lack of understanding of the complexity of the change process on the part of policy-makers and developers and the failure by them to get more substantially involved in supporting the dissemination phase.

Major curriculum reform in the form of Curriculum 2005 is being introduced in South Africa. What does this involve and what are the implications for implementation? Curriculum 2005 requires two major shifts at a classroom level for teachers. First, it is to be outcomes based with a strong emphasis on the development of skills and attitudes. For teachers this requires a change towards more complex and demanding teaching methodologies, away from the easier traditional, transmission-orientated teaching based on content-laden textbooks to match the fixed curriculum. Secondly, it involves a collapse of subject disciplines into eight integrated learning areas. Teachers trained to teach physical science, for example, will now be required to develop and teach integrated science learning programmes involving biology and earth sciences as well. This has major implications for the implementation of the new curriculum and the resulting gap between intent and practice.

The non-governmental organisations (NGOs) working in the educational field in South Africa have done valuable work to bring about innovation and change within the tight constraints of a fixed syllabus and present a ray of hope to us in an otherwise bleak situation. They have worked quite effectively, particularly in formerly black schools, to develop professional attitudes and practices amongst an embattled teaching force. The Science Education Project (SEP) was foremost in this endeavour in the field of science education (Rogan & Gray 1998). Macdonald (1993) provides valuable insight into the collective work. There are many valuable lessons to be learned from the NGO work for anyone involved in the business of implementing curriculum change and the professional development of teachers, particularly for those working to develop and implement Curriculum 2005.

It is from experience with the SEP and other work that I offer some thoughts on the issues inherent in implementing curriculum change in the schools. I spent five intense years (1980–4) working closely with science teachers in the KwaZulu-Natal schools in and around Durban to implement changes inherent in the SEP, its methods, materials and ways of working with teachers. This on-the-ground experience has taught me a great deal about some of the complexities of involving teachers in curriculum innovation in any significant way. Besides SEP, the more recent experience of developing and trialing the materials and methods of the Science Through Applications Project (Gray 1997; Gray & Ramahlape 1997; Clark 1997; 1998) in a wide range of schools in the Western Cape has shown that the lessons of the SEP KwaZulu-Natal experience, and the issues involved in bringing about change in education in a South African context, are as pertinent today as they were then. Teacher-driven curriculum change involves issues such as: the professional empowerment of teachers, ownership of the innovation and the implementation process, sustainability of the innovative process, ongoing professional development, the role of outsiders in the process and implementation strategies.

The Science Education Project (SEP) and its implementation in KwaZulu-Natal schools

The initial task for SEP was to develop science curriculum materials and in-service support methods that would be relevant to the context. Science teaching in the majority of schools in South Africa in the early 1980s was characterised by large classes, under-prepared teachers, poor facilities and a lack of even the most basic tools for the task. Transmission, content-orientated teaching that did not encourage questions dominated and the administrative system was authoritarian, top-down in nature and discouraged any form of professional initiative. Teachers were also 'trapped' in a model of education and teaching that was severely limited in its vision and professional collaboration was virtually non-existent.

After three years of development and trialing, the final SEP 'package' comprised: (i) transportable kits of apparatus for group work by pupils in classrooms, (ii) pupil guide materials, (iii) structured teacher guide materials, and (iv) some understanding of strategies that could prove useful for supporting teachers. In the light of the situation in the schools, SEP decided in 1980 to get fully involved, as an NGO, in the dissemination process.

In the KwaZulu-Natal schools I chose to adopt a bottom-up strategy, consulting first with principals and teachers – those who would be most affected by the innovation and who would ultimately determine what happens in the classroom. The following five years saw a holistic support programme evolve and extend to include 38 schools and over 150 teachers. 'Ownership' of the innovation and the implementation process was a key determinant of what happened. A significant development in the whole process was the establishment of the 'zone programme' whereby teachers in a geographically determined cluster of schools met together for professional purposes on a regular basis. The zone programme arose out of two frustrations that were being felt at the time: (i) 'old' SEP teachers were wanting new courses to sustain their professional interest and involvement in the programme, and (ii) the need to develop structures that could provide for sustainable support beyond the life of the NGO which should, in principle, withdraw at some time anyway. The whole zone system was teacher-driven and teacher-led with a zone leader and deputy elected on an annual basis.

Several internal and external evaluation studies were carried out. Amongst other things, these revealed some success in terms of improved classroom practice as well as professional engagement and development by teachers as a whole. At a classroom level there was evidence of improved examination performance, more pupils opting to take Physical Science at the Grade 10 level, more practical work being done and improved teacher and pupil attitudes towards the subject. Of more significance, however, was substantial evidence that a greater sense of professional worth and identity was established that had been largely absent before. A number of teachers became quite involved, at leadership and other levels, in the local science teacher association.

However, there is another side to the 'achievements coin' that also needs to be clearly stated. Whilst there were many real gains that were accomplished in the years under discussion, there were also many moments and episodes of considerable frustration and disappointment for the implementers. Much of this can be attributed to poor administration in the schools and the low morale and commitment of teachers in a very depressed system that was part of the reality in 'black' education and which had its roots in the Apartheid system. Part of it could also be attributed to the complex political 'game' that was being played out and which would perhaps not normally be the case in any 'normal' situation where it was acceptable to work in co-operation with, and have the support of, the education authorities. The insecure funding base of an NGO operation also took its toll. It was demanding work that frequently tested the resolve and commitment of those responsible for overseeing and developing the programme. A mini-thesis (Gray 1990) documents much of the work in this period.

Lessons about implementing curriculum reform that emerge from the SEP KwaZulu-Natal experience

The whole experience proved to be an extremely valuable lesson on the complexities of trying to bring about change in education. Out of it there were a number of notable elements in the whole implementation process that I feel contributed significantly to what was achieved and which I feel are worth consideration by anyone engaged in curriculum development, in-service education or the continuing professional development of teachers. These are described below.

The immediate availability of appropriate support materials

The kits, teachers' guide materials and pupil worksheets were a very significant positive factor in what was achieved. These concrete forms of support were appropriate to the context and related directly to expressed needs of teachers. In this way they provided some immediate and real support and, in many ways, served as very useful 'bait' for the initial engagement of teachers and something around which we could start to build the programme and process.

I am aware of the arguments against the use of structured curriculum materials for curriculum innovation, most of which centre around their potential for deskilling teachers, ownership issues and the need to involve teachers from the start in the process of developing the curricula and materials. Whilst involvement of teachers in developing their own curriculum and materials from the outset is an ideal, I believe that one's ability to get a process going is dependant on the context in which change is being sought. In the context of KwaZulu-Natal (and I believe most other 'developing' world contexts), the immediate availability of appropriate curriculum materials in support of the innovation can answer some of the most urgent and immediate needs of teachers and with it greatly facilitate the engagement process. Through the materials, teachers are more easily able to engage professionally with the curriculum, and feel the immediate support through which they can develop confidence to take it further. In such situations, I believe, the advantages to be gained through the use of prepared and structured guide materials far outweigh the disadvantages.

If one follows this route the issue then centres around the extent to which the materials become fixed as a resource for teaching or are used as a catalyst and starting point for further development where the methods and materials developed become more personalised. I feel that there is a real need to be realistic about where teachers are and what is possible in a context and not to get carried away in fantasies from the ivory tower or armchair world.

The importance of a holistic approach to in-service support and development

There are many factors that impact on the life of teachers and their ability to accommodate and deal with the proposed change. Fullan (1982) identifies and discusses some of these. Each context will be different and the balance of factors will be different. However, the implementation strategy adopted needs to recognise that any single factor carries the potential to block, or significantly retard, the proposed innovation. It therefore becomes imperative to develop support programmes that are holistic in conception. Much of the success of the SEP in the KwaZulu-Natal schools can, I think, be attributed to this. Some of the support strategies used include:

- use of appropriate materials,
- in-service courses/workshops (multi-purpose, centre and school-based),
- school visiting,
- administrative facilitation and back-up,
- development of structures to provide for sustainable support,
- equipment management systems, and
- promotion of 'ownership' of the innovation and the dissemination process.

Working in context

In-service courses and workshops are frequently conducted in centres where the facilities are vastly different to the under-resourced schools in which the teachers operate. This resource gap clearly has implications for the acceptability of the innovation by teachers in their working context. In the case of the SEP, centre-based workshops/courses were conducted in a room with no basic facilities, which in many ways mirrored the situation in which the teachers taught. SEP teachers were able, for example, to see that the organisation for hands-on practical work by a large group of pupils was possible in a basic classroom.

Follow-through school visits

In the case of the SEP the school visiting component of the in-service support programme was unquestionably a most valuable means of bringing about real change. The on-site school visits meant support in the working context of the teacher. The credibility of the implementer was considerably enhanced through situations such as team-teaching or the modelling of a lesson *in situ* for reflective discussion. Teachers attending centre-based courses also felt that their problems were better understood.

School visits were able to fulfil a host of other important functions such as:

- providing moral support and addressing problems,
- facilitating project administrative arrangements,
- maintaining impetus and creating a positive pressure for effort in a very run-down system, and
- providing feedback for reflection and for decisions to be made about the overall implementation programme.

However, the expansion of the project led to less school visiting and with it a noticeable reduction in the effectiveness of the programme in terms of building confidence, sense of purpose and adaptation to change by new recruits coming into the programme. Amongst other things it resulted, in 1982, in a significant change in the way schools were equipped. The heavy demand on resources that school visits requires is a major problem for anyone introducing innovation. However, it is invaluable and as far as possible attempts should be made to incorporate some form of in-school support into the programme. Skill and sensitivity on the part of the implementer are required as teachers generally work in a very private world, often behind closed classroom doors, and many may feel 'exposed'. They need to feel comfortable with, and confident in, the person supporting them.

Reflective, sensitive, 'process approach' to the development of the programme

Many in-service teacher education (INSET) or dissemination programmes, particularly when launched from a departmental base, tend to adopt a 'blueprint approach' with regard to how the programme should be structured and run. Whilst it may be necessary to start off with some plan, there are many risks associated with a 'blueprint approach'. In the case of the SEP, the implementation programme was continuously evaluated and changed on the basis of feedback and critical reflection. Teachers were also continuously, and deliberately, involved in decisions about the nature of the support needed and the overall development of the programme.

Development of 'ownership' of the innovation and the implementation process by teachers

The implementation strategies adopted in KwaZulu-Natal schools was premised on the belief that teachers were more likely to implement the envisaged changes if they were part of the decision-making processes. I believe that this aspect of the process, namely, the development of 'ownership' of both the innovation and the ongoing development process, was the key to much of the commitment secured from teachers to the work, the ongoing development of the innovation as well as their general professional involvement. Through it teachers were able to feel some degree of professional empowerment in a system that systematically sought to disempower them at every turn.

There were a number of elements of the programme that contributed to the development of this sense of 'ownership' and empowerment. These included:

- Voluntary participation in the programme – this was significant in the South African context.
- The mode of working with teachers – this was collaborative, collegial and reflective. This was easier for an outsider (working in this instance in an NGO from a university base) and was quite foreign in a top-down authoritarian system where teachers were usually instructed to attend in-service courses and then became recipients in the process. An annual mid-term evaluation meeting formed an important part of this particular process. It was used for joint reflection and forward planning. Crucial strategic decisions that affected the general development of the programme were taken with the whole teacher body at this event: for example in 1981 to establish the teachers' committee and in 1982 to establish the zone programme.
- The increasing and significant involvement of teachers in designing and delivering in-service courses and workshops, particularly with the advent of the zone programme – use was also made of peers as role models in a number of different ways. The strategy tried to dispel the notion of the outside 'expert' and to help teachers acknowledge (and believe in) their own expertise as well as to work towards a position of collective self-sufficiency. Contrary to standard practice I tried, through this move, to shift the responsibility and initiative for ongoing professional development onto the practitioners themselves.
- The teachers' committee, (established June 1981) – this allowed for the sharing of decisions and frustrations and provided a forum in which strategic decisions could be taken. This element of professional practice was totally foreign to teachers who were seldom, if ever, consulted by the authorities about what they did, let alone made part of the decision-making process. Representatives from this committee were part of the selection committee for the departmental seconded post (1983). This was quite a new development as teachers were for the first time involved in a decision about a more senior departmental appointment.
- The development of the zone system – the zone system was an innovation in itself and contributed significantly to both 'ownership' as well as a means of providing a structure and mechanism for the provision of ongoing support. (This was later further secured institutionally through the establishment of a seconded departmental post for a person to work as an implementer in support of the zone leaders and the zone system.) Through the system teachers were much more substantially placed in charge of their own situation. Its greatest asset was the space that it provided for teachers to exercise leadership and initiative and to develop – both professionally and personally. A number of teachers blossomed in this respect and have

since moved onwards and upwards in a number of different ways. In time each zone developed its own identity and character, which was related to the personalities involved and the context. They spawned a number of very successful initiatives, such as inter-school science olympiads, common exams and curriculum writing groups. The zone programme also marked an important shift away from centre-based courses and workshops towards more local, teacher-driven, school-based programmes.

• The zone system, in essence, is nothing more than a system to facilitate collective work on a local level. If supported, I believe, it can play an invaluable role for a host of important professional activities that teachers continuously engage in. In the case of Curriculum 2005, such locally based collectives could easily be used to develop local learning programmes.

Role of the outside agent

The role of the outside agent might be different in different contexts but, because of the political situation in South Africa at that time, such an intervenor was able to play a very important role. NGOs were generally able to operate and establish trust and co-operation with teachers in situations where the education authorities found it impossible.

For the SEP programme, the teachers recognised the skills and experience brought to the programme by the outside agent. The university base also provided some degree of credibility to the innovation. As outsiders, the more flexible position enabled us to act as catalysts and to provide options for consideration in a manner that bureaucratic institutions such as the education authorities could not.

There are clearly disadvantages associated with initiating programmes from the outside. Many of these centre around motives for intervention and change and the issue of 'ownership'. However, my sense of it is that the advantages far outweigh the disadvantages in a 'developing world' context (and often others) and non-engagement for the above reason may often be an excuse for not getting involved at all. The issue then becomes the manner in which the outsiders become involved and how the innovation and implementation process is managed. I believe too, that outside agents should operate and plan in a way that reduces the vulnerability of the programme to their departure (and usually funding) and that they should always be working towards redundancy. A weakness in the operation of a number of NGOs in the South African situation was that money was often too freely available and that they lived and operated in a manner that was not sustainable. Teachers would often go for the glitter and not the gold.

The 1994 election brought a legitimate government into power. It now becomes much more possible for state departments and outside agencies such as NGOs and tertiary institutions to form strategic partnerships. This has particular significance for those wanting to introduce curriculum reform. In terms of the scale of the problem in the South African context, the state is the only body that has the resources to deal with something as big as curriculum reform. It makes sense for them to use outside resources to help. However, the nature of the collaboration and strategic partnership will have to be carefully worked out if the system is to derive the benefits associated with the involvement of outside agencies.

Role and nature of the project leader

The skill of the person introducing the innovation and leading the implementation and development process is vital for success and should not be underestimated. Unfortunately, as with any innovation or exercise involving human relationships, many of the desirable attributes are closely related to personality, though some are skills that can be developed over time. Essentially, it is important that teachers are able to relate to the person, be able to acknowledge and value what he/she has to offer and build up trust and a healthy working relationship. Amongst other things, I believe that the person needs to have a solid background in the subject and its pedagogy. Teachers need to feel confident in the person, and that they have something to learn from him or her. The person also needs to be able to listen and acknowledge the grounded contextual experience and understanding of the teachers. The project leader should also play a decreasing role to minimise the inherent dangers of dependence. In this respect, skill and sensitivity are needed when working in a system that has not made it easy for a teacher to take responsibility and undertake leadership roles.

Concluding comments

As indicated at the start, the key issue when implementing curriculum reform is the gap between curriculum intent and curriculum in practice. The changes envisaged by Curriculum 2005 are major and will be difficult for even our most experienced teachers to implement, not to mention the vast majority who teach in difficult circumstances, often with minimal appropriate training. The above lessons have been gained out of fairly intensive on-the-ground work with teachers trying to effect a much less difficult change. What I have tried to show are some of the difficulties and complexities involved in trying to narrow the gap.

11

New paradigms in provision for special educational needs: South Africa and Scotland in comparative perspective

*LILIAN LOMOFSKY, GEORGE THOMSON, ANDRÉ GOUWS
AND LEVI ENGELBRECHT*

In this chapter, we examine the extent to which new paradigms have influenced and informed policies and provision for supporting learners with special educational needs. To do this we consider the education systems of South Africa and Scotland in comparative perspective – the former is in the process of transformation; the latter is a more developed system. The chapter starts with a description of the two educational contexts, continues by examining the policy framework in each setting in respect of provision for special educational needs, and concludes by examining training issues in higher education in the Western Cape (one of nine provinces in the Republic of South Africa) and Scotland (one of four constituent countries making up Britain).

Features of the educational systems

Republic of South Africa

Since the election of South Africa's first democratic government in 1994, the general education system in South Africa has been in the process of being transformed into a unitary non-racial department. Under the previous system of Apartheid, separate education for each of the various ethnic groups (white, Indian, coloured and black)[1] required a complex structure consisting of seventeen different education systems, all under central government control. This led to discriminatory practices and all educational institutions (schools, colleges and universities) were segregated along racial lines. There was much duplication of functions, responsibility and services, as well as vast disparities in per capita funding in different education departments (Du Toit 1996). In the new dispensation, education has been reorganised into nine provincial education departments and one unified national department, all of which are non-racial.

In order to redress the injustices of the past, in South Africa's Constitution the education section of the Bill of Rights states that 'all learners have a right to basic education including adult basic education and further education' (Republic of South Africa 1996a:291). In accordance with this, the South African Schools Act (Department of Education 1996d) legislates for compulsory education for learners from the year of their seventh birthday until the age of fifteen or the ninth grade (present Standard 7), whichever occurs first. Additionally, the Minister 'will determine the ages of compulsory attendance at school for learners with special educational needs'.

Thus, the rights of all children are protected, including children with special educational needs, by ensuring that seven years of primary education and a further two years in secondary school are compulsory. In the secondary schools, however, there will be provision for a further three years up to Grade 12 (present Standard 10). The Department of Education is basing its forward thinking on the Draft Provisional structure of the National Qualifications Framework (NQF), which comprises eight qualification levels. Level 1 will be the General Education Certificate, which will be awarded after the acquisition of required credits at the end of the compulsory schooling phase – pre-school plus nine years to Grade 9 – or it may be awarded through ABET (adult basic education and training). Levels 2 to 4 will comprise: (i) a senior secondary school programme up to Grade 12, (ii) general and specific programmes offered in the college sector, and (iii) programmes offered in regional training centres such as through workplace training.

The total population of South Africa is in the region of 38 million. The total number of pupils who should have been in school (estimated) in 1987 was 9 762 100 (SAIRR, Survey 1987/88 cited in Moulder 1991:31). Of these 68 per cent (6 661 226) were at school and the remaining 32 per cent (3 100 874) were out of school, the latter being mostly black and coloured pupils.

Compulsory education will incorporate a vast number of school-age children who are not currently at school. This will include many disaffected youth and school dropouts, some of whom have not progressed beyond Sub A (Grade 1), who would be requiring re-admission to the education system.

These children will have special educational needs that require learning support beyond that which is traditionally available in the regular classroom in ordinary (not special) South African schools. Within the new unitary system, the demand to meet the special educational needs of all children with the provision of support services on an equitable basis is great.

From Table 11.1 it can be seen that the number of dropouts from Grade 1 (Sub A) in black primary education between 1984 and 1990 was 1 252 936. However only 0,6 are provided for and this indicates that the deficit for black children is most severe. For coloured and Indian children it increases to 12,9 per cent and 7,7 per cent (provided for) respectively whereas white children are moderately provided for at 58 per cent. When translated into figures for special educational needs, for every 100 children a conservative estimate is that 75 are black, 12 are white, 10 are coloured and 3 are Indian. These figures illustrate that it is the disadvantaged who are unassisted and under-resourced (Donald 1994:146). In addition, as Table 11.2 shows, there is an unequal distribution of children in special schools/classes across these racial groupings.

Table 11.1: Dropout rates in black primary education, 1984–90

Enrolment, Sub A (Grade 1)	1984	1985	1986	1987
	1 029 799	1 041 551	1 067 992	1 134 116
	1988	**1989**	**1990**	**Total**
	1 168 204	1 183 570	1 218 606	7 843 838
Dropout, Sub A (Grade 1)	**1984**	**1985**	**1986**	**1987**
	161 678	160 339	165 539	171 252
	1988	**1989**	**1990**	**Total**
	189 249	197 656	207 163	1 252 936
Percent of enrolment	**1984**	**1985**	**1986**	**1987**
	15,7	15,4	15,5	15,1
	1988	**1989**	**1990**	**Total**
	16,2	16,7	17,0	16,0

Source: C. Verwey, P. E. Carstens and A. du Plessis, *Education & Manpower Production*, No. 4 (Research Institute for Educational Planning, University of the Orange Free State, Bloemfontein, 1984) in Donald (1993:147).

Table 11.2: Number of pupils in special schools as a ratio of enrolment for the various race groups, 1990

Race	Number of pupils in special education	Total enrolment	Ratio
Whites	14 969	932 181	1:62
Indians	5 580	233 101	1:42
Coloureds	6 558	841 387	1:128
Blacks	9 811	8 143 217	1:830

Scotland

In common with the other three component parts of Britain, Scotland enjoys an educational system that provides for universal and compulsory education over the age range 5–16 years. Within the Scottish system, there are seven years of primary school education followed by four years of secondary schooling. Whilst the statutory school leaving age is sixteen plus, the reality is that increasing proportions of pupils remain at school for up to two further years, a phenomenon that in part reflects the problem of youth unemployment in recent years, but also reinforces a Scottish tradition of staying on to access the national examinations of the Scottish Examinations Board (SEB) at 'Higher' Grade with a view to entering advanced, post-school education. Pupils at the Secondary 4 (S4) stage present for the SEB examinations at Standard Grade (Foundation, General or Credit) as well as for modular certificates awarded by the Scottish Vocational Educational Council (SCOTVEC). These latter awards are also available to pupils at S5 and S6 stages.[2]

With a population of around five million and a school age population of just under one million, Scotland is administered by 32 all-purpose authorities. 'Education' is one of a number of regionally-based services whose funding is derived in part from regionally-raised funds via the Council Tax and a share of the central government Exchequer grant, which is allocated by formula through the Scottish Office. The Scottish Office Education and Industry Department (SOEID) is responsible for the implementation of government policy in respect of education. The prime act that underpins education in Scotland is the Education (Scotland) Act 1980 as amended. In general terms, the similarities with the legislation covering other parts of Britain are greater than the differences, although concerning provision for special educational needs, the subtle differences are of greater significance, particularly concerning parental wishes.

145

The policy framework in respect of special educational needs

The Republic of South Africa

In this section we consider the history of policy and provision to meet special educational needs in South African, then for comparison, outline the situation in Scotland.

In the context of this chapter's focus on the comparative nature of thinking about special educational needs, it is apparent that educational thinking in South Africa has followed the dominant international trends and initially emulated the American model by creating categories of 'exceptionality' for physical, sensory or cognitive disabilities. In the past, the problems in the South African educational system were compounded by the separation of schools according to racial groupings – leaving a legacy of division and inequity to add to the other burdens weighing on the new transitional process within contemporary South Africa.

Two major commissions on policies and practices in relation to special education were sponsored by the National Party government. First, the Murray Report (1969), an enquiry into children with minimal brain dysfunction, recommended facilities for specialised services which were for white children only, and excluded the multitude of learners with disabilities from other races. In contrast, the De Lange Report (1981) included recommendations on children with special educational needs. It advocated a single unitary education department and moved away from the strict categorisation and labelling of children with disabilities towards the broader focus on children with special educational needs. Clearly this was a movement away from categorisation of learners with intrinsic disabilities towards understanding individual children in terms of specific behaviours and needs. It also allowed for more flexibility and motility by favouring placement of children with special educational needs in mainstream schools. These recommendations were for all learners. The De Lange Report (1981) deplored the inadequate facilities for blacks, and was concerned with the needs of learners who were environmentally deprived. There was a shift of emphasis from the medical model, which assumed that special educational need is created where there is a deficit or disability within or intrinsic to the learner, towards recognising the extrinsic or the environmental factors which adversely affect a child's education. In this regard the De Lange Report (1981) echoed much of the philosophy of the Warnock Report (Department of Education and Science 1978) in Britain, and represented an enlightened approach to education in the Apartheid era. Sadly, by the time of the National Education Policy Investigation (NEPI 1992) was published eleven years later, the rhetoric had not been translated into reality.

The Human Sciences Research Council (HSRC) *Report on Education for the Black Disabled* (1987) reflected on the extremely high incidence of disability in the black population group, which has been attributed to factors associated with environmental disadvantage, such as poverty, lack of awareness and access to medical and health care facilities, exposure to political violence and a lack of opportunities for learning. Educational disadvantage in the South African context refers to a school system in which problems have been both structural and systemic in nature. Structural educational factors are overcrowded classrooms, underqualified teachers (who themselves were victims of Apartheid), and lack of textbooks and stationery, equipment and resources. Systemic factors are an authoritarian ethos and rigid process of teaching, no provision for special education and lack of learning support personnel, and problems in regular basic education.

When children are exposed to deprivation and disadvantage in a hostile environment, 'risk' factors that lead to learning and behaviour problems increase. In this context, these learning and behaviour problems are viewed as the reciprocal product of individual predisposition and the nature of the environment (Adelman 1992; NEPI 1992; Donald 1993). Thus, where the earliest definitions excluded environmental, cultural and economic disadvantage, they can no longer be applicable to South Africa where people are being viewed in the context in which they are taught and expected to learn – in relationship to the school, family and interrelationships with the community. Because of the interactive effects of intrinsic and extrinsic factors, research studies have indicated that special educational need was being generated at double the rate of that in more developed countries and the incidence of learners with special educational needs (LSEN) at a real estimate is between 40 and 50 per cent (HSRC 1987; NEPI 1992; Donald 1993) as compared to the 20 per cent in more developed countries.

Learners with special educational needs in South Africa have traditionally been classified into categories based on medical and standardised intelligence tests. Access to educational services was based on the categories ascribed to the learners. Access to such facilities was further complicated during the Apartheid years, since most of the special schools were reserved for white students with learning difficulties. There were very few schools, if any, allocated to black learners, but since the early 1990s some of these white schools opened their doors to black children with special educational needs. The dynamic reorganisation of the education system has been a long and slow process partly because of limited resources and partly due to the fact that the education authorities have decided to consult widely and to ensure the participation of all stakeholders in educational policy formulation.

The focus of the proposed changes to the South African general education system has been on the rationalisation of the fundamental structures of schools such as pupil/teacher ratios and the improvement of physical facilities designed to eradicate the inequalities of Apartheid policies.

The Department of Education's *White Paper on Education and Training* (1995) emphasises the philosophy of the South African education system as gearing towards equality, access, redress and quality education for all children. It further recognises that the practical implementation of such a philosophy requires revision and redistribution of resources to eradicate previous injustices. Unfortunately, there is a big discrepancy between government-stated policy and the actual provision of services. Although the current government inherited the inequalities in provision of services in meeting special needs, it has acknowledged these deficiencies and the need to redeploy and redistribute existing resources and services to the neglected and deprived regions. Schools in the (black) ex-Department of Education and Training (DET) have had involuntary mainstreaming imposed on them through 'neglect'. This means that teachers and learners with special educational needs in these schools have had to cope with a multiplicity of learning and educational needs, in the majority of cases, with no support.

Services were well provided for in the more advantaged sectors, which were also minority groups, and unfortunately grossly neglected in the majority sectors where they were most needed (Kriegler & Skuy 1996; NEPI 1992). For example, specialised support for children in the mainstream with difficulties in learning and behaviour was available mainly for white children. For black children the only service that was introduced was a system of teacher support, called Panels for Identification, Diagnosis and Assessment (the PIDA system) in mainstream black schools. This service was imposed on regular class teachers who were inadequately equipped and lacked the back-up support. (Lomofsky & Mvambi 1988; Green *et al.* 1992). There are estimates (Skuy & Partington 1990; Donald 1993) which suggest that South Africa has nationally made provision for only one per cent of learners with special educational needs. This is slightly higher in the Western Cape since provision of services for LSEN is about two per cent (Theron 1996, personal communication). Although the figures are dated, they indicate that there are gross inequalities in provision of educational support services among the different groups, and that blacks are largely disadvantaged.

In most developed countries, since the 1970s, there has been a movement towards the integration of special education into the mainstream, but the radical restructuring of the mainstream is dependent on the reconceptualisation of the relationship between special education and the nature of the mainstream.

148

This indicates more than special education being integrated into mainstream classes in ordinary schools but is a moral issue of 'human values' as embodied in the Salamanca Statement (UNESCO;1994), which in 'asserting inclusion as a right' sees inclusion as a part of the creation of an inclusive society (Clark *et al.* 1997). The implication of 'inclusive education' is that learners with special needs have the right to be educated alongside their peers in ordinary schools and the emphasis falls on the system meeting the special needs of the child rather than excluding the learner to suit the needs of the system (Donald *et al.* 1997). This philosophical position prevails in both countries, but the situation in South Africa is more complex than in Scotland. Inclusive education presupposes the availability of strong and adequate educational support services. In South Africa this may be the situation for the small minority advantaged sector, but does not apply to the majority of black learners with extrinsically generated special educational needs, who are already mainstreamed in ordinary schools where educational support services are almost non-existent.

Even if the government should decide to opt for a policy of inclusive education for all learners, it will be incumbent on them to redress past deficiencies by providing appropriate support services for learners with special educational needs. This ideology is resulting in policies for LSEN that are still being developed in the face of limited financial resources.

NEPI (1992), a project of the National Education Co-ordinating Committee (NECC), was set up to investigate policy options under the banner of People's Education. This was an African National Congress (ANC) initiative to inform education policy in preparation for the new dispensation. In developing policy options, NEPI (1992) was guided by the following principles, which also have particular significance in the *Support Services* report (NEPI 1992): basic human rights to education, a unitary system, non-racism and non-sexism (non-discrimination), redress and democracy. These principles have been identified in the Department of Education's White Paper (1995) as essential to drive national policy for the reconstruction and development of education and training.

In a comparative perspective these principles and values are common ideologies in the education systems in both these countries, the difference being that they are a novel and recent development in South African constitutional law, whereas in Scotland they are entrenched in legislative and educational policy. Due to major historical differences in policy development and the social and contextual factors between South Africa and Scotland, variations in interpretation in relation to general provision and special education are evident in administration and practice.

- Human rights: The right to basic education and quality education for all in South Africa is a recent phenomenon and though legislated (*South African Schools Act*, 1996) is not yet fully enforced, whereas it is entrenched in the Scottish education system, although quality education is still differentially available.
- Unitary system: South Africa requires a unitary system of governance and the integration of all support services into the mainstream. In Scotland, the former has been the status quo, and the latter is under review in the current situation.
- Non-racism, non-sexism and non-discrimination of race, gender, class, ability and a basic right to education for all children indicates that state schools in South Africa should be open to all children of school-going age, including those with special needs. Non-discrimination on the grounds of race is more of an issue in South Africa than it is in Scotland.
- Redress of educational inequalities: in South Africa, from a historical perspective, support services should be allocated to those most in need and priority should be given to marginalised youth, learners with special needs, those adversely affected by violence and those who have limited access to quality education. Issues of redress in Scotland also apply but may differ in nature and severity; for example, the educational provision in more isolated rural districts may be under-resourced.
- Democracy: The rights of all parents, teachers and students, and others with special needs should be encouraged. Structures and mechanisms should be set up to ensure accountability in both South Africa and Scotland.

The NEPI Report (1992) recommended a framework for the provision of support services which would be holistic and integrated and require interdisciplinary and intersectoral collaboration between the various sectors, incorporating school health, social work, specialised education, vocational and general guidance and counselling and other psychological services. The rationale for recommending the re-organisation of Education Support Services was to redress inadequacies of the past by making provision for prevention and health promotion which could operate in addition to a curative mode (Lazarus & Donald 1995).

This recommendation has been adopted in the government's *White Paper on Education and Training* (1995:28): 'The Ministry of Education intends to explore a holistic and integrated approach to Education Support Services in collaboration with the Provincial Ministries of Education and in consultation with the Ministries of Health, Welfare and Population Development, and Labour. The inclusive integrated approach recognizes that issues of health, social, psychological, academic and vocational development and, support services for all learners with special educational needs in mainstream schools are all inter-related.'

This is also compatible with the vision of the government-appointed National Commission on Special Needs in Education and Training (NCS-NET) and the National Committee on Education Support Services (NCESS), which is in progress at the time of writing, to provide an ecosystemic, holistic and integrated service for all learners with special educational needs.

Scotland

As indicated above, the component parts of Britain enjoy separate educational systems. However, from an international perspective, these differences are less significant than the similarities. For this reason, whilst what follows refers to specific 'Scottish' legislation, in the main, the principles are generalised across Britain.

The Education (Scotland) Act, 1981 (the amending legislation to the prime Act) implemented certain proposals made by the Warnock Committee (Department of Education and Science 1978) affecting pupils with special educational needs. The principal aims of the legislation were:

- to de-categorise handicaps;
- to substitute the concept 'special educational needs' in place of the previous nine statutory categories of handicap;
- to ensure parental participation in all aspects of decision-making concerning their children's education;
- to stress the *educational needs* aspect;
- to introduce a formal document – the Record of Needs – as the basis upon which the child/pupil's special educational needs would be identified, assessed and provided for, all in the context of parents' participation and agreement.

From a comparative perspective, all of the above factors are common to the education systems of South Africa and Scotland. The one aspect that differs significantly is that to date, in South Africa, there is no stipulation for legal documentation such as a 'Record of Needs' or 'statementing'. There is, however, an expectation that an Individual Education Programme will be devised, but again this is not obligatory.

The Record (or Statement) of Special Educational Needs has the status of a legal document in Scotland. Contentiously, there are parts of the Record which are exempted from parental appeal. Whilst parents can appeal against the placement recommendations contained in the document, they are denied any right of appeal against an education authority's failure to deliver or put into place the measures set in the Record to meet the child's needs. This continues to create tension between parents and education authorities. The effects of the legislation on provision for special educational needs have been evaluated by one of the authors and his colleagues (Thomson *et al.* 1989; Riddell *et al.* 1992); we shall return to them later in this chapter.

Since 1987, a major reform of the curriculum has been underway. In that year the Scottish Office Education Department (SOED) published its statement on the framework of the curriculum covering the age range 5–14 (Scottish Office Education Department 1987). The subsequent publication of specific curricular guidelines took place, with the whole initiative being referred to as the 5–14 Development Programme. A feature of each of the curricular guidelines has been the guaranteeing to all pupils of access to an appropriate curriculum. Each guideline document includes specific reference on how to deliver the curriculum to pupils with special educational needs. This educational development has been the subject of an independent evaluation by a research group co-ordinated by the Scottish Council for Research in Education (1994), a component study of which has focused on the needs of pupils at either end of the ability spectrum (Thomson *et al.* 1995).

It could be argued that the so-called 'post-Warnock legislation' derives from at least two major philosophical or theoretical perspectives. At a general level, there is that perspective which indicates a major paradigmatic shift from a deficit model of adjustment, towards a system model of change. In the former, special educational needs are seen to derive from a within-individual pathology; in the latter, special educational needs derive from the difficulties encountered by the individual in interacting with her or his environment and hence it is the system which is required to adapt and to accommodate the individual. For some time now, this view has been represented widely in the literature of contemporary educational psychology of which Apter (1982) and Campion (1985) would be illustrative examples.

At a more particular level, Kirp's (1982) analysis of British, compared with United States, special education highlights a significant difference in the philosophical approaches to provision for special educational needs in both countries. Here, the distinctions between legislation for Scotland as compared with that for England and Wales are irrelevant. In Kirp's view, a range of policy options is available when an educational system seeks to provide for special educational needs. In the United States, legalisation is the preferred option, and concepts such as civil and individual rights, and due processes of law dominate. These reflect, in Kirp's view, a cultural tradition of individualism by which the United States is stereotyped. In contrast, British practice is

152

dominated by what Kirp calls 'professionalisation', wherein strategically placed or dominant professional groups control or act as 'gatekeepers' to procedures, processes, resources, etc.

This then sets the policy context in which South Africa and Scotland set their provision for special educational needs. We now turn our attention to consider how training professionals to work in this sector is delivered in higher education institutions.

Professional preparation of teachers in provision for special educational needs

The South African experience

From the above overview of the major paradigmatic and policy shifts in specialised education, it is clear that the school system must change to enable it to respond to the educational needs of all children, including those with special needs. Amongst other things, this shift is to be accompanied by teacher education reform to equip mainstream teachers and special educators with appropriate knowledge and understanding for the revised role envisaged for them (as well as the building of the necessary support systems).

In view of the 'cascade of services' (Lazarus & Donald 1995) to be rendered to learners with special educational needs (LSEN), the following educational needs (in ascending order of importance) for teachers can be identified:

- mainstream teachers with basic skills acquired during pre-service teacher education involving the identification of LSEN and the infusion of intervention strategies into mainstream classroom practice;
- mainstream teachers with extra expertise acquired through in-service training to form a core team to provide support to both mainstream teachers and parents;
- medium-skilled teachers at educational support centres to work on an itinerant basis to support teachers and support teams, to present in-service training programmes and organise prevention strategies, and to play an advocacy role in communities; and
- highly skilled special educators to provide specialised assessments, diagnosis and interventions, and to consult with, train and support medium-skilled teams.

For each of these categories of teachers, there are differing professional developmental needs with distinctively different training implications. Let us consider each of these in turn.

For teachers in the mainstream, the key to teacher education reform is to develop the confidence of teachers so that they feel that they can accomplish this task. This can be developed through effective pre-service and in-service programmes and by ensuring organisational support. At the pre-service level, the implication of providing basic education for all children in mainstream schools is that all teachers should be provided with the requisite knowledge and skills to enable them to respond to special needs in the classroom. Such material can be provided as a freestanding, accredited course or elements of it can be integrated into the relevant pre-service teacher education courses.

Pre-service education programmes target the limited number of teachers who are annually introduced into the school system to satisfy the needs of attrition or to meet the demands of additional enrolments. The greater challenge lies in preparing in-service teachers to enable schools to be responsive to the specific needs of learners. It requires a change in existing thinking and practice of teachers and of those who provide them with support. In this regard, it is possible to identify several possible models of in-service training on special needs. At one level, there are exclusive, short courses on special needs that can be organised at regional level. At a somewhat more advanced level, there are part-time courses, leading to accreditation, which can be offered through tertiary institutions. These can be exclusive 'credit' courses or can be offered as a component of other courses. They can also be offered on a distance learning basis. Moving to another level, there are school-based in-service training programmes, encouraging a whole-school approach. This can be an effective strategy. School-based in-service training seems to be an evolving and emerging as a favoured model, whereas the first three methods listed above are well established.

Turning to the professional developmental needs of special educators, a different set of priorities present themselves. The number of special schools and special classes may start declining both in developed and developing countries, but for different reasons. In developed countries, the downward population trend that affects school enrolments, as well as the policy shift towards the promotion of varying initiatives in mainstreaming or integration into regular education, such as inclusive schooling, are contributory factors. In developing countries, with the main emphasis on access and correcting historical imbalances such as existed in South Africa throughout the Apartheid years, primary basic education is prioritised at the expense of specialised education. Whatever the circumstances, the redefinition of the role of special educators requires conventional training programmes to be changed. The following trends seem to be emerging certainly in the South African context.

First, there appears to be a shift towards giving a broader base to the classic single disability teacher education programme. Courses now include a core course on all disabilities as well as specialisation in one type of disability. A second discernible trend is in the training of support teachers in more than one disability, especially for service in rural areas in developing countries. This enables them to provide peer support to 'cluster schools'. Special schools redefine their roles to serve as resource centres for integration programmes for special educators with the objective of providing them with the skills to work with mainstream teachers and to organise training programmes for them.

A third initiative can be seen in the existence of special needs elements being provided as a component of ongoing in-service training programmes for teachers. The content depends on the available time or the possibility of extending the content and duration of such programmes. An awareness-level module that sensitises mainstream teachers to special needs issues is the minimum that should be included.

Scottish experience

Historically, the professional preparation of teachers for the educational system in Scotland was undertaken in mono-technic 'colleges of education' with the 'older' universities reserving their involvement in teacher education to postgraduate and research aspects. Because of governmental policies to increase participation rates in higher education amongst the age cohort, throughout the 1980s and 1990s, such colleges either affiliated themselves to or became integral faculties of adjacent universities. This moved the universities from the somewhat peripheral positions they had previously occupied, to one that was more centralist. This pattern is gaining momentum at the time of writing.

When considering the training of teachers in the Scottish context, there are a number of important and relevant factors to bear in mind. The first is unique in Britain – all teachers are required statutorily to be registered with the General Teaching Council for Scotland (GTC) before they can take up a teaching post in the public sector.

Increasingly, schools in the private sector are making GTC registration a condition of employment.[3] A second point to emphasise is that teaching in Scotland is an all-graduate profession in which the GTC advises the SOEID on standards and, indeed, on matters concerning supply of teachers, etc. This means that there is scrutiny by external agencies such as the GTC and SOEID of the programmes offered by the training outlets. A third point to stress in the context of training teachers to support children with special educational needs is that the principle of *inclusion* is very much a central tenet – although the extent to which pupils with special educational needs are indeed educated within mainstream settings remains a moot point. A *final* point to emphasise is that notwithstanding a series of volume cuts on the funding of education and indeed other social services, the issues and problems which might plague the delivery of education in Scotland pale to a degree of insignificance when compared with the problems presenting themselves to the South African system at this transitional point in its development when matters of equity, *inter alia*, require urgent attention.

With the above general comments in mind, it is worth indicating a few general statistics concerning the Scottish situation. As at September 1996 (the date of the annual schools' census), the school age population (age 5 to 18) stood at 758 315 pupils attending schools in the public sector. Of those, 441 691 (58,2 per cent) were in primary schools and 316 624 (41,8 per cent) in the secondary sector. Full-time equivalent (FTE) teachers in the primary sector numbered 22 481, yielding a pupil:teacher ratio of 1:19,6. In comparison, there were 24 265 teachers in the secondary sector with a pupil:teacher ratio of 1:13. Bearing in mind the situation in Scotland where children with special educational needs may have these needs 'recorded' in line with relevant statute, about 18 100 or close to 2,4 per cent of the school population, were so 'recorded' – of those 5 400 (29,8 per cent) attended mainstream classes with the remainder attending either special schools or units attached to primary or secondary schools. Such data must be treated with caution, however, since they do not take account of those individual pupils with special educational needs whose needs have not given rise to the opening of a Record of Needs. They do, of course, provide some idea of the dimensions of the population for whom specifically trained staff are required to deliver support.

In common with¹ South Africa, a 'cascade of services' is provided. All teachers in training will at some stage of their pre-service training receive input on the nature and extent of special educational needs. However, this will tend to be sketchy at best and limited to the point of non-existence, at worst. The major emphasis on training lies at the post-experience stage with a range of professional development needs catered for in a highly articulated structure of post-experience training under the Scottish Credit Accumulation and Transfer Scheme (SCOTCAT). This allows for all participating institutions to recognise each other's courses and award 'points' to enable students to gain a clear idea of what they are being credited with and whatever they require to 'earn' to gain an award at either Certificate, Diploma or Masters levels. That is to say, the system permits multiple access and exit points for an individual teacher in the educational system. In terms of content, notwithstanding the principle of de-categorisation of handicap, courses at each of the three levels of award tend to be directed at specific aspects of special educational need, provision and support.

In common with practice throughout Britain, education authorities in Scotland have a statutory requirement to provide for their area an educational psychology service whose functions are broadly defined in statute to study children with special educational needs, and to provide advice, guidance, etc. to parents, teachers and other professionals on how to support such pupils, etc. British experience is one in which educational psychologists find themselves occupying a bureaucratic role sometimes at odds with their professional identity. Nevertheless, the practice of educational psychology certainly testifies to the shifting paradigm referred to earlier in which issues such as consultancy work with 'front line' professionals in the delivery of services is the preferred mode of working. Educational psychologists represent one of the most highly trained professional groups in the education service. They are required to possess an Honours degree in Psychology and, before training at Masters level in Educational Psychology, are normally expected to have two years' relevant experience in working with children and young people (normally as teachers but not exclusively so). After training, they are employed at a training grade for two further years before gaining Charter status of the British Psychological Society. In Scotland, there are presently 320 such psychologists. The current average ratio for psychologists serving children 18 years 11 months and younger is 1:3839, with the target of 1:3600 in reach.

Reference has been made earlier in this section, and elsewhere in this chapter, to the statutory requirement to 'record' children with special educational needs. This has proved to be a somewhat problematic area of educational provision, with difficulties exacerbated by the variability of practice across the country in the administration of the procedures. Current developmental thinking on this suggests a shift away from the uni-dimensionality of the 'continuum of needs' towards a multi-axial approach in which account has to be taken of *types* of educational support available to a school and the *levels* of educational needs of a given pupil. There is a widely held view on these points though terminology may differ from commentator to commentator; for example, Center (1987) proposed a model for delivering special education services that embraces eight levels of service delivery. Mitchell & Ryba (1994) echoing this view, described a more parsimonious model. In Scotland, Cross *et al.* (1994) argue for an approach to recording special educational needs which takes account of dimensions of needs and provision.

Drawing upon data gathered in the context of research on incidence levels as well as taking account of current literature on the issue, it is argued that thinking about support for pupils with special needs involves consideration of at least six distinct aspects, each of equal importance. In addition, instead of thinking about 'special educational needs', it is perhaps more relevant to consider 'a pupil's educational support needs'. This term is used deliberately to move the emphasis away from the within-child model of a pathology towards a systems-based approach that stresses the extent to which the context has to adjust or change. The six strands conceptualised are indicated below:

- the physical environment;
- the nature of the curriculum and how it is delivered;
- the level of pupil support needs;
- access to specialised resources;
- access to specialised support agents or agencies; and
- the mode of communication.

Further, it is possible to grade the level of need on each of these variables along a continuum. Drawing upon research evidence, a 4 x 6 matrix is shown as Figure 11.1 (see pp 160–161). In this matrix, the cell descriptors provide an operational basis on which decisions may be taken regarding the support for a pupil with special educational needs. It is offered at this time as a relevant illustration from the Scottish context on how thinking and practice has developed on the issue of delivering services to pupils with special educational needs. It is also offered as a potential 'audit tool' for any educational context where pressures are such that criteria are required to be established so that scarce resources might be optimally deployed to support pupils with special educational needs.

Conclusion and discussion

In this chapter we have provided an overview of the policies and provision which exist for children with special educational needs in South Africa and Scotland. Clearly there are major differences between these two contexts, but a number of issues and concerns are common to both. Looking at the situation in terms of what might be regarded as concerns and priorities for a transitional educational system, we offer the following discussion.

In South Africa, provision for special educational needs has been peripheral and marginalised in relation to general education. The present priority is that it should take a more central position. To date, the priority in all provinces has been the rationalisation and redistribution of teachers in general education, where vast discrepancies in teacher:pupil ratios are evident, for example in white schools the average ratio is 1:18, whereas the average ratio for black schools ranges from 1:40 to 1:60 (Green 1991). The recently stipulated target is a ratio of 1:40 for all primary schools and 1:35 for secondary schools. To date this has not yet been achieved. Clearly, even if this target were to be achieved, it would compare unfavourably with the Scottish experience as was shown by the ratios reported for Scotland.

In South Africa, there are no official figures at the time of writing for the number of specialist personnel. A situational analysis by NCSNET/NCESS is in progress. The situation in South Africa concerning educational psychologists and other educational support personnel is as bad as it is for teaching staff and compares, again, unfavourably with the experience in a more developed system. Kriegler & Farman (1995) state that even if services, resources and personnel that were reserved for whites were redistributed, the overall ratio of professionals to pupils would remain at an unrealistic level of 1:12 000.

Despite the gross disparities in provision, both systems present some interesting similarities, albeit with differences in emphasis. For example, both systems have similar ideologies in relation to rights, equity, redress, non-discrimination and democracy. Both systems pay special attention to the rights of parents and the community to participate in school governance. In South Africa, 'non-discrimination' is happening at two levels in respect of the issue of 'integration'. At one level, integration refers to the abandonment of the previous Apartheid regime whereby there were different departments of education for the different racial groups. On the other hand, there is a growing practice of ensuring the inclusion of children with special educational needs into the mainstream of education. Whilst this is enshrined in the *South African Schools Act*, 1996, it is by no means, yet, a universal phenomenon. In Scotland whilst the same philosophy of 'inclusion' prevails, the universal realisation of this has not yet been achieved, as Thomson *et al.* (1995) have shown.

Approaches and techniques in provision for special educational needs which are imported from Western societies may not always be appropriate to the learners' needs in developing or transitional societies such as South Africa; therefore in the current training of support professionals and other personnel there is a need to develop a sensitivity towards the needs of (disadvantaged) black pupils with regard to assessment, curriculum issues and the learning context.

Figure 11.1: A level-of-needs matrix

Needs relating to:	Level A Needs	Level B Needs	Level C Needs	Level D Needs
The physical environment	The ordinary class/school environment is appropriate	Some special features are needed in the class/school accommodation, e.g. access to a resource base may be required for the delivery of structured programmes, etc. for some of the time. Provision of ramps and other aids.	A specialist facility may be required, e.g. a resource base/unit within a mainstream school may be required for a substantial portion of the pupil's time in school. Major structural alterations required.	A highly specialised environment, e.g. a special unit/school is required for all the time the pupil is in school to deal with a combination of profound sensory loss, physical disability and/or disruptive behaviour.
The curriculum and how it is delivered	Ordinary curriculum with minor features of differentiation in relation to '5–14' guidelines, such as specific objectives for reading, listening, etc. Alternative methods of presentation within the group.	Significant differentiation is needed in ONE or some areas of the '5–14' curriculum such as require structured and clearly targeted programmes in learning and/or behaviour which are subject to termly review.	Very substantial and specialised differentiation is needed in a wide area of the '5–14' curriculum, such as require weekly review and consultation with agent(s) external to the school on an individualised teaching plan.	The curriculum which the child follows is radically different from that provided in the mainstream in that it requires daily review and consultation with agent(s) external to the school in order to establish the pre-requisites for learning, e.g. cognitive and sensory development.
The level of pupil support required	Levels of pupil support/contact in individual/group settings which are normally available with short periods of up to 3 hours per week contact with classroom aide in small group of 4/5 pupils.	Direct individual support by Learning Support staff in small group of 4/5 pupils. Use of scribe/reader. Short-term behaviour support to avoid causing stress to self/others.	Enhanced level of individual pupil/aide contact required for some of the time, e.g. primary care needs (soiling, catheterisation, etc.), behaviour support.	Pupil requires enhanced level of teacher and/or aide contact continuously. Extended primary care needs, continuous behaviour support, longer-term life plan of total care needs.

Access to specialised resources, facilities and technologies	Ordinarily available resources, facilities and/or technology shared with groups of up to 4/5 pupils on a time-limited basis, e.g. word processors/PCs.	Ordinarily available resources, facilities and/or technology required by the pupil individually, on a time-limited basis, e.g. word processors/PCs.	Highly specialised resources, facilities or technology not normally available and deployed/ designed for the pupil's specific use on a time-limited basis.	Highly specialised resources, facilities or technology not normally available and deployed/ designed for the pupil's specific use on a continuous basis.
Access to specialised support agent(s)	Needs identified and monitored by class teacher and within-school support staff, e.g. Learning Support in mainstream setting. Advice only from other external agent(s), e.g. RAPS, speech and language therapy, behaviour support, sensory-impaired service, etc.	Agreed and monitored support and advice with clear objectives delivered by teacher and support staff deployed to support/ teach pupil, e.g. RAPS, speech and language therapy, occupational therapy, physiotherapy, sensory-impaired service, behaviour support .	Agreed, monitored and delivered support on a regular basis of up to 2 hours per week to small groups of 4/5 pupils by specialist agent(s) as in Level B.	Agreed, monitored and delivered support on an intensive basis of up to 5 hours per week on an individualised basis in a specialised setting, e.g. unit, base or special school by specialist agent(s) as in Level B.
Mode of communication	Ordinary oral/aural and written appropriate with support from relevant aids		Highly specialised methods are required by the pupil, e.g. sign language, braille etc	

Endnotes

1. This terminology is used only insofar as it reflects on the previous Apartheid system in education and in no way represents the views of the authors themselves, who are wholly committed to the principles of non-discrimination.

2. For a detailed critique of the Scottish educational system, see McPherson & Raab (1988). Since 1 April 1997, SCOTVEC and SEB have amalgamated to form the Scottish Qualifications Authority (SQA), which is responsible for the full range of national awards within the Scottish educational system, except for the university sector.

3. The model of the GTC is in varying degrees being adopted in other parts of the Commonwealth – in certain Provinces in Canada, in Australia and in South Africa. Elsewhere in the European Union, the concept of registration has been adopted.

12

How silent was my voice: four decades of a 'coloured' female teacher's experiences

EDITH JANTJES

For as long as I can remember, the passion for learning has been the single most constant force in my life. There were many experiences that contributed to uncertainties about life in South Africa – before, during and even after the era of Apartheid. There were also many personal changes that sometimes shattered my need to learn. But no power has succeeded in obliterating or suppressing for long, this deep-rooted urge to learn.

During the past forty years, as a 'coloured' teacher in South Africa, this passion changed from a desire to learn for personal growth, to an urge to learn in order to become a more effective teacher and to motivate youth and older persons; thus showing them that learning is rewarding.

With time it became clear that having the urge to learn was not enough to open the doors to the learning process itself. There were so many obstacles that threatened to close the doors; yet, that passion to learn somehow always resurfaced. What contributed to the resurfacing of this passion to learn?

The early years of my teaching life, when fear of dominant authorities silenced my voice, my growth as a teacher was inhibited by an absence of other educators' views and insights to illuminate my troubled thinking processes. It was not the lack of knowledge or ignorance as such that was the cause of this helplessness, but rather a lack of opportunity to communicate verbally with other educators. But despite this 'quiet' start, I did develop a greater understanding of the issues and grew as a teacher, as I started to communicate with others.

Career choices in the 1950s

During the 1950s in Apartheid South Africa, a coloured female had limited career choices. If her father's income allowed it, and she loved books, or if she acquired one of the rare scholarships available, she would become either a teacher or a nurse. Mostly this career training would start after having passed Standard Eight – the then Junior Certificate school leaving examination, and the trained nurse or teacher would then occupy the lowest ranks in that profession. As I have always loved books, and as I had won a scholarship at the end of my Standard Six year, my career decision was almost inevitable.

Of the two career choices, I preferred to teach. A further impetus was my great fascination with the magic of the human mind. As a child, when I first learned that wisdom comes from one's 'brain box', I marvelled at my father's magic 'brain box'. To me, as his five-year-old and youngest daughter, he had all the wisdom in the world. Whatever my young mind could not fathom – my father knew so well, not only would he use words to unravel the confusion, but he would illustrate by sketches and real smart humour. He would, for instance, draw a tennis court, place the opponents in a single match and we clearly understood why a ball was 'out' and which had been 'in', in a doubles match – just like that, without even thinking. Or, while playing his violin, and singing, we would learn to appreciate both the light classics of Jeanette MacDonald and Nelson Eddy, as well as dance to the rhythms of Fred Astaire and Ginger Rodgers.

And so I became a primary school teacher, placed in the lowest category in the hierarchy of teaching.

What is teaching?

The first moment in 1956, when I was left alone with my first class of forty-odd Sub B (Grade 2) little children, I was shaking. Those eager eyes seemed not only to look through me, but to rely on me. For what? Oh yes I was their teacher, so I had to teach them. What did that mean? Did I have to teach them all the 'knowledge' in the syllabus, explain and illustrate it as my father had done, and as I had been taught at the teacher training college? Was that it? My father had taught us what we wanted to know, and what he thought we should know to become morally good people. It was real fun. School 'knowledge' as I analysed it, was not wisdom that children eagerly wanted to learn, nor was it knowledge that would make them morally good people. It certainly was not relaxing and fun.

By then I had learnt that school knowledge was what certain educators 'told' teachers to teach, and I used to wonder how they thought that out. All I knew was that unless I taught that knowledge so well that the children could repeat and know it well, I would not become a permanently appointed teacher. Teaching, I firmly told myself, was conveying 'knowledge' to these children, a knowledge which my 'bosses' in education had told me was good for them.

Year after year my learners did reasonably well – very few failed their examinations. But still I asked myself many questions. Was I a good teacher? Did I teach only in the classrooms during the times allotted to the subject matter slots on the timetable? Does a teacher ever stop teaching even when she is not working at school?

Does a teacher teach only in the classroom?

I had started teaching in Port Elizabeth, in the Eastern Cape at a primary school which was a mission school, under the auspices of the church where I worshipped. Soon I learned that a teacher's work did not belong to the classroom only, but involved numerous other forms of teaching after school. It was here that the opportunity to develop moral character took place – in the Sunday School, the church choir, the Girls' and Boys' Brigade, the Youth meetings. And I was happy that I was fulfilling the role of my life's great teacher – my late father – as well as adhering to the tenets of my Christian faith.

To do my job well I separated teaching school knowledge or content in the classroom (to enable children to pass the examinations), from teaching moral education to build character through the numerous social and religious organizations in our community.

I soon learnt that compartmentalising teaching did not work. In the classroom we all had to learn to be caring and kind, and to complete all our work. Learners had to think for themselves about the answers to questions, and to be responsible for their own learning – or was it memorising – in order to pass each standard. In the community we all needed knowledge to understand the world of which we were a part. It was so frightening to try to teach everything. To whom could I talk about my own confusion so that I could understand the mission and nature of my career? If I talked to the school principal, or was rebellious enough to ask the school inspector a question, I could lose my job, and my fountain of wisdom – my father – was no longer there.

And so I turned to books – just as my father had taught us. Once we could understand the written word, he used the books he had acquired for us in the home, to show us how to direct our own independent inquiries to sources that would satisfy our individual pursuits. It was rather lonely, and the answers took a long to come. Often it was too difficult, for it was like a blind journey, in the secret of our minds, and no one could tell where the end would be and what would be waiting here.

What does the acquisition of knowledge involve?

The puzzle was far from being solved for me. In fact, in many ways it is still puzzling. If success with classroom teaching also needs moral education, and if effective teaching in the community depends on a knowledge base, why not combine the two at school and in community teaching? At that time, I did not know about all the many books on education, so the first source I studied was Whitehead's *Aims of education* (1949). I learned from Whitehead a totally different perspective on teaching. Firstly I had to grapple with his notion that teaching is understood in terms of both verbal and non verbal communion between the teacher and the learner – an active rather than a passive experience! And, that this 'communion' does not mean the acquisition of knowledge alone. Whitehead taught me that the mission of education is also the "acquisition of the art of the utilization of knowledge". It is an art which is much more than the proliferation of 'inert ideas' which are simply told and "received without being utilized, or tested, or thrown into fresh combinations" (Whitehead 1949:13–36; Jantjes 1987:15–16).

Many, many years later, Whitehead's teaching was echoed in the 'verbal and non verbal communion' between me – a fifty-year old graduate student working on my Ph.D in the United States (USA), and one of my most inspiring formal teachers – Benjamin Bloom, when he taught us that teaching was the utilisation, application, critique, and testing of knowledge in every institution of one's society, including the development of one's own status. But, more of this experience later. Filled with fear of seeming to be rebellious and without knowing whom to trust and talk to about my real concerns, I struggled with these new ideas, and with their application in my teaching.

My task became clearer when I stumbled on another source, cited by Whitehead, namely Gilman (1898). I learned that all of the teacher teaches all of the learner. Most pertinently, that teaching should aim at developing character. Teaching is not so much imparting knowledge; it is more about whetting the appetite of the learners, developing powers and moral forces, and exhibiting methods to do so (Jantjes 1987:16). Gilman (1898 cited in Whitehead 1949) is emphatic about the development of character – to him the aims of teaching involve the development of the character of the learners by the character of the teacher, and that this development should prepare learners for the service of society; learners that are thoughtful and progressive guides in whatever act or thought they may be engaged. This aim of teaching has also been echoed by the philosopher, Martin Buber (see Kohn 1991:497). According to him "education worthy of the name is essentially education of character".

During the 1950s however, it was the study of Whitehead that shed much treasured light on the development of my own understanding of my career. Sadly, my understanding became much clearer in my mind than it did in practice, and in Apartheid South Africa, grappling with the ongoing development of my own career it became a lonely, fearful process.

Reflections: What is learning?

To come to grips with my many concerns about learning I started reflecting on my own learning process. It was a startling discovery to find that all the mathematics and science that I had loved so well, and had spent voluntary time doing at high school (even when I had no homework in these subjects) I had completely forgotten by the time I became a teacher. So many of my peers at high school had argued over borrowing my science and mathematics homework books. Yet a few years later I could not remember most of those subject matters. What does it then benefit a learner to learn content and to achieve exceptionally well in examinations? In fact why learn content at all? I was shocked that I had dared to think such a thought, even though it was just in the secrecy of my mind. And, oh, I just loved the human mind more and more. It was one's own private world, only God knew what happened in that 'magic brain box'.

One thing I knew most emphatically, I could never verbalise this question about school content to anyone – it would be tantamount to heresy. Still, there I was with a blank about most of the past content I had understood so well. Why teach at all?

But there was another side to it. I not only remembered passionately the English literature I had studied at school, but I actually kept a poetry anthology at my bedside, next to my Bible, and these books were not there for display – I read them even when I was tired. And, years before I had had no idea that one could read poetry for leisure reading. So what was different about the content of English literature? My love for reading my Bible was part of my father's and my Dutch grandmother's daily teaching – the Bible contains the moral codes of behaviour which guide my life. But that was not so with English literature. Besides, my mathematics and science teachers at high school were just as brilliant as my English teacher, or could it have been that this English teacher at Paterson High School in Port Elizabeth in 1952, already had a premonition that, as a political activist, while he was still allowed to teach and live in South Africa, it was his calling to challenge the minds of the non-white youth he taught? Perhaps this English teacher, Dennis Brutus was as optimistic in the early 50s as Colin Eglin was in the 70s, that through education, he would be preparing his young learners for a South African society that would one day move away from a racially separated society to a sharing society – socially, economically, culturally and educationally (Starcke 1978:84).

Whatever it was that inspired Dennis Brutus as a teacher, in his teaching there was a difference. Not only was this English teacher a brilliant scholar and writer, he did certain things differently. What was it? It was not just that his amazingly retentive mind could quote verbatim, accurate excerpts from different texts, with precise referencing to pagination, chapter or acts and scenes, and publication details – no, there was something else.

There was the misty morning in 1952 in Port Elizabeth, when Brutus walked into Standard Nine classroom, gently punched a few of us on our shoulders, and whisked us out of the classroom, onto the top of the wall at the entrance of the school, overlooking the bay. We were to use adjectives, adverbs, punctuation, action verbs, imagery, other figures of speech, and intersperse short and long sentences, to describe the effects of the mist on the harbour. We had to return to class, and communicate verbally and nonverbally our impressions of the misty cloud hovering over the bay, to the rest of our classmates. (What a pity I had to leave school that year to train as a primary school teacher.)

Then, there was our school magazine, when we saw our own compositions – first neatly typed, and then in print – we could write, we could compose verse! And, it was our own juggling with words that stared back at us.

And the many dramatisations of Shakespeare in our own idiom in class – with our own improvised props, and the varied shared 'communions' of our own young experiences which unmistakably related to characters and themes in poetry, drama, short stories and novels, that made literature so relevant and meaningful. Our own experiences were like the experiences of characters in the works of great writers.

It took me a long time to realise the difference between that learning process and the other subject matters I had learned. Literature was part of our lives, part of the world outside the classroom, real and exciting, yet most firmly intertwined with classroom work.

Whitehead and Gilman certainly became just as real to me. The problem was how to incorporate this understanding of learning in my own teaching without letting my academic superiors know what I was doing?

Is there a causal relationship between teaching and learning?

To many of us the good things come late in life, while some good ones sadly never happen. My desire to study at university came very late in my life, but it did happen and my appetite for ongoing learning remained huge.

It was, possibly, not unexpected that I chose to major in English, in order to teach English, and that I pursued the study of History in order to understand our world much better. There was, however, another reason for further studies in History, despite the fact that at high school I had always hated South African history, which to me was the glorification of the British and the Afrikaners, and the defamation of the character of all the other people in South Africa. I resolved to study History after my encounter with another inspiring teacher at the University of the Western Cape, an Afrikaner, Gerhard Duvenage. He taught us, his undergraduate students, to think deeply about the reality of Cicero's wisdom: that unless we understood and examined what happened before we were born, we would remain forever children (Duvenage 1973). I studied and taught English with a relish that gained me the title 'workaholic'.

By then my disenchantment with teaching had gained other dimensions. I had taught all levels at primary school, at high school, and at teacher training college. But what did educators do? In my various administrative duties I had access to many records, including the 'green books' with neat rows of test scores. What was horrifying was that the achievement levels of children very seldom changed over the years. As I compared children's test achievements, or learning capacities, I found that they remained mostly at the same achievement level when they left school, as they were when they were admitted to the school four, six, seven or more years before. What did we educators do to alter children's learning abilities? What does school 'knowledge' do to improve children's capacity to develop and learn and to have more positive feelings about themselves as learners? It was fine if a child started school as an 'A' achiever and left school as such, but for the 'E' and 'F' achievers, they invariably ended school as drop outs.

Did teaching cause learning? Is there a causal relationship between what we teach and children's ability to learn, long after they had left our classes and have learned the subject matter we taught them? If there were a causal relationship between teaching and learning, why did children, after twelve and more years of subject-matter learning, not develop their abilities to learn other work, other than subject matter at school? Should the ability to learn content then not affect the ability to learn in general?

I was further outraged when as Head of the Department of English at the college of education where I taught, I had assisted an older Afrikaans-speaking student to improve remarkably at English. When the school inspectors 'tested' him and others for the final oral examination, I was told he had to remain at the level he was at the beginning of the year of his further study. Why? "It was not possible for an Afrikaans speaking adult to improve so remarkably within one year!" Yet, this student's 'appetite for English had been whetted', he could converse in English with confidence, he read beyond the prescribed works – a rare achievement – all demonstrations of changes in his interaction with English!

Why do some of the authorities complacently accept that learning levels should remain static? Have the experiences during the processes of teaching and learning subjects no influence over the development of other skills and abilities of learners? The disillusionment with my career drove me to such depths of despair that I wondered why we had schools at all. When I am sick, I reasoned, I go to a trained physician in the institution of medicine, and after my encounter I am not left in that sick state. Yet, within the institution of education, many learners' learning abilities remained at the same level of achievement after many encounters with trained educators. It was disturbing that students seemed happy to be learning subject matter as it was given to them, and to forget it after their examinations. Why were they not keen to argue, explore, debate, analyse and even produce new and innovative ideas about the knowledge they had learned? And, why did this not seem unusual and odd to so many educators with whom I worked? I was completely non-plussed.

The dependence between teaching and learning: from teaching to 'studenting' and then to learning

Good things were to happen to me, at the most appropriate time. Just when I thought I would never see light in my confused mind, I found myself on the staff at the University of the Western Cape (UWC), in the Faculty of Education, and two years later, at the 'ripe' or 'old' age of fifty, as a recipient of an Educational Opportunities Council scholarship, I was sitting at the feet of Benjamin Bloom in the USA. These are experiences I would not exchange, not even for the monetary wealth we teachers so often long for. The learning processes as a faculty member at UWC, and as a graduate student at Northwestern University almost literally 'lifted the lid of my mind' and admitted me freely, as a spontaneous passenger on an on-going learning expedition.

In my first graduate class, with Bloom as the teacher, for a while I wondered if I were close to heaven. It was just too good to be really happening. Bloom was articulating all of these secret fears and thoughts I had had, in describing past research on teaching and learning. He and many other educators had been researching "The alterable variables and the Two sigma problem" (Bloom 1984), for more than fifty years, in many countries in the world. The predictability of learning achievement had not only been researched and challenged, there were proven strategies that could be applied to alter children's learning achievement and mental processes and abilities, long after school content had been forgotten. Subject matter was used as a vehicle for social dialogical interaction and mental pursuit. At last I could talk about all my concerns freely, openly, anytime, anywhere and with anyone. I could question researchers and research findings, contest any generalizations.

More than that, I thanked God for the newly found consolation and encouragement – my mind had not played tricks with me during all those past years. Spiritually I had searched for a place in a world of advanced, developed and active thinking, where I could confidently and fearlessly articulate my thoughts in vigorous and illuminating discourse.

Motivated by Bloom and Robert Menges, my academic adviser and keen scholar and scientific writer, a great deal of my search was rewarded. As I could articulate my thoughts fearlessly, my learning process was no longer a lonely, mental pursuit. It had become an active and interactive and extended, delightful and illuminating journey. Much more, it had become excitingly challenging, as well as challenged.

The understanding of my mission and its application had become fused. The process was reinforced by numerous works of educators and thinkers, such as Fenstermacher (1986), in particular his assertion that there is a dependence between teaching and learning, and not a causal relationship, and how this "ontological dependence" (his words) manifests itself. For Fenstermacher the observed variations in learning that follow the observed variations of teaching, are the outcomes of the teacher's attempts to improve the learner's abilities and capacities to be a learner (Jantjes 1987:23). The teacher's role is to initiate the process of learning. Knowledge, in Fenstermacher's theory has a much wider purpose – the teacher provides the means, or leads the learner to an understanding of knowledge, not as an end in itself, but to enable the learner to become a student who can thereafter gain independent access to any knowledge. To Fenstermacher

> ...to educate a fellow human being is to provide that person with the means to structure his or her own experiences in ways that keep on expanding what the person knows, has reasons to doubt or believe, and understands, as well as the person's capacity for autonomous and authentic action, and the person's sense of a place in history. It is not supplying the knowledge, the reasonable beliefs, but rather supplying the means to gain access to and continue the enlargement of knowledge, of understanding. (Fenstermacher 1986:46; Jantjes 1987:26)

My mission – of helping to liberate the human mind – to guide learners to develop mental powers and moral forces in order to utilise knowledge and to develop character, had become more attainable than ever before. Teaching knowledge, I understood, is not a means to get a learner to become a specialist in that knowledge in a prescribed way; rather the understanding of knowledge should increase the learner's capacity to understand much more than that knowledge. In the process the learner should gain some influence over the art of living, to become an individual in pursuit of his or her own interests, curiosity, and meaning in life.

The mission of my own career was no longer a troubled course – I had found direction, though late in my career.

Political and mental liberation

Back in South Africa, as a disadvantaged educator, teaching mainly disadvantaged students, teacher education had become a challenging dialogue. There was so much to share and learn from colleagues as well as students. To inspire and motivate pre- and in-service teachers to teach each learner to make the best of themselves – despite the political 'labels' and barriers forced on them – turned me into a committed 'educational activist'.

I was most enthusiastic to share the results of my doctoral research in the USA on Bloom's "Alterable Variables" (1984). But this turned out to be a further challenge for me when I learned that many of my colleagues had different views on Benjamin Bloom and in fact I soon shared Bloom's tag, of being 'a Positivist'. If it had not been for the collegial and collaborative debates with colleagues in the Department of Didactics at UWC, in particular with the then chairperson of the Department, Dirk Meerkotter, I might have crept back into my shell of silence. Instead I embraced critique, and in consequence my learning process continued.

As I listened to the many stories of my disadvantaged students, I realised how essential it is to analyse knowledge on different levels, to find out whether it is oppressive or exploitative, whether it misrepresents or marginalises particular views of the world, or whether it provides a deeper understanding of how our and our students' world is constructed (McLaren 1989:183). With my peers I started reinventing myself in order to learn how to become a liberating educator. And I welcomed our staff development seminars as a means to engage in mutual (though often scary) discussion. I was happy to continue to reform myself as a teacher, to talk, argue, debate, seek others' points of view, and when necessary to disagree with anyone, in writing and in discussion. To me this was the practical process of liberation of my own mind, and it rubbed off onto my students at all levels.

I think it was my enthusiasm that indicated to my students that I was sincere about our mutual development. I became eager to create conditions in class for them to speak to the themes of their own lives. Education, for me had become a process of illumination, which is more than just an intellectual task. It had become a real process of knowing both reality and how reality is composed. Teaching and learning are not absolute. With ongoing interaction and communion between the learning process and the reality of changing societies, there can never be an end point in the development of the teacher.

Teaching and learning had become for me a means of inquiry, critique, construction and reconstruction. Gradually my idiom became a language of hope and possibility (Giroux 1983:103) for both my students and myself in my regular classes, at in-service levels and in the various community-based and research projects undertaken. Learning was being made relevant, critical, and transformative, the basis for social transformation, for helping so many other disadvantaged persons to become involved in building a better world for themselves.

Changing through the experience of 'voice'

Now, after forty years of teaching and learning, it has become possible to understand how and why to use the knowledge of how society works in the classrooms. It has become possible to enjoy working at school, in the classroom as well as in community activities outside the classroom. For learning has truly become an ongoing process, always challenged by the process of my own growth, my own formation. It means also learning from practice, but from practice in community with many actors, and not being afraid of bringing social practice into the classroom.

It does not mean talking *to* students, and talking *to* peers. What it does mean is talking *with* them, and not fearing to challenge and be challenged. The moment when I became liberated from the fears of letting my voice be heard was really the moment I became a learner as well as a teacher.

Conclusions: the relationship between my own development as a teacher, and the growth of my students

As a pragmatist my concerns are with the outcomes, the results of my teaching work. The burning question after four teaching-packed decades, working full time, part time and in many places and capacities, is: 'Have I served my students and education meaningfully, or not?' and 'Is there a relationship between my own development and feelings as a teacher, and the growth of my students?'

Retrospectively the processes of analysis and comparison can be attempted by investigating the actual students I taught. Mostly they were disadvantaged students from disadvantaged environments in Apartheid South Africa. So I ask myself more specifically: 'What kind of adults/people have they become after leaving school? Have I contributed in some way to their lives as successful, independent adults, or not?'

Sadly, the ten years as a primary school teacher, did not yield actual feedback by past students that demonstrated that I had made a meaningful impact on their lives. In this regard I refer to the qualities that Freire links to the production of knowledge, namely abilities of creating, recreating, critical reflection, curiosity. Qualities that are enabling and that lead to "ultimate participation in society's historical process" (Freire 1970:12).

Contrary to this lack of observed outcomes, as well as voluntary communication by the past students I taught at primary schools, I have received ongoing reports, and seen the changes in many students taught at high school, tertiary levels, in-service and basic adult education workshops. Boldly they contact me telephonically, in writing, through messages via my own children, and in greeting cards, long after the content of the subject matters I taught them have been forgotten. They describe how classroom experiences have enabled them to reflect on both their history and cultural experiences as disadvantaged and formerly disadvantaged persons. They testify how they have been enabled to participate in the production of new and transformed knowledge.

There is, for instance Saleem, the advocate, who is now a director and partner in a formidable legal firm in Cape Town, who repeatedly acknowledges that if I had not enabled him to debate, argue, reason logically and express his own views time and time again in English classes, he would never have realized how powerfully eloquent he really is. There is Eugene, one of three brothers in the sub economic gangster-dominated township of Manenberg in Cape Town, whom most teachers at the particular school refused to teach in 1976, who declares over and over again that not only did I teach him to 'juggle with words' in creative writing exercises, but I also enabled him to understand the difference between 'credit' and 'debit' in Accountancy classes. Eugene is in the trucking business, writes his own specifications and interviews the 'top' persons in an organisation, and also does community policing. He now insists that he must 'protect' me.

When Namibia gained independence, I was invited in 1989 to a week of workshops with subject advisors and administrators, exposing them to Bloom's "Alterable Variables" and "automaticity in reading". The purpose was to assist educators to make learning and teaching more relevant to society's needs and the invitation was prompted by past students of mine.

Silence versus voice

Reflection on the development of so many of my students, led me to realize the role that my own voice played in my students' growth: the years as a primary school teacher, during the years of fearful subjugation, when my own voice was 'quiet', a culture of silence prevailed. I compared these years to the time when I had acquired a voice, had communication and dialogue with students, peers and teachers.

In analysing my teaching at primary school, I must come to terms with the assessment of my classroom pedagogy. It corresponds with the time when we in South Africa, as disadvantaged persons, were dominated into silence, when the power elite had totally imposed its will and culture of silence onto a vast sector of the oppressed masses.

It was also my understanding with that 'knowledge' which I was compelled to pass onto my primary school learners, that mystified and legitimized given political belief systems, even though silently in my own mind I had questioned my teaching, I was a victim of hegemony. For this kind of teaching typified Freire's notion of a 'banking' approach to education that so dominated my teaching at primary school. I did not talk and speak as a teacher about things in which I believed, instead, the 'I' that taught was dominated and subordinate, and I perpetuated this ideological manipulation onto my learners.

They were the passive recipients of knowledge presented as objective facts, originally transferred to me by many teachers (except those I mention in this chapter), and then transferred to my primary school learners by me – knowledge as absolute truth. No wonder most of my primary school learners' creative abilities were stifled by me, even perhaps inhibited, as they were taught merely to memorize knowledge without critical reflection and questioning.

In concluding this story, which is mainly personal and in a way autobiographical, I have presented a self-analysis of my own teaching and learning experiences. The emphasis has been on the many changes of my identity through the various stages of personal assertion and growth. The processes of introspection and retrospection demonstrate the force of *self* in developing a critical consciousness, and the enabling role of dialogue – ongoing shared dialogue – in the process of improving my own situation as well as helping disadvantaged persons to improve, and if necessary transform their view of the world and their situations.

SECTION FOUR

Changing teaching and learning practices in adult and higher education

Introduction

In both Britain and South Africa, higher education is in a state of flux because of the insufficient resources available for teaching and the substantial increases in the numbers of students from a wider range of backgrounds. While the scale of the problem facing the two countries is very different, in both situations the proposed solutions stress the importance of more systematic preparation of students, more effective teaching through both traditional and innovative methods, and greater use of resource-based learning materials. In Britain, there is increasing discussion of the possibilities of electronic transfer between institutions, but this is still not an immediate reality. In the South African context, the historic imbalances in educational provision have the highest priority, while teaching is substantially affected by problems of second language learning.

In Britain, the Dearing Report (Dearing Committee 1997) has drawn attention to the need to make greater and more systematic use of innovative teaching methods. The lack of training of academic staff, even in traditional methods of teaching, creates a substantial problem when new methods are urgently required, and so the Dearing Report has suggested that all lecturers should undergo both initial and subsequent training, with teaching quality being assured through membership of a professional body – the Institute for Learning and Teaching in Higher Education.

In South Africa, the *Draft White Paper on Higher Education* (Department of Education 1997j) has presented a blueprint for the transformation of higher education, which also indicates some of the implications for teaching and learning. There are, however, serious tensions in what has been proposed. There is a need to widen access to higher education, while producing high quality graduates, and yet many young people seek entry from inadequate levels of school achievement. There have also been demands to make higher education more related to the needs of industry. One suggestion has been the extension of the competency or outcomes-based model – Curriculum 2005 – into higher education, but that would constrain the efforts of staff to educate students to think for themselves. Yet South Africa needs many more critical, reflective graduates to lead the transformation of its society.

The chapters in this section address these suggestions and dilemmas in the light of both research findings and recent developments in teaching and learning at the University of the Western Cape. Entwistle compares the changes in higher education in Britain with the conclusions of the White Paper, and introduces research findings to indicate the kinds of learning that will be required of future graduates in both countries. These findings highlight the advantages of deep approaches to learning which lead to personal understanding and ready transfer of knowledge into new contexts and problems. They also suggest ways in which teaching and the whole learning environment affect the quality of learning, and the difficulties which can be anticipated in persuading staff to change their fundamental beliefs about teaching.

The subsequent chapters summarise a series of innovative approaches to teaching carried out at the University of the Western Cape. Linder and Marshall explain how an introductory Physics programme has been fundamentally changed to make the material relevant and interesting, while increasing the intellectual challenge it offers to the students. The course has evolved over several years and shows how imaginative methods can be used to meet some of the demands of the White Paper, and how the systematic application of research findings can guide practice. Such changes can, however, be expected to be effective only where the lecturers have a conception of teaching which focuses on the learner, rather than simply on presenting information within the traditional framework of the discipline.

The chapter by Bak again indicates how innovative methods of teaching not only improve the quality and enjoyment of learning, but also respond to the needs of society. The consideration of metatheory within a post-graduate degree in education may seem far removed from the everyday concerns of school teachers, but this course encourages the students to think critically and independently about the issues facing education in South Africa. The development of this type of thinking will be crucial if teachers are to counteract the prevailing rejection in schools of expert advice that is seen as hegemonic discourse. The ability to weigh such advice in terms of its evidence and its logic provides a focus for this metatheory course. The use of resource-based methods, combined with periodic lectures and tutorials, also indicates in practical terms how to design a course for the academic development of teachers in a context of limited resources and with difficulties in attending regular classes.

The final chapter by Geidt takes up a similar theme by showing how students in continuing education can be encouraged to develop an understanding of research skills, and the uses and misuses of evidence, both in the press and in discussions within their own community.

The teaching innovations presented in this section have been chosen to illustrate changes that have already been made, and to provide guidelines for future progress, but the reports on this work also contain warnings about the difficulties in store, as the higher education system tries to respond through new ways of teaching and learning to demands for redress and transformation within the new South Africa.

Nelleke Bak and Noel Entwistle

13

Teaching for learning as higher education changes

NOEL ENTWISTLE

This chapter examines some of the changes that are taking place in higher education in both Britain and South Africa and the ways in which these affect teaching and learning. These changes derive from attempts to rapidly increase the proportion of the age group entering higher education at a time when governments are unable to provide any real increase in funding. The changes are also directed towards more equitable access opportunities and a more economical use of allocated funds while maintaining, if not improving, the quality of teaching and learning. There is a growing realisation that the continued use of traditional teaching methods in this changed climate will lead to a breakdown in the system. In both countries, the suggested solutions involve greater use of both resource-based learning and distance learning supported by information technology.

One of the weaknesses of higher education in the past has been a failure to draw on relevant research findings to inform decisions. While academic staff build their courses on research findings in their own discipline, they rarely are well informed about research on teaching and learning. Indeed, many of them have only a rudimentary grasp of the basic principles of teaching. They do have what might be called 'craft knowledge' (Van Driel *et al.* 1997) which is passed on by word of mouth, but few have seriously studied pedagogical aspects of their profession. This lack of a professional knowledge of teaching and learning inevitably impedes change. In a situation where radical change is essential, traditional attitudes have to be modified to allow new methods even to gain a foothold. This is not to say that research findings provide the whole answer, but to ignore them at a time when new approaches to teaching are urgently needed seems perverse.

This chapter considers the current situation in the two countries and draws on research into student learning to indicate ways in which the innovations being considered might best be implemented. Higher education can be seen as a series of systems – at national level, as a set of institutions, and then within each institution and each department (Biggs 1994). The system operating within an institution presents the student with a learning environment in which knowledge and skills have to be acquired and demonstrated under specific conditions. This environment is made up of teaching and assessment practices, together with the assignments and learning resources that form part of the course. Every component of this environment affects both the learning process and the quality and longevity of the knowledge that is acquired (Eizenberg 1988). This view of teaching and learning will be elaborated through relevant research evidence and considered in relation to the specific changes being suggested.

Predictions of learning outcomes cannot be precise because of the complexity and variability of learning environments and their differential effects on individual students (Entwistle 1997c). Nevertheless, the research evidence does offer principles and guidelines that can be used, along with professional experience and judgement, to plan changes with more confidence.

The changing context of higher education in Britain

The populist and monetarist policies of the Conservative governments from 1979 to 1997 fundamentally affected the nature of the whole education system in Britain. These demanded greater efficiency and effectiveness of teaching, together with more accountability and openness, while substantially increasing the proportion of the age group entering higher education. A change in the funding system abolished the 'binary divide' between universities and polytechnics, thus creating a much larger and more diverse university system. Besides bringing the proportion of the age group entering higher education more into line with other equivalent countries, the government was anxious to widen access for under-represented social groups, as well as for students with physical handicaps. Universities were also expected to make provision for mature students by allowing them to retrain and study for additional professional qualifications.

Staff have thus been faced not only with larger numbers but also a higher proportion of students less well prepared for university than previously. Many schools still have little experience in preparing pupils to study in university, and indeed have to put all their efforts into helping the majority to achieve reasonable levels in the various external examinations. Such schools are thus allowing a larger proportion of students to reach higher education, but leaving universities with more problems in teaching them.

The mechanisms used to induce change included both manipulation of the funding procedures and the introduction of quality assurance in various forms. Funding of student numbers was used initially to encourage institutions to accept substantially more students, and then to prevent further expansion. At the same time, the 'efficiency gains' required of all higher education institutions have progressively decreased the unit of resource available for teaching.

The efficiency with which institutions were managed and governed was, until recently, overseen by a quality audit from the Higher Education Quality Council, while the effectiveness of teaching within departments was judged through systems set up by the funding councils. Recently, a Quality Assurance Agency has been set up to develop less intrusive and time-consuming approaches. As the monetary rewards for excellence in research have substantially outweighed those for teaching, this system has distorted the balance of effort between teaching and research throughout the British system, to the detriment of teaching. Nevertheless, quality assessment has raised the profile of teaching within institutions, and has made the procedures through which quality is assured more transparent and effective.

Typically, quality in teaching is secured by appraising the performance of individual academic staff every two years. Appraisal interviews are conducted by the head of department, or another senior member of the department, who also examines a self-report on the whole range of activities. Each interview leads to an action report, agreed by the individual concerned, which specifies any changes required or training to be received. While these reports are expected to include improvements in teaching, actions concerning research or the allocation of teaching have been more common, particularly in the older universities. The quality of teaching within departments is usually judged by a faculty committee, which examines departmental procedures. The committee considers how feedback on courses is obtained from students and whether such feedback, and comments from external examiners, have led to changes. At university level, a committee will then ensure that faculties have been following institutional policies on quality assurance.

These policies on quality assurance, however, have not been well articulated, particularly at national level. And, at both national and institutional level, the procedures introduced have imposed an altogether excessive bureaucratic burden on staff. Quality assurance procedures have, to a large extent, eliminated weak management and teaching practices, but they have also severely damaged staff morale. The additional demands for evidence of effective teaching came just as pressures were also building up from increased student numbers and the Research Assessment Exercise.

Day-to-day working life for academic staff in Britain has changed substantially, with typically a much greater marking load and larger tutorial groups. The number of hours spent in face-to-face teaching depends on the way in which departments have responded to the challenge of larger numbers. In some departments, there are more tutorial classes to teach, as well as larger ones; in others, graduate students and other part-time teachers have been brought in to keep teaching loads at reasonable levels.

Although the need to think radically about the methods used in teaching has been widely recognised, the response so far has been limited. Departments have been expected not just to find better ways of dealing with larger numbers but also to help under-prepared students. Some universities have provided imaginative induction schemes, but few university-wide policies have been developed. It had been anticipated that greater use would be made of resource-based and technology-based learning to cope with the increased numbers. While this has happened to some extent, the changes have been neither systematic nor sufficiently widespread. Substantial changes may, however, be imminent with the recent publication of the report of the National Committee of Inquiry into Higher Education (Dearing Committee 1997), chaired by Sir Ron Dearing.

Students and learning: Conclusions of the Dearing Committee

The main conclusions of the Dearing Committee relating to teaching and learning anticipate changes in the learning environment in higher education, with less reliance on lectures and face-to-face tuition generally, and with greater use of independent learning through resource-based and computer-based learning materials. The report argued that newly appointed academic staff should be trained to teach, and that there should be a national system of qualifications through which staff could demonstrate their competence. It also criticised the lack of systematic research into the changes being introduced into higher education. To tackle this problem it suggested establishing an Institute for Learning and Teaching in Higher Education. This new organisation would accredit staff training, establish quality control of computer-based learning materials, plan and fund systematic research and development work, and disseminate its findings. The first of these functions has already been accepted by the Committee of Vice-Chancellors and Principals, but there appears to be a continuing reluctance to invest in systematic research and development work.

Redress and transformation: *The Draft White Paper on Higher Education*

The situation facing South African higher education has been described in detail in the report of the National Commission on Higher Education, which formed the basis for government proposals contained in the *Draft White Paper on Higher Education* (Department of Education, 1997j). The two terms *redress* and *transformation* encapsulate the main proposals – to redress the historic imbalance between educational provision for whites, compared with coloured and black students, and the transformation of the whole educational system to provide an education designed for the needs of the twenty-first century. The stages from primary through to post-graduate are to become fully articulated within an overall system which gives fair access to all.

The conditions under which black children were educated at school meant that even those who obtained the matriculation requirements for entry into higher education were prevented from coping effectively with courses designed for students coming from schools in the white sector. Progress through the educational system was also difficult due to the lack of places in technikons and in teacher training, nursing, agricultural and other colleges. Such inadequate preparation for university is made more difficult as instruction is almost entirely in English or Afrikaans, either of which is a second language (or even third) for most black and many coloured students. These problems are now being accentuated by increased movement between areas of the country, drawing many young people, without either money or accommodation, to study in the major cities. The composition of student bodies in all universities is in the process of rapid change at a time when no additional resources are available. The speed and scale of these changes thus create substantial threats to the whole higher education system.

The White Paper envisages a substantial increase in the number of places available at non-university tertiary institutions, but nevertheless recognises that methods of teaching will have to change radically to cope with the demand for advanced education of various kinds. The proposed solution, not yet fully worked out, would require much greater use of resource-based learning for students within contact universities, and of technology-based learning for students working on their own. The government plans to create a single body responsible for producing materials for distance learning in higher education and co-ordinating the production of resource-based learning materials through regional learning centres.

Much of the rhetoric from both the Curriculum 2005 for schools and the White Paper is redolent of two rather different ideologies within educational thinking, which can be found in many other countries as well. There is an attempt to blur the distinction between education and training, so as to increase the status of the latter. This move is intended to make education more directly relevant to the vocational and labour needs of the economy. In itself, this seems to be a long overdue change, but it has also altered thinking about education. An 'outcome-based education', with precise specification of what students should learn, can create severe restrictions on freedom for both teachers and students. However, both Curriculum 2005 and the White Paper call for the development of skills such as 'learning to learn' and envisage methods of teaching which encourage group learning and openness in teaching. The curious incompatibility between these two ideologies of teaching can be seen more clearly by looking at recent conceptualisations of student learning and teaching in higher education.

Contrasting approaches to studying

Over the last twenty years, a substantial literature on student learning has been built up from studies originating in Sweden and Britain (see Marton *et al.* 1984) and subsequently developed extensively in Australasia (see Biggs 1987, 1993). This literature now offers to staff in higher education a coherent set of concepts with which to describe important qualitative differences in the ways in which students study. These differences can be seen as individual variations in student characteristics and personal history, but they also depend on the ways in which students perceive teaching and the whole learning environment (Entwistle 1997c).

Staff often underestimate the substantial differences in the knowledge base which students have when starting any course. Even when they have comparable qualifications, these differences remain and affect how well they subsequently learn. Beyond these differences in knowledge, students also differ markedly in their reasons for continuing into higher education. Beaty has described these differences in terms of *learning orientations* (Beaty *et al.* 1997) which identify not just vocational, academic, personal and social orientations, but, in addition, within the first three, a variation in the focus of interest – either *intrinsic* interest in the actual content of the course or an *extrinsic* concern with the qualification or with simply continuing up the educational 'ladder' without any clear goal.

Säljö distinguished contrasting conceptions of learning within a hierarchy which described how adults varied in their beliefs about what was involved in learning (see Marton & Säljö 1997). The fundamental difference was between those who saw learning as essentially accumulating knowledge in an unreflective way, ready to reproduce it as required, and those who believed that learning depended on understanding the material for themselves, and so transforming the material presented in interaction with their own prior knowledge, experience and feelings.

The concept that has had most continuing impact on teaching and learning in higher education describes the very different ways in which students tackle specific study tasks – their *approaches to studying*. Marton originally introduced this concept to summarise what he found to be surprisingly different ways in which students went about reading an academic article (Marton & Säljö 1976b), but subsequently its meaning was extended to cover a range of different academic tasks (see Entwistle 1997d). Students approach tasks with different intentions, either to reproduce the material without much internal processing (*surface approach*) or to understand the material for themselves (*deep approach*). The surface approach often derives from habitual ways of studying acquired at school and an instrumental attitude to the course material, while the deep approach depends on having adequate prior knowledge, but also on a transformational view of learning and an intrinsic interest in the material. Naturally, students are also *strategic* in their approach to studying (Ramsden 1981), adapting their approach to the specific assessment requirements, and this tendency explains the ways in which teaching and the learning environment so markedly affect the quality of learning outcomes.

Relating teaching to learning

The research on student learning initially described, admittedly in an oversimplified way, the way the approach to studying affected learning outcomes. The next step was to investigate how teaching and assessment influenced approaches to studying, and hence learning outcomes. It soon became clear that it was possible to change the average level of these approaches by manipulating the method of assessment. Where students knew they would be given fact-based multiple choice tests, their approaches shifted away from deep towards surface, and when essay-type examinations were expected the reverse was true (Thomas & Bain 1984). Subsequently, it was found that 'freedom in learning' – having some opportunity to choose certain courses, topics and methods of learning – encouraged a deep approach, while a heavy workload, and the lack of time for independent study that this implies, pushed students into surface approaches.

Of course, the method and style of teaching also affects approaches to studying. While lectures have been criticised for inducing passive learning, there are lecturers who are able to transform students' approaches by providing a vicarious experience of relevance (Hodgson 1997). Clarity, level, pace and structure are widely seen as affecting how well lectures are rated, but it seems to be the quality of explanations, and the lecturer's enthusiasm for the subject matter and perceived empathy towards the students, which most strongly induce a deep approach (Entwistle 1997d).

The essence of this approach to lecturing is to engage the students in the academic enterprise, and the same effect can be produced in small group discussions, and in resource-based learning. It is not so much the method, but the way in which that method is implemented which most directly affects the quality of learning. It is pointless looking in isolation at the effects of any particular teaching method, or indeed at the form of assessment or any other aspect of the learning environment. Outcomes of learning depend on the *combined* effects of each component of the whole learning environment (Eizenberg 1988). In other words, we are dealing with a system of which teaching is an important contribution, but no more than that.

A systems approach to teaching and learning in higher education

If we go on to consider how to devise learning environments which will produce the outcomes that are intended, we need to look first at the different functions which those environments should provide for students. These are listed in Table 13.1. The point to emphasise in looking at these functions is that each of them can be provided in different ways. Given the circumstances of a particular course, at a particular level, we must decide how best to provide each function. It may be that some of the first series of functions can be provided effectively and economically by good lectures, but perhaps equally well by resource-based materials of high quality. Overall, however, students must have opportunities to try out their understanding on other people – staff or students – both in writing and through discussions, and good feedback is essential if they are to be able to monitor the effectiveness of their understanding. Table 13.1 provides a checklist for the design of curricular provision, with decisions about specific teaching and assessment procedures being taken in the context of the overall learning environment.

There is also the question of timing. It is difficult enough for a student to cope with the transition from a school-based system of learning, under the immediate control of a teacher, to the greater independence demanded in higher education. To move from school directly to resource-based learning

Table 13.1: Main functions to be provided by learning environments

Orienting	Setting the scene; explaining what is required and why.
Motivating	Pointing up relevance; evoking and sustaining interest.
Presenting	Introducing new knowledge within a clear, supportive structure.
Clarifying	Explaining thoroughly and providing remedial support.
Exemplifying	Using relevant and varied examples to develop concepts.
Modelling	Showing how to think and reason within the discipline.
Elaborating	Introducing additional material to develop more detailed knowledge.
Practising	Developing skills and becoming familiar with procedures.
Consolidating	Encouraging development and testing of personal understanding.
Confirming	Ensuring adequacy of knowledge and understanding reached.

implies a substantial discontinuity of experience that is unlikely to be effective. Students entering higher education need the maximum amount of support, both in developing appropriate skills in learning, and in dealing with new concepts. Provision for study skills support is best carried out within departments, perhaps with general resource-based materials to introduce ideas on effective studying (which lecturers are typically not equipped to give).

Contrasting conceptions of teaching

While it is easy to use the research evidence to demonstrate the advantages of more innovative approaches to teaching, it is much more difficult to persuade lecturers actually to adopt them. Academic staff, on the whole, have had little or no systematic training in teaching, and lack any conceptual basis through which to consider their classroom experiences (Van Driel *et al.* 1997). Many colleagues have a conception of teaching, based solely on their own experiences as students, and see traditional methods as unproblematic. Recent research has been exploring the variations that exist among lecturers in their conceptions of teaching (see, for example, Prosser *et al.* 1994). A broad distinction emerges from this work between lecturers who focus on institutional and teacher requirements (covering the syllabus and producing results) and those who also put considerable emphasis on student learning and development. This dichotomy also reflects differing emphases on transmitting information and encouraging understanding (Entwistle 1997d).

Not only are lecturers' conceptions of teaching related directly to the methods of teaching they adopt (at least where they have sufficient freedom in determining those methods), but the conceptions also seem to influence their attitudes towards staff development and to innovative approaches to teaching and learning. Recent evidence of the links between conceptions of teaching and attitudes to innovation can be found in a study carried out in the Netherlands (Van Driel *et al.* 1997). The researchers initially described three contrasting conceptions of teaching, of which the extremes fitted closely the dichotomy described above. The intermediate category they called 'student directing'.

The main purpose of this study was to monitor the implementation of an innovation intended to promote self-regulated learning and meta-cognitive strategies in studying. Staff who viewed teaching as 'transmitting information' were least likely to change their methods. The 'student-directing' lecturers were generally willing to change, but they did not seem to appreciate the necessary relationship between meta-cognitive skills and self-regulation. In addition, they did not have sufficient confidence in the students' ability to learn independently and to thus relinquish their role in directing that learning. Only the lecturers who saw teaching in terms of 'encouraging learning' were ready to adopt the innovation in the way it was intended. For the vast majority of the staff, then, it seemed that their underlying conceptions of teaching limited their willingness to carry through the innovation in the way it was intended.

The interplay of theory and practice in transforming education

This brief review of the literature on student learning indicates that there is a developing consensus about the relationships between teaching and learning. The research shows that a deep approach, so necessary for the development of understanding, depends not just on the student's prior educational history, but on the whole learning environment provided by the course of study.

The research findings, however, are general while the implementation has to be specific, taking account of differing cultural, social and historical contexts. The specific suggestions made, for example, by the Dearing Committee (which were informed by research on student learning) cannot therefore be applied directly to the South African context. The research will have to be re-evaluated to decide what specific implications follow. It is, however, clear in general terms that there will have to be more support for students in developing the skills of independent learning and greater use of both resource-based and technology-based learning materials.

The need for such changes has now been accepted at national level in both Britain and South Africa, but difficulties in implementing any radical change are formidable. Not only is such change being demanded without additional resources, but it is being required of staff who lack any strong educational background. Different methods can be required of lecturers, but unless they fully understand what these new approaches can achieve, any implementation is likely to be both half-hearted and ineffective. A fundamental alteration in emphasis is needed to move from teaching a set syllabus in traditional ways to innovative efforts to support the development of learning skills which will allow knowledge to be updated continuously throughout life.

Any such change in conceptions of teaching cannot be achieved easily or quickly, and systematic research is needed to ensure that policy decisions are soundly based. This research will have to examine not just the best ways of teaching for conceptual understanding but also the procedures in staff development which are most likely to produce conceptual change. These are issues that face South Africa and Britain alike, and the sharing of experiences and ideas should be mutually beneficial.

14

Innovation in undergraduate science teaching and learning: a case study in introductory physics

CEDRIC LINDER AND DELIA MARSHALL

The democratisation of South Africa, as well as trends in higher education worldwide, have necessitated a re-examination of the purposes of higher education and of current practices in South Africa's tertiary institutions. As in other countries worldwide, there is an emphasis on widening access and increasing student diversity. In South Africa, there are the additional challenges of how higher education can best serve the aims of national reconstruction and development while also attending to the needs and growth of a democratic society. In this respect, the South African *Draft White Paper on Higher Education* (Department of Education 1997j) has provided a framework for addressing such transformation issues. The Draft White Paper highlights labour market needs as well as the need for higher education to develop critical, reflective learners.

The Draft White Paper poses significant challenges for all involved in higher education, especially the science sector. This is because the undergraduate science sector has been built on a view of teaching and learning which is based on a model of extensive specialisation for the preparation for graduate research career-paths.

This approach is attracting criticism internationally since it is based upon an enormous content coverage which often leads to limited meaningful learning, and leaves little or no time for exploration of issues such as the nature of science, the methods of science and science's impact on everyday life. All science graduates need a more holistic education – be they scientists, politicians, managers, civil servants, business people, journalists, etc. – to be able to contribute meaningfully to society. Having a sound subject-specific knowledge base is insufficient; there is also the need to be able think critically about related issues in wider contexts. The challenge does not end here. Besides fostering critical reflective learning, attention must also be given to developing associated life-long learning skills, such as group work and communication skills.

Besides implications for *curriculum reform* in undergraduate programmes, the Draft White Paper also has implications for how *widening* access might be facilitated. It recognises the articulation gap between the demands of higher education programmes and the preparedness of many school-leavers for academic study, and strongly supports the integration of academic development approaches into mainstream programmes. In our opinion, this 'articulation gap' is often not merely a deficit in *skills* or *content knowledge*, but includes a *view of learning* that limits students to superficial, rote-learning approaches. Therefore, getting students to think not only about the content of what they are learning, but also about the *nature of their learning* (often called meta-cognition) should become an essential and integral part of the science curriculum.

In the next section, we describe how we have developed strategies to promote some of the ideas presented above within the context of a large introductory Physics class that includes students from diverse backgrounds.

The course design

In 1992, we decided to offer a new Introductory Physics course for non-Physics majors at the University of the Western Cape. Our aim was to generate a curriculum that would include strategies to address some of the issues described earlier. To achieve this we decided to develop a curriculum that would drastically reduce formal mathematical calculation, and dramatically increase student participation in the teaching and learning of the course.

Our decision to shift away from the more traditional approach was influenced by local and international research outcomes. We had just completed a study into our students' conceptions of learning (Linder 1996) and found that just over 40 per cent of our first-year students equated learning Physics with rote memorisation of derivations, formulae and problem-solving methods. Most of these students did not even read their prescribed textbooks, but simply memorised the derivations, formulae and problem-solving methodologies from the notes that they had taken during lectures. Such 'surface' approaches to undergraduate Physics learning are typically found in many junior undergraduate Physics classes worldwide (for example, see Arons 1979, 1983; Dahlgren &

Marton 1978; Hewitt 1983; McDermott 1991; Lin 1982; Lundgren 1977). Hence, we decided that another important focus of the course would be to challenge students to think about their own learning. We then decided to begin the course with topics which had not been part of their secondary school science curriculum to see if we could limit the likelihood of students immediately adopting the rote-learning approach that so many of them had become familiar with at school. So, instead of starting the course with the traditional 'revision' of vectors as a forerunner to classical mechanics, so typical of many first-year Introductory Physics courses, we began the course with a four-week section on modern Physics.

By 1996, having tried out a range of innovations with a former colleague, Greg Hillhouse (see Linder & Hillhouse 1996), we generated a series of explicit teaching and learning strategies which we infused into our course design. Although we need to list these strategies as separate entities to illustrate what we were trying to do, we did not develop or use them in this way; they are all essentially mutually interactive. These strategies tried to promote:

1. in-class learner activity;
2. communication and group work skills;
3. the development of a coherent overview of the concepts related to the course;
4. reflection on learning;
5. the development of an independent, critical attitude.

In the next section, we will give a brief description of these strategies. At the end of each description, an example of how students said they experienced the strategy is given (drawn from typical descriptions obtained from many interviews and anonymous student course-evaluations).

Strategies to promote learner activity

'Check-your-neighbour' in-class discussion

The course usually has about 200 students enrolled in it. These students are divided into two lecture groups, each of which is taught by one of the authors. The aim of this strategy was to limit the passive teacher-driven 'chalk-and talk' teaching and to promote both thinking and communication. This 'check-your-neighbour' strategy effectively split lecture periods into smaller teaching clips, which included students sitting next to one another being asked to think and discuss concepts, issues and problem-solving and so generating 'verbal interpretations' (Arons 1990) of their understanding. An example of how students described experiencing this strategy is:

> By checking my neighbour I didn't have to accept what the lecturer 'printed in my head', but had the opportunity to hear out my friend's point of view.

Using students extensively in class demonstration and modelling of physical situations

This strategy involved inviting students to participate in metaphoric illustrations through role-playing. It was used to help foster students' reflection on their learning and at the same time to help facilitate complex conceptualisation. (Baird & Northfield 1992, reporting on Australian PEEL project experiences, also found this strategy useful in instances where science processes are 'essentially unobservable or complicated'.) An example of what we mean by 'metaphoric role-playing illustrations' is having groups of male and female students standing together in groups to represent nuclei. The males represent neutrons and the females, protons – both males and females are nucleons. It is then possible to illustrate how types of atom are uniquely determined by the number of protons (females) only, and by interchanging males and females, how certain types of radiation change the fundamental properties of a nucleus.

> Using my friends in class demonstrations helped me a lot because when there is a problem concerning what was illustrated I remember it easily because I imagine who was used at the time.

Discouraging in-class note-taking

This strategy involved discouraging students from coming to our lectures to make notes of our teacher-talk. Instead, we encouraged them to think about what was being taught and to verbalise their thoughts. Our aim was continuously to make it explicit what type of learning we were expecting them to do – to *engage* with the course material in such a way so as to attempt to *make sense of things*. We also wanted our students to reflect on their sense-making *after lectures*, and to then summarise this sense-making. We considered this an important aspect of developing our students as independent and autonomous learners.

> Now I first read, attend lectures, read again and thereafter write down what I have understood so far in physics. Before it was a simple matter of repeating what I had learnt by heart.

Strategies to promote communication and group work skills.
Making peer discussion an integral part of the course

Once students had engaged in 'check-your-neighbour' discussion around some issue, groups of students were asked to share their conclusions with the rest of the class. Other groups were then asked to comment on whether they agreed or disagreed, and why.

> Working in our groups has made learning to understand things much better for me, instead of learning in parrot fashion. I've learnt to question, reason things out, not just accept them.

Encouraging a co-operative, 'peer-to-independent' model of articulating ideas

This strategy is an extension of the 'check-your-neighbour' and 'making peer discussion an integral part of the course' strategies. It was used mainly during tutorial periods where students are divided into co-operative learning groups to do end-of-chapter problems (which are mainly qualitative in nature). The idea was firstly for the students to discuss the problems amongst each other and then, once they felt that they had fully explored their understanding with each another, independently to write down a full account of that under-standing in the most coherent way which they could.

> I found working with others very helpful because, not only for physics, it improved my communication skills. Most of all I can now determine for myself whether I understand a particular concept or not by discussing it.

Having small groups of students make presentations to the class

To develop students' presentation skills, co-operative learning groups were established, and the groups were given a selection of titles to choose from for ten-minute class presentations. The topics were associated with the course topics but had not been dealt with in any formal sense in class.

Strategies to promote developing a coherent overview of the concepts related to the course

These strategies were all aimed at helping students develop a 'well-structured knowledge base', one of the factors that previous research indicates helps foster a 'deep' learning approach (Biggs 1989).

Concept-mapping as a way of constructing a holistic conceptual overview

The concept-mapping that we taught was based on the Ausubel-Novak-Gowin theory of developing meaningful learning (Novak & Gowin 1984). The aim was to assist students in thinking about hierarchies of propositional conceptual connections so as to construct holistic conceptual overviews.

We also found that concept-mapping was a useful way for students to shift from *verbalising* to *writing* their explanations of conceptual connections.

> Concept map drawing has changed the way I try to understand a chapter. Somehow I studied all my educational life learning things off by heart and not understanding the concepts or the facts whatsoever, which I feel was such a waste. But this concept mapping has made me realise that if you understand you will not forget.

Linking different parts of the course

This strategy involved an explicit focus on linking different physics topics and concepts with each other. (Research with first-year physics students by White *et al.* 1995, highlighted how students have difficulty doing this linking on their own.) The linking of topics was not teacher 'chalk-and-talk' driven, but rather in-class questions were posed to encouraged reflection and exploration on such linkages.

Emphasis on verbalising qualitative reasoning

The strategy introduces students to a problem-solving approach that requires the verbalisation of conceptual meaning rather than 'putting-numbers-into-formulae' solutions. Here we expected the students verbally to reason out problems, which could have been solved using a formula through an appropriate framework of fundamental concepts.

> I like this strategy he's taking – of us knowing exactly what's going on, rather than just taking the equations. I think it's interesting to know what is happening first, before you just, like, answer the questions with equations.

Strategies to promote reflections on learning

Introducing discussions on learning as part of the curriculum

This strategy involved making *meta-cognition* explicit on an ongoing basis. The opportunities for this explicitness usually arose in situations where students, based upon their school experiences, would have resorted to rote-learning procedures or definitions. The students were then encouraged to reflect on their 'old' learning approaches, and on how these differed from the 'new' sense-making approach that the course emphasised.

> By learning to think properly and constructively, one can make proper decisions. Talking about learning in class opens up one's eyes to all the things that go on around us.

Using cartoons to stimulate reflection on the meaning of learning

Often, instead of discussing meta-cognitive issues with students, cartoons were used to evoke further meaningful reflection of these issues. The cartoons were shown to students and the students' responses during the year indicated that, as their meta-cognition evolved, so their appreciation of the humour, represented by the cartoons, increased.

> At school, we had cold, hard facts in physics. The [cartoons] you showed us in class were interesting because they made me think about study theories critically, and so I began to try to understand better.

Using pop-music to stimulate reflection on the meaning of higher education

The words of 'popular' songs, with which the students could identify, were modified slightly to get students to reflect on the meaning of higher education. The altered words of the songs were given to the students and the original songs played to them during class. For example, the words of Queen's 'I want to break free' were re-written to associate the song with wanting to break free from rote learning. This strategy is closely linked to the *promoting reflection on the relevance and value of what is taught* strategy (see later) in that it sought reflection on aims and attitudes in relation to university education – what Beaty and her colleagues have called 'learning orientations' (Beaty *et al.* 1997).

> The songs, they made me feel that someone other than my friends and parents were trying to open my eyes to learning.

Embedding the Physics taught in everyday examples

This strategy entailed relating what was being taught to a variety of common everyday contexts. The strategy is so explicit that virtually all the teaching evolves around this strategy. Its aim is to contextualise the subject matter in such a way that the interest, relevance and motivation dynamics of the course are enhanced.

I live science – whatever I do, I have a scientific explanation – whether I am walking in a circle, or baking bread, or taking a shower.

Placing Physics content in much broader societal, historical and environmental contexts

This strategy had the curriculum emphasising the integration of Science with wider issues and values so that we could encourage the students to think critically, to form opinions and to make choices that contribute to their quality of life. The Physics topics were embedded, wherever possible, in personal and societal contexts relevant to the students. This turned out to be an excellent strategy to stimulate in-lecture student participation. For example, when dealing with modern Physics topics, we discussed issues like nuclear weapon creation and its consequences, from Hiroshima and Nagasaki to present-day proliferation; the physical and social dimensions of nuclear power stations; accelerators; Tokomaks; and medical and food preservation uses of radiation.

> I've learnt about things that occurred which I once didn't even think about… it makes you use your brain and be a human being, not a zombie studying notes but not seeing the reason for it.

Strategies to develop an independent, critical attitude

Fostering reflection on the nature of the discipline

Research on student learning has indicated that 'emphasising and modelling the way of thinking characteristic of that discipline' can have an important influence on the quality of student learning (Entwistle 1995). Within the Physics education community, there is growing concern that Introductory Physics courses tend to present Physics as a body of facts and theories instead of developing in students an awareness of the nature of Science (for example, Helm 1996; Hilborn 1988; Linder 1992; Leach *et al.* 1996). This strategy, therefore, involved getting students to think about the *nature of scientific knowledge* by having a focus in lectures on the role of models in constructing scientific understanding, or clarifying thinking, about physical phenomena. For example, we began the course with an exploration of students' conceptions of the nature of Science with respect to issues such as the methods of scientific enquiry, paradigms and modelling. Then, throughout the course we would refer back to these issues.

> Like Newton's Laws – at school, they'd give you formulas and you had to cram the formulas. It was a question of cramming because you didn't know how it came

about. Or how to explain the origin of it, or the person who developed the formula – what reasoning he was using, what procedure did he use. So I would say that the learning in [this course] is basing itself on the scientific method... how those scientists were thinking, how they were viewing the thing, and how they came to reason in that way.

Making it explicit that the primary aim of the course was the development of reflective, critical thinking

This strategy involved discussing regularly with our students what the aim of the course was – definitely not an acquisition of facts to be learnt for examinations and tests, but the development of reflective, critical thinking which would be a life-long skill development.

> This is the first course I have come across which has taught me so much, in terms of life skills, studying, and most importantly how to think critically. I think that this is also the first time that I have learnt physics even though I did it at school.

Promoting reflection on the relevance and value of what is taught

The strategy involved generating in-class discussions about issues such as what the students expected to get in return for their university fees, and how their understanding of Physics impacted on their self-image as informed citizens exercising their rights in a modern democracy, in particular vis à vis socio-political decisions which need an informed and evaluative scientific perspective.

> [The lecturer] is not afraid of speaking to the students about how they feel about their society. But other lecturers just concentrate on the textbook – they never tell you, 'Look, you must be able to make decisions for your children in the future!'

The impact of the teaching and learning innovations

We have described teaching and learning innovations which we developed to try to transform the way students experience the learning of Physics. We were interested in the impact of these strategies on our students' learning in several respects.

Firstly, since a central aim of the course was to develop a sound *understanding of Physics concepts*, we conducted a comparative study with first-year 'mainstream' students. This study indicated that this aim had indeed been achieved with our students. (Full details of this comparative study are given by Linder & Hillhouse 1996.)

Secondly, we needed to find out if the meta-cognitive dynamic had affected the students' learning. To do so we conducted a study using a learning inventory – the Approaches to Studying Inventory (Entwistle & Ramsden 1983) and student interviews. Analysis of both showed that the students had changed the way they learned their Physics, reflecting a shift towards 'deep', sense-making learning from 'surface' memorisation/recall-based learning. These changes in students' approaches to learning were very positive since international studies indicate that the learning approach which students adopt is a crucial aspect of academic success (see, for example, Marton & Säljö 1976a, 1976b, 1997; Trigwell & Prosser 1991) and of self-direction for life-long learning (see, for example, Candy 1991). Furthermore, allied to students' changes in approach to learning were changes in their views of knowledge and of learning, which we characterised as shifts in epistemological perspective. In essence, students were moving away from an association of knowledge with the *recall of taught facts* to an association of knowledge with coherence, every-day experience and personal significance (see Linder & Marshall 1996 for full details of this study).

Discussion

Despite the positive feedback from students about the teaching and learning innovations, and the positive impact that these appeared to have on the students' learning, the process of implementing the innovations was not always easy. Perhaps our biggest challenge involved issues of legitimacy – from the perspective both of colleagues and students. Our colleagues' perspective remains complex. Inevitably, there are some reservations about teaching Physics effectively with a limited amount of mathematical framing. Furthermore, securing the legitimacy of other innovations that are linked with developing critical, reflective learners would seem to depend on profound beliefs about the nature of scientific knowledge and the consequent purpose of higher education, an issue which perhaps is going to be the most difficult one for Science educators to deal with in our transformation process.

Securing legitimacy from the students' perspective was a different type of challenge. In adopting non-traditional approaches to Physics teaching and learning, we soon realised that students needed to be able to perceive our teaching as 'legitimate' Physics teaching. This was particularly challenging when they were being asked to take the risk of relinquishing their familiar, memorisation-based modes of learning. For example, this student describes how he experienced this challenge:

When I went to the lecture for the first time, and Prof. said, 'You don't need to take notes', I thought, 'I don't think he knows what he's saying!' He said, 'This course is about understanding, not just calculations'. I said, 'In Physics?!?!' Well, you know, I had to give him the chance to go on and clarify what he was talking about. But as the time went on, I could see what he really meant. We come out of lectures with *nothing written, but with minds full of understanding.*

It is not easy to explain how we established this legitimacy; part of it came from making students explicitly aware of the course focus on having them become more critical, reflective learners. Another part came from making them aware that we were interested in them *as people* (having the responsibility of making a constructive contribution to society). In this regard, we felt that the strategies were likely to have a significant impact on the students' learning only if they could appreciate the benefit or 'fruitfulness' of learning Physics in this way (see Gunstone 1992). So, we stressed the 'fruitfulness' of a reflective and critical approach to Physics learning in two respects.

Firstly, we emphasised a reflective and critical approach to Physics learning in terms of making sense of everyday phenomena, and also through being empowered to make better life-choices. A significant decision, we realised, was to begin the course with topics that had potential for initiating class discussion and generating perceived relevance. Secondly, we ensured that there was congruency between our espoused course objectives and our assessment demands.

Another important issue is the development of students' *intellectual autonomy and independence.* For that, the ability to be aware of, and to reflect on, one's own learning is clearly required. Therefore, it would seem that fostering students' reflection on learning (meta-cognition) needs to be an essential part of any academic development initiative. In this regard, we have become convinced that fostering reflection on learning is a far more important foundation for students' intellectual autonomy and independence than the more technical and traditional 'study skills' approaches (focusing on issues like effective note-taking skills, time-management, etc.) which have become the hallmark of many 'bridging' or academic development programmes. This claim is borne out in research on student learning (see, for example, Martin & Ramsden 1987).

In summary, we have argued that higher education entails more than an understanding of one's discipline – it entails an ability to go beyond that, to see one's discipline in a wider context, and to be critically reflective about it. Therefore, we believe that Science courses should not merely be *content-orientated,* but should also have a focus on the nature of Science, on Science's impact on society, and students' reflection on their own learning. Our case-study

experiences have demonstrated to us that active learning and student participation can be achieved, even in large classes.

They also highlighted strongly for us the need for a systemic approach to
innovation. A common vision of the purposes of a Science higher education is
required within faculties and departments if meaningful change is to be
effected. If there is commitment to developing students' wider abilities,
beyond the confines of subject boundaries, to their critical and reflective abilities, as well as life skills such as group work and communication skills – then
these objectives need to be incorporated into undergraduate programmes in a
co-ordinated and coherent manner. Whether the recommendations of the
Draft White Paper will lead to meaningful changes in teaching and learning
practices in Science higher education, or merely to an instrumental 'repackag-
ing' of existing curricula in new guises, remains to be seen.

15

Organising learning in large group teaching

NELLEKE BAK

Challenges for higher education in South Africa

The *Draft White Paper on Higher Education* (Department of Education 1997j) aims to restructure higher education in South Africa along lines of equity and quality, in an attempt to redress past injustices of exclusion based on race. 'There is a need for the expansion of the higher education system if it is to meet the imperatives of equity, redress and development. This will require expanding enrolments to accommodate increased student demand and to cater for a far more diverse student body' (*ibid.* para. 2.4). The new policy aims to 'generate new models of teaching and learning to accommodate a larger and more diverse student population' (*ibid.* para. 1.10). While no one would disagree with the noble aims of the document, there are a number of challenges and potential tensions that arise. Coupled to the call for expansion and diversity in higher education, the Draft White Paper stresses the need for pursuing quality, for 'maintaining and applying academic and educational standards' (*ibid.* para. 1.19). That the double call for expansion and diversity on the one hand and the pursuit of quality on the other are in tension is borne out in the document where access to higher education for a greater and more diverse student body is balanced with a call for higher rates of success for this student body: 'Ensuring equity of access must be complemented by a concern for equity of outcomes' (*ibid.* para. 2.12). In short, higher education must develop teaching and learning strategies that will ensure an increased yield of quality students drawn from a large and diverse student body.

This in itself is a daunting enough task for teachers in higher education, but coupled to a matching decline in funds for higher education and a large and diverse student body that is in general seriously under-prepared for academic study, the task becomes even more demanding. Just how academic quality, or good teaching and learning, might be pursued in a context of large group teaching with limited funds is the focus of this chapter.

One way of trying to understand what is meant by the call for higher education to 'be more responsive to societal interests and needs' (*ibid.* para. 1.11) is to articulate what these needs may be. The needs of political and economic communities may be for 'useful' knowledge (i.e. knowledge that has vocational currency). Furthermore, there is the need for greater access to higher education of students who have been denied this (historically). The group of historically disadvantaged students is not a homogeneous one – within the group are differences of language, culture, quality of schooling and economic power. So, not only is there a demand for greater number of historically disadvantaged students to have access, but they will bring with them greater diversity. With the change towards a democratic government in 1994, there has also been a sense of redress in the form of 'entitlement' to higher education by historically disadvantaged students (Morrow 1996a; 1996b). On the other hand, the academic community's task is to ensure that these graduates are academically competent. This implies a knowledge of the discipline – the content, the appropriate skills associated with the discipline, an understanding of the context in which the discipline knowledge is developed and a responsible use of that knowledge. The challenge facing higher education institutions in South Africa is to organise knowledge (through specific learning and teaching strategies) in such a way that students become informed, competent and responsible participants in the specific discipline area.

The Ministry of Education's response to this challenge is as follows: 'The Ministry believes that distance education based on the principles of open learning and resource-based learning, has a crucial role to play in meeting the challenge of greater access and enhanced quality in a context of resource constraints and a diverse student body' (Department of Education 1997j: para. 2.34). This chapter examines an attempt to use resource-based learning as a strategy to cope with a large and fairly diverse class of Honours students doing a course in Metatheory in Education at the University of the Western Cape (UWC).

First, it is important to have greater clarity on what is meant by access. Morrow (1992) makes a distinction between formal and epistemological access. Formal access has to do with legal registration at the institution – questions of entry qualification, student fees and the physical location of the institution arise here. However, once the students have been formally admitted into the institution, there is the further question of how to engage students into the knowledge of the course for which they have legally registered. This initiation into the discourse and practices of the discipline is the area of epistemological access. This chapter focuses on the broadening of this latter form of access.

To broaden epistemological access is the area of teaching and learning strategies. Questions here are raised about how to teach the particular students in the course in order to enable them to become informed participants in the discourse and practices of the subject on offer. To rephrase the challenge posed by the Draft White Paper (Department of Education 1997j:para. 2.6): How can epistemological access be broadened to a large and diverse student body in order to 'contribute to the development of the analytical, intellectual, cultural and ethical skills and competencies necessary for participation in the knowledge society'?

Metatheory

The course I shall discuss as an example of an attempt to respond to this challenge is a B.Ed course called Metatheory. It is one of the compulsory courses in a two-year part-time postgraduate Honours degree in Education. On average, it has 220 students, most of whom are working teachers studying part-time. The majority of students are about 25 to 40 years old, with about 50 per cent being women. In the last few years, more and more African students have enrolled so that in 1997 about 60 per cent were African students.[1] In 1994 the course was redesigned, as a move towards a notion of resource-based learning. One of the reasons for this change was to accommodate students from further afield. Instead of meeting for one-and-a-half hours every week for 15 weeks, contact time was reduced to four contact sessions of 3 hours each over the 15-week semester period.

The course itself is a sophisticated philosophical analysis of three main theoretical frameworks in terms of which knowledge and practices of education are conceived. In general, the purpose is to articulate, examine, engage with and raise critical questions about the concepts that underlie particular perspectives on education. In particular, students are expected to be able to understand that there are different interpretations and perceptions of education, to articulate what these are, to understand the underlying assumptions that shape practices and perceptions, and to recognise *why* aspects of these perceptions may be problematic or fruitful. Students must be able to construct arguments and see how evidence is used. This implies an understanding of the history of the practice, the changes in concepts that shape practices and the reasons for the changes.

Challenges facing Metatheory

Metatheory has tried to address the challenges raised in the Draft White Paper. There are general as well as specific challenges that face both teachers and learners in Metatheory. One of the general challenges is coping with large classes of about 220 postgraduate students. Traditionally postgraduate teaching and learning are conceived of as small group, face-to-face seminars, where learners can ask questions and engage in conversation with the lecturer. Perhaps this is the ideal situation, but it is just not feasible given the growing number of students in higher education. Another hampering factor is very limited resources: there is little money to employ full-time administrative assistance, to employ more tutors and to develop learning resources. A further difficulty facing teachers and learners is the initial lack of a shared knowledge base of education. Given that students come from a diversity of academic backgrounds, there is no common content and skills base on which teachers can readily draw. Furthermore, a major difficulty for teachers and learners in Metatheory is that some students are academically under-prepared for postgraduate work. Others, as second- or third- (or even fourth) language English speakers, find reading and writing in English difficult, which is exacerbated by philosophical nuances in conceptual meaning. One of the last general challenges facing teachers at UWC is that the university in the 1980s declared that the 'doors of learning shall be opened', in keeping with the manifesto of the African National Congress (ANC). This has generated in some students expectations not only of access but also of success (Morrow 1994; 1996b). This perception of attaining postgraduate degrees rests on a conception of political entitlement, rather than on a notion of academic work as epistemological labour and developing competence.

These are general challenges that face most teachers and learners in higher education in South Africa currently, but there are also specific challenges that face teachers and learners of Metatheory. One of the difficulties around epistemological access is the task of enabling students to become participants in and users of a shared disciplinary practice that is initially beyond their reach. Teachers need to help students acquire the language (the grammar, images, rules and logic) of the specialist practice. Teaching is a recognition that learners, by definition, do not yet speak the discourse. Students need to become participants in the academic conversation that informs practices of education. In other words, they need to learn to speak about education in more precise and thoughtful ways. The problem in teaching is often that academics use the discourse as a 'natural' language, but to students it is an unfamiliar and often seemingly inaccessible language. Good teaching, seen as an initiation into a specialist discourse, is perceived as a matter of broadening epistemological access. What this implies is that good teaching and learning are not just a matter of developing academic skills, but also a matter of developing communicative skills.

The notion of epistemological access needs to be coupled to the notion of epistemological labour. What this means is that the task of teachers is to make the knowledge and language 'clear', but to clarify does not necessarily mean to make the knowledge 'easy'. To learn to speak the language or, put differently, to learn to speak about a topic with understanding and confidence, requires effort on the part of the learner. Some students, when faced with the task of learning the language, repeat the words without understanding them. This is often an entrenched approach to learning by students who have, through impoverished schooling, been drilled in rote learning and memorisation, coupled with a notion of education as repeating what the 'experts' say. However, an interesting countermove to a rejection of rote learning, prevalent in Bantu education, is an automatic rejection of 'expert' or 'hegemonic' discourse. Arising out of the protest move against Bantu Education is the move to view all 'expert' discourse with suspicion precisely because of its entrenched dominance. This approach to learning is usually reflected in an 'outsider's' rejection of the discourse and an unwillingness to engage with, or 'legitimise', the discourse. The challenge for teachers on the Metatheory course is to initiate learners into the discourse, help them become informed participants and, perhaps paradoxically, help them to develop a critical reflection of the very language they have been using. To learn to reflect critically does not necessarily mean to reject the concepts used, but it does mean to contribute to the development of the discourse and, where necessary, to change it. Even for postgraduate learners this can be a very unsettling approach to learning: the notion of becoming acquainted with the discourse, and then challenging it. To some students it may seem pointless to struggle to get into the language of a particular framework of education, only to 'reject' it later.

Another difficulty for teachers and learners of the course is to establish a notion of a 'community of learners' despite the large, diverse class that meets only occasionally. The question to address is how the participants in the course can establish an idea of an academic community when the learners largely work in isolation. The notion of learning that drives this challenge is one that learners learn by engaging in a dynamic conversation, through which they develop an ability to construct sense within the field of knowledge being taught.

Postgraduate students already have some experience of studying, but other pressures come to bear on them. They are often part-time students, coping with demands of work and family commitments and with limited time for studying. Given the limited contact time of the Metatheory course, a large challenge is to help students to learn *how* to learn on their own and *how* to cope with outside pressures that impact on their studies, so the Metatheory course is not just a matter of clarifying the discourse of education, but also helping students to engage with that discourse. This means that the teachers (and designers) of the course need to address the question of epistemological access on a number of levels: organising the presentation of knowledge so that students can start to engage with it, organising the learning practices of the learners, and constructing a specific learning environment for the particular students of the course.

In summary, the challenges that face Metatheory are the large number of students in the course, limited funding, the lack of a shared knowledge base of students entering the course, students' different approaches to learning, at times students' unrealistic expectations from the course, students struggling with both English as a language and the language of academic conventions and logic, the limited contact time in the course and learners learning mostly in isolation.

The design of a learning environment in Metatheory

A course that hopes to address these challenges needs to be well designed and have embedded learner support systems and an efficient and effective administration. I must state at the outset that the Metatheory course does not claim to have all three of these requirements in place, but I shall discuss some of the features in the design of the course that try to address some of the challenges outlined.

One of the major moves in the restructuring of the course in 1994 was towards resource-based learning, where the main resources are print-based. These include a course guidebook, a set of readings, a set of general instructions and notes on the three assignments. The course guidebook helps the learner come to grips with the set readings, and highlights key themes that run through each of the theoretical frameworks discussed. It tries to anticipate queries that learners may have, addresses some of the difficulties by means of examples and explanation and tries to set up a kind of dialogue with the learner. In effect, this text becomes the teacher with whom the learner engages in conversation. The text, first of all, invites learners to become co-speakers of that particular discourse and then later it encourages the learners to look at the discourse from a critical perspective and to raise some penetrating questions about it. Furthermore, the text, reflecting a clear and systematic line of argument itself, encourages students to construct their arguments in a similar way. It provides a coherent narrative structure within which the details of the course are located. The intelligible structure of the text provides a principle of relevance in terms of which certain details are highlighted and others backgrounded. In this way the text not only initiates students into the discourse of the discipline, but also into the practices of academic writing and thinking through resource-based learning.

In effect, what resource-based learning aims at is a one-to-one interaction between learner and teacher/text, no matter how large the class. Each learner has her/his own text with which to engage. Of course, resource-based learning *in itself* is not a solution; it needs to be seen as part of a constructed environment that encourages learning or, put differently, broadens epistemological access. One of the advantages of a print-based course is that it makes the teaching/learning practice far more visible and open to analysis than is generally the case in face-to-face teaching.

Metatheory also has face-to-face teaching, but these contact sessions are limited to four a semester. They are each three hours long and divided roughly half into a plenary session with the lecturer, and half into smaller tutorial groups of about 20 students with a tutor. The purpose of the contact sessions is to *support* the learning encouraged by the set text. The purpose of the plenary session is to 'demonstrate' the discourse-in-action, to motivate and encourage. The lecturer's task here is not to plod through the text; rather it is to make the language come alive with examples and vigour.

Whereas in the plenary session (and in the text) the lecturer vicariously frames meaning for the students, in the tutorials, through group discussions, there is a more collective framing of meaning. The principle of learning that steers tutorials is the notion of learning through doing, or learning through speaking the language of the particular theoretical framework under discussion. It is a notion of learning based on a concept of *practice*. The language into which students are initiated is a system of meaning, with particular conventions and uses. In order to understand these, students must *practise* the language. To 'know' one of the discourses is seen not only as having specific items (such as concepts or facts) stored in one's head, but as having the capability of producing argument within a powerful or prestigious discourse. To learn to do this entails doing it – having the space in which to try out the discourse and see where it takes one and how it shapes one's interpretation of education. Metatheory tutorials aim to provide such spaces where tutors guide the conversation of the students. In effect, students are expected not only to learn *about* particular concepts that shape educational thinking and practices, but also to think *with* these concepts – to use them as tools to construct 'new' interpretations. Whereas students watched discourse in action in the plenary session, they are encouraged to speak it themselves in the tutorials.

An extension of the concept of learning-through-doing is in the set of written assignments. A number of teaching considerations come to the fore in the framing of the assignments. First of all, the three set assignments, one on each of the major theoretical frameworks discussed in the course, all focus on the same theme, for example, on practices of teaching, on the meaning of critical thinking or on the notion of 'research' in education. The reason for setting the three assignments on the same theme is two-fold: to draw links between the different theoretical frameworks and to reinforce the notion of the course as developing a coherent and systematic line of argument. Furthermore, this highlights to students that educational issues are interpreted in terms of particular theoretical frameworks – the same issue in different frameworks gives rise to different responses.

The second teaching consideration that is embedded in the structuring of the assignments is that the assignment topic is always posed as a question, mostly a question that elicits a 'yes' or 'no' response. Examples are: 'Does all learning contribute to emancipation?', 'Can a theory of learning avoid being ideological?' or 'Is learning a concept the same as learning a rule?'. The reason for structuring the question in this way is again two-fold: it makes the student aware that there are different positions that can be adopted to the problem, and, at the same time, it forces the student to adopt a particular position and defend it. Furthermore, the structure of the question requires students to give reasons for adopting that position – in other words, to construct an argument within a powerful discourse. The notion of posing a problem question as an assignment implies that teaching and learning are seen as a matter of developing an 'informed voice' in the ongoing conversation about education. Not only are students required to be familiar with the central concepts and ideas of the main theoretical frameworks (the 'informed' part of their development towards academic competence), but also to be able to argue for their choice of judging one position to develop a more illuminating understanding of the problem at hand (the 'own voice' part of what it is to be academically competent). The learning-through-doing notion that drives the assignments is one that tries to steer away from merely paraphrasing the discourse of a particular position, to encouraging the student to *work* with the concepts in order to clarify the problem posed by the assignment question.

This touches on the way in which the teachers of the Metatheory course view the task of philosophy of education. The problem questions focus on *actual* problems in educational practices. In Dworkin's words (1993:29), it is a course that connects theory with practice 'from the inside out', that is, it

211

begins with a *practical* problem and then asks which general philosophical or conceptual issues need to be confronted in order to resolve these practical problems. The assignments call for an argumentative essay (rather than a survey or overview of available literature) that engages theoretical issues but *begins* with and remains *disciplined* by a subject of practical importance.

To argue for a particular approach to the problem with an 'informed voice' is no mean task. Epistemological access entails helping students to develop such an academic skill. One way in which the course tries to do this is to have a set of assessment criteria for each assignment. For the first one, a rudimentary set of five criteria is given to students, including 'Is the question answered?', 'Does the essay have a clear structure and direction?' and 'Does the essay conform to accepted conventions of presentation?'. The second assignment extends the initial list to include more sophisticated criteria, such as 'Does the Abstract reveal the structure, direction and argument of the essay?'. The final assignment again extends this second list to include even more complex criteria such as 'Does the writer develop a critical understanding of the issues?'. The reason for this incremental aspect in the assessment of students' written work is based on the notion of learning as a process of ever-increasing skill development. Moreover, by building up on the set of criteria, students practise academic conventions – the academic tasks set in the preceding assignment need to be demonstrated again in subsequent written work and in the final exam.

If one conceives of learning as developing an informed voice through academic exercise, then one must also see learning as a process that is not necessarily linear. Coupled with the idea of philosophy of education as a skill of working *with* concepts, trying out new interpretations, the notion of learning must have space in which students can learn through trying out innovative approaches, and possibly through seeing that some of these approaches are inadequate. The assessment structure must have 'safe spaces' for students to try out ways of working with concepts. If not, it will discourage students from seeing learning as working with concepts and will tempt them into paraphrasing the 'received ideas'. As I noted earlier on, the familiarity with the given discourse is an important part of learning, which comes with *using* the concepts. An important subsequent part of learning is to be able to raise critical questions about the given discourse and to explore some ways in which to adapt, extend or change it. This is an area of 'risk taking' for students, and if seen as an important part of learning, the assessment must *support*, rather than discourage, learners in taking conceptual risks. The Metatheory course tries to create such a safe space by steering away from 'continuous assessment' in which every exercise counts, and where students are discouraged from taking risks. The course has a rule that states that if the exam mark is higher than the course work mark (a total of the three assignments with heavier weighting for each subsequent assignment), the exam mark will count as the final mark; if the exam mark is lower than the course work mark, then a proportionate average of the two will count as the final mark. In effect, this means that the course work mark can never count *against* the student (and in this way invites the student to take risks in her or his learning). It does, however, act as an 'insurance' if the student does not perform well in the exam (and in this way, it 'rewards' work done during the semester).

In conclusion, the structure of the learning environment in Metatheory is an attempt to address the challenge to broaden epistemological access to large classes in a context of limited funds, while trying to maintain quality of the academic enterprise. Whether it has succeeded in doing so, needs to be the focus of a much longer study. However, indications are that while learners at first struggle to come to grips with the texts, they are able to develop, through extensive reading, guided reflection, regular writing and limited formal contact sessions, academic competence. The resource-based learning approach adopted in the Metatheory course seems to be worth pursuing as an attempt to face the challenges posed in the Draft White Paper. In the meantime, it has opened up discussion within the Faculty of Education at UWC about new ways to develop teaching and learning strategies in higher education.

Endnote

1. 'African' students until 1989 had very limited formal access to UWC, which was officially designated as a university for 'coloured' students. Since 1989, when the policy was abandoned by UWC in spite of government decree, the number of African students has risen to about 70 per cent of students enrolled in the Arts and Education faculties (Radcliffe 1996).

16

Using research processes to guide the transformation of community-based learning in South Africa[1]

Jonathan Geidt

A central tenet underlying academic traditions in South Africa is an assumption that research is for postgraduates. Anybody embarking on a research project, it is believed, must have studied with success to a point at least beyond first degree level. The grounds for supporting this view appear to be obvious. They are, that research uses resources that consume time and money, that doing research is complicated and involves activities and skills not easily learned, that aspiring researchers are confronted with a host of practical challenges, and finally that success or failure involves prestige for the department concerned. So, there seem to be enough reasons to stop people with little experience of academic studying from being thrown into the academic deep end. That is how it is seen.

Other people think that research is too useful a learning tool to be left to an aristocracy of established academics. The case hinges on what is meant by this important-sounding word. If 'research' was opened up and some aspects of it freed from institutional rites of passage, more people would be able to do it. Learning to do research could then become a practical and enjoyable way of learning how to learn. This already happens in the United States, where I have heard that one has to dodge down alleys to escape the questioning of high school investigators!

My contention is that moving towards the adoption of a more plebeian view of research will also help to build bridges between the differently resourced communities of South Africa. The evidence I use comes from the research course that I teach. This forms part of the Certificate for Educators of Adults at the Centre for Adult Continuing Education (CACE), designed for non-graduate adult educators, now known as Education and Training Development Practitioners (ETDPs). All South Africa's new democratic institutions need people who have a working knowledge of research and its limitations. This is particularly true of community-based organisations (CBOs), most of whom operate within acute constraints of a lack of resources of all kinds. Few locally educated ETDPs working in CBOs have had any exposure to research, know what it is used for, or even know what the word means.

It is, of course, pointless to expect the same level or kind of work from non-graduate as from postgraduate programmes – what is taught and practised has to be adapted to the needs and contexts of students – but, if traditional attitudes to learning can be overcome and adult students who have not been to university are treated as apprentice researchers, exciting things can happen. One might call it barefoot research with unpredictable spin-offs.

The chapter is divided into two sections. The first section describes the course with particular reference to learning skills and practices. The second section looks at the significance of such courses to community education and development.

A description of the CACE certificate research course

CACE is part of the University of the Western Cape. The Certificate for Educators of Adults is an outreach course for non-graduates working in community organisations in the provinces of the Western and Northern Cape. It lasts two years and is delivered part-time through a mix of study-weekends (lasting two-and-a-half days) and local study-groups. Work is assessed by assignments and exams. Applicants are accepted with Standard 8 or 9 (Standard 10 being matric) if they have adult education related organisational experience. The overall aim of the course is to help learners succeed in their own contexts by developing their capacities to engage in organisational policy, planning and evaluation processes, and they also increasingly need to access further academically related studies.

The Certificate is taught through a series of five residential study-weekends. Only some of this time is spent on teaching workshops related to the research part of the programme. As well as research methods, the curriculum includes adult learning and facilitation, organising skills, education for development, design and facilitation of workshops, contextual studies, social awareness programmes focusing on race class and gender issues, and an introduction to word processing. The research course forms the central part of the second year.

Most (but not all) learners live in under-resourced localities disadvantaged by South Africa's distorted society. Motivation they have, but to achieve success they need structured planning. Second-language learning and the problems inherited from a politically engineered second- or third-class education means that they are under-prepared for the demands of their first year of studying. Yet, in most cases these are mature adults with families, working in community organisations whose aims are broadly to do with social repair and development of the community. Certificate students are interesting people. Given the appropriate research skills, a majority of them could make knowledgeable contributions to the recorded information about their communities.

The research course was developed through the twin processes of interrogating aims and learning from mistakes. In 1991, we thought that full-blown academic research would be too much to expect, so we encouraged students to create oral history. There were presentations about the potential role of oral history in South Africa and, after being shown how to interview, students had to go out and get 'ordinary' people to talk about their lives. Many of the resulting narratives proved to be interesting, but they were framed in reports that in most instances lacked an interpretative focus.

In 1993, we took the decision to do 'real' research. We naïvely and vaguely believed that research would 'empower' learners and their communities and we hoped that the strong political motivations that had brought people to the course would carry them through the practical and conceptual problems that we anticipated. Students were given workshops about the nature of research, how to choose a research topic and how to conduct questionnaires. Again, the written reports were disappointing. A few performed adequately; the rest, in spite of high levels of commitment, were unable to formulate clear research proposals. Final reports failed to lay out evidence or to present arguments.

Until 1994, most South African schools made pervasive use of rote learning – the method that adult students instinctively revert to when asked to perform tasks that involve written information. This above all else explains why we encountered so many difficulties (for a discussion of the central position of rote learning under Apartheid see Geidt 1996:17–18). It may help at this point to summarise some of the things that a majority of students, many of them ETDP practitioners, were unable to do:

- discuss a research project in ways that recognised the position of a researcher;
- distinguish between the status of different kinds of information – the researcher's views from those of others, opinions from established facts, evidence from arguments;

- relate personal experiences to documentary evidence and
- write clear reports about what they had seen or done
- take responsibility for learning.

Educational progress is not made by avoiding weaknesses. Obvious lessons from 1993 were that research proposals have to be produced in good time and that people with limited experience of studying are more likely to sustain progress if they work within structured schedules. It seemed that an important feature of research has to do with learning how to separate and re-integrate writing with other activities that mature students may be able to do quite well – when interviewing, for example, a student has to plan appropriate questions, choose a respondent, ask the questions, listen to and note down a summary of the answers, write a draft that interprets what happened and discuss this draft with other people.

During the processes of monitoring and counselling we came to realise that the didactically channelled processes students carry out are valuable in themselves as a fertile and productive learning resource. To gather and record information about the research project topic need not be the principal aim of the exercise, but the means by which learning outcomes are achieved. While the topic provides students with motivation, from a teaching-learning standpoint it is a secondary consideration. We decided to stop treating a taught research course as if the primary concern was with content – what to research – since this approach presented non-graduate students with a host of choices in an unfamiliar discourse to which they were unable to respond.

Practical step-by step processes – how to research – became the 1995 focus. We produced a carefully articulated plan of activities that gave students an experience of using different methods within their own organisations. Research proposals were 'forced' by making everyone answer an open-ended questionnaire and assignments that involved laid-out tasks had to be handed in at every study-weekend. Answers to the question 'What is research?' were discovered through a series of how-to explanations centring on a tripartite structure of planning, doing and writing. Research sessions became practical discussions. Honest writing was encouraged by stressing the importance of distinguishing a researcher's interpretation from an accurately reported respondent's opinion.

In 1997, a teaching text was introduced (*Research Methods for Adult Educators*, Geidt 1997) which describes the 1995 course structures and experiences. Successive chapters elaborate the original study-weekend programme. Shortened versions of student assignments are used to illustrate different aspects of practical community research and these form a dialogue with didactic sections and suggested activities for small groups. The idea behind this format is that students who lack confidence are encouraged into taking action. Over-confidence (a frequent problem to begin with) can also be restrained by cautionary tales, as in the following honest description by a team of two 1995 students:

> Our questions were not answered the way we would have liked them to be. Perhaps they were not clear and direct enough... [We believe] we found an answer to our main question, but it was disguised between lots of facts. (Beauzick & Van Rooyen, in Geidt 1997:84).

The 1997 version of the course had four aims (Geidt 1997):

1. to enable learners to obtain and report important or interesting information clearly to an audience;
2. to enable learners to use some of the research methods commonly used in the social sciences;
3. to give learners a fuller understanding of the subject they chose to research; and
4. to enable learners to understand what 'doing research' meant and what it involved.

An outline of the programme is given below. At least two research workshops take place at each study-weekend. Back-up is provided by locally organised tutor-led study-group sessions for discussing the practical assignments. These eventually form part of final research reports.

What is research?	Documents and libraries
	Writing a project proposal
	How to interview
	Reporting a meeting
	Creating a questionnaire
	Presenting findings
	Writing a final report

What kind of practical skills are learned on the above programme? I list below some of the activities – practical and conceptual – that students carried out during the course of the programme with varying degrees of success. Each item could, of course, be broken down into an impossibly large number of component activities.

Planning meetings.	*Structuring conversations.*
Listening to conversations.	*Observing behaviour in social situations.*
Selecting appropriate questions.	*Finding and using documents.*
Using a word processor.	*Taking notes.*
Writing structured reports.	*Talking about written reports.*
Presenting ideas to an audience.	*Differentiating between different kinds*
Distinguishing between opinions.	*of information.*
Making judgements.	*Reviewing progress.*

It is not possible from the evidence of assessment marks and statements by students to make pronouncements about the extent to which particular practices are learned. The component bits of research fit specific research contexts and individual needs. There is a range of different activities involved in classroom and community – each student has a different background and every research project makes unique demands. Some learning changes are attitudinal. In general one can say that on a course of this type learners develop or strengthen a large number of interrelated practice-based skills and attitudes and that the extent to which any of them is developed depends, first, on the educational profile and motivation of the student and, second, on the context and scope of the project.

It is also inappropriate to judge the written projects in relation to research published in academic journals. While there have been a large number of excellently described narratives and four or five projects that are on a par with good work produced for the third year of a degree course, most students do not reach these levels. However, within the context of the four aims, surprisingly large gains are made in terms of learning outcomes. A majority writes structured, interesting reports. Concentrating on practical details seems to enable students to escape from the rhetorical opinions many of them express about their topics before they start, and helps them bring the objects of their research into clearer perspective. Almost everyone on the course expressed positive sentiments about his or her achievements. At the 1995 CACE/University of Linkoping Conference (Adult Education in Reconstruction and Development: Lessons from the South and North) twelve of the 1995 intake successfully gave verbal presentations and three had reports of their work published in the conference proceedings. The topics presented are given below.

> Remedial & adaptation classes in Heideveld primary schools
> The education of Cape Town City centre street children
> Why children do not attend Educare classes
> Why men do not attend literacy classes in Mitchells Plain
> The liaison between Health Services in Montagu and Ashton
> Attitudes to teenage pregnancies in Site C Khayelitsha
> The political aims and objectives of members of the Atlantis Transitional Council
> An evaluation of the Breast Feeding policy of Saint Mary's Hospital
> The causes of drug abuse in a school in Zoleni
> Attitudes towards TB in an informal settlement at Worcester
> Child abuse in Leonsdale, Elsies River
> The economic progress of the Namaqualand Diamond quartzite Mining Community

Bearing in mind the reservations expressed above, there is nevertheless plenty of evidence to suggest that by the end of the course students are more adept at debating issues and distinguishing between points of view. Many also move towards accepting degrees of uncertainty. All students are asked to write an evaluation under the heading of 'Personal conclusion'. Some of the statements indicate that research has led to substantial learning changes. As an example, the following extract is taken from a statement written by Lisanne le Roux from Namaqualand in the Northern Cape (in Geidt 1997:92).

What doing this research has taught me:
If I reflect upon the past 8 months I admit that I have become a wiser person. During the project I really got to know and understand people. Probably the biggest lesson I learnt is that one should not conduct research just to prove preconceived ideas and expectations. I have also realised that if people don't want to change their outlook on life not even legislation will be able to force them. When I started my research in March I had no idea in which direction I was heading. I believed that because we had a new government which did not discriminate, racial discrimination in our small village was definitely a thing of the past. I discovered that people are still not able to live freely in an area of their own choice and that this decision is based on skin colour. Many people answered dishonestly when questioned about their feelings and thoughts regarding 'black people'. As a researcher one has to adopt an attitude of subtlety and humility. I found that people were generally very suspicious when I was conducting an interview. Many of the older people thought that I was just inquisitive. You should not be rigid in your questioning but sit down and let the conversation flow; by doing this you will get information which you have not asked for. Older people tend to be more honest

with their answers regarding the issue of not letting 'black people' live in their areas. A certain gentleman told me directly: 'Oh no, no, my child, we've always been afraid of black people, why should we now live next to them?'

Shortly after completing the course, Lisanne le Roux took a job as an adult education organiser in the Springbok region. Some of the points she makes were also made by other students. Her reflection suggests, among other things, that learning to do research encourages students to adopt a deep approach to learning, that is to say: 'active learning processes which concentrate on both ideas and evidence' (Entwistle 1997a:10).

It is precisely because of the wide-ranging nature of what has to be done that research processes can be used as fertile ground for developing learning activities. All of Kolb's (1984) cycle of learning stages are brought into play – experiencing, reflecting, theorising and testing – but one has to be cautious. The long-term impact of any course depends for every learner on an indeterminate number of largely unpredictable factors. Each person takes away his or her own distinct experience to be modified and blended with a different set of contexts. Evidence from elsewhere confirms that the long-term effects and possible community impacts of adult education courses may be different to the immediate reactions of individuals as reported in evaluations (Ottoson 1997:92–108). This is not to deny the existence of long-term impacts.

Discussion: The community context of social research

In spite of running a course on the subject, it was only in 1995 that we started to question what research is in terms of functions and benefits. If someone in 1993 had asked me to define research, I would have replied along the following lines:

A. Research extends the boundaries of empirically-based knowledge about and for the world
Research seemed to be a self-evident, pre-determined, fixed entity with forbidding international connotations. The problem for us was that experience seemed to demonstrate that non-graduates – in our case politically involved ETDP practitioners in oppressed communities – lacked the academic experience and training to be successful at the elevated activities implied by A. It began to look as if running research courses for Certificate students was not the most effective way to spend time and money.

The turning point came when we realised that all research does not have to be A. Research need not be invested with globally significant expectations. Practising research does more than prepare people to use an academic discourse – other kinds of research may have different purposes. In the light of our experiences, I would in 1997 put forward a broader description of research.

B. Research means finding out and recording things (and ideas about things) in carefully articulated ways

B is a less prescriptive statement than A, but does not exclude the possibility of A. If our pre-1994 experiences confirm that adult learners at lower than tertiary levels in the educational hierarchy cannot do A, our post-1994 experiences show that they can do B, providing the processes are clearly described, discussed and rehearsed.

Looked at from the perspective of the individual learner, substantial benefits are to be derived from learning how to tackle the kinds of problem that occur when one has to implement, discuss and write up a B-type research project.

It is generally accepted, however, that learning processes cannot be understood without taking into account learning contexts. Collins *et al.* (1989: 453–494) following Wilson (1983:77–79) argued that structured 'learning environments' support learners facing the challenges of participating in a new culture through 'cognitive apprenticeships' fundamentally situated in a community of practice. Successful learning is not determined by individual factors alone but by participation in, and access to, communities of learning practice. Thorpe & Thompson (1993:5) reach a similar conclusion when describing the performance of students – they prefer to use the term 'study practices' rather than 'study skills' since 'study practices [suggest] the social context within which communication is learned'. As Field & Schuller (1997:17–18) put it, 'learning is something which involves, draws on and also forms relationships'. From a social perspective then, one assumes (and hopes) that research-related skills learned within a classroom context are transferred to the community organisation contexts where many of the ETDP apprentice researchers work. I will now discuss the reasons why this is important and why it does not happen very often.

Consider the typical primary research situation. When researchers ask people questions, information flows in one direction only. In most typical teaching situations, on the other hand, (leaving complications to do with distance education and the uses of texts and teaching resources aside) information flows in both directions and the student stands to gain from what happens. Little wonder that many people are unwilling to participate in research projects as respondents – the researcher gains everything and they get nothing.

Social research is most frequently carried out with two audiences in mind: funders and the academic community as a whole. If one excludes the long-term, and I believe fairly exceptional, possibility that the research product might be used for the benefit of the researched community, the gain in terms of information, skills and social prestige is clearly to the researcher, the researcher's community and the funder. Generally speaking, it has to be said that university-based social research enhances those who are already in dominant positions.

The problem is most acute and least acceptable in developing contexts. In these circumstances an academic researcher is distanced from the community she or he is researching. The researcher's community is privileged, skilled and wealthy; the researched community is none of these things. The researcher's community depends on a culture of academic literacy with rich resources of information technology; the researched community has neither the resources nor the organisational culture of contexts and relationships to be able to use those resources. To outrageously simplify some complex and extended debates, two kinds of questions have over-riding importance for the ontological standing of social research. They are:

1. Questions of method: how do we bridge the gap between the different cultural worlds of researcher and respondent in terms of education, language, habits and cultural assumptions?
2. Questions of ethics: how do we use work by researchers in ways that will benefit the community being investigated?

These kinds of concerns were first raised by the social anthropologist Malinowski in the 1920s. Action research, participant research and the development of the qualitative, ethnographic investigative techniques of participant observation and oral history are all, in different ways, attempts to face up to a predicament which is endemic to research situations in developing contexts.

It will be recalled that an aim of the Certificate course as a whole is to help ETDP practitioners to succeed in their own contexts by developing strategic planning skills. Put simply, doing research helps students to conceptualise, plan, obtain evidence, record and structure information. A taught research course for non-graduates with prior experience of the communities they research is different to ethnography. Ethnographers are academics who live for a time in the researched community in order to study it. Nor can the course be described as 'an alternative system of knowledge production' (Tandon 1988: 18) since learning to use orthodox research methods is a central feature. It is also different to most action research. Feminist writers influenced by the ideas of Derrida and Foucault have attempted to define new action research technologies that 'seek to empower individuals and communities in ways that lead to social change' (Joyappa & Martin 1996: 1–14; see also Code 1991). The action researcher is an academic from a different community who is often committed to a pre-existing political position. There are, however, similarities with some versions of participant research, particularly in those cases where the researcher determines the methods rather than the assumptions, but the differences are substantial: in the Certificate methods are a primary concern rather than a means to an end.

In the CACE Certificate course, and others like it, the student researcher's community is also the researched community. The crucial point is that since this is a taught research course, a dialogue between teacher and student enables communication to take place in both directions, that is to say between the teacher-researcher's academic community and the student-researcher's researched community. Potentially, then, both communities can benefit: information about the researched community flows out; information about skilled practices flows in and can be used by the student researcher and others to reconsider known community problems.

The function of research implied by the aims of the Certificate course is consonant with the view of Habermas (1984) rather than of Foucault. Habermas's central enlightenment ideal is that social emancipation can be approached through clear communicative practice. Our course attempts to enable students to (re)interpret a chosen social context in honest, systematic and accurate ways and to provide a tool with potential for personal growth. This may suggest ideas for social change in the researched community.

Conclusions

Mythological attitudes sustain the idea that research can only be done by acknowledged experts at the upper end of the academic hierarchy. Subotzky *et al.* (1997) give extensive evidence of the harmful and pervasive influence of this myth in South Africa's 'historically black universities' where in many instances the very prospect of doing research is so daunting that postgraduates and teaching staff do little of it. A more open and practical attitude is needed. The expectations that people have of research findings can often be scaled down in favour of the learning functions of research processes.

If taught research courses were to become a more important component of adult education, a research-friendly culture would begin to extend knowledge about the ability to use some of the resources that South Africa's oppressed communities so desperately need. Walters (1996:67) suggests that 'the power of the [ETDP] concept at present lies in the fact that opportunities are being created for practitioners to live in the gaps between sectors and traditions of education and training'. If ETDP apprentice researchers learn to use carefully described techniques, research becomes something that can be applied to and for local communities. Our experience at CACE indicates, however, that although research findings are unpredictable, the benefits to be derived from learning to do research are more certain. Non-graduate research courses can be used to teach people how to identify, discuss and reformulate their problems.

Endnote

1. The following people participated in various ways in helping to design the research course described in this article: Beverley Thaver, Daniel Moshenberg, Mignonne Breier, George Subotzky, Salma Ismael, Angela Schaffer, Lucy Alexander and the participants of a workshop at the fourth conference on 'Learning and Research in Working Life' at Steyr, Austria held in July 1996.

SECTION FIVE

Diversity and social cohesion in education

Introduction

Each section of this book focuses on a series of interconnected questions prominent on the agendas of educational policy and practice across a wide range of societies in the contemporary world – questions which require the attention of theorists and researchers as well as policy-makers and practitioners if public debate and democratic decision-making are to be fully informed. Each nexus of questions addressed presents itself in strong form in the new South Africa, not least because each exhibits differing aspects of the tension between the claims of social equity and the demands for economic development. This tension lies at the heart of debates over the aims, form and function of public education in modern democratic societies, with successive educational 'reforms' claiming to optimise achievement of whichever demand is currently dominant whilst also accommodating the competing claim. Nowhere is that tension more acute than in the South Africa of today, with obstacles to its resolution exacerbated by the radical diversity between citizens present there on every dimension of salience to the provision of equitable and effective public education and to the achievement of democratic citizenship. It is therefore fitting that the final section in this volume be concerned with education's role in promoting respect for cultural diversity in the building of an equitable and cohesive society.

Worldwide at the end of the twentieth century, following decolonisation, large-scale migration, reconfiguration of international alliances, liberal secularisation, and accelerating technological and social change with consequent disruption to traditional social structures and patterns of personal life, nation-states and the citizens who make them up have become particularly sensitive to their sources of identity. In proportion as these were ignored or suppressed in the past, or even too lightly surrendered, anxiety is evident that a valued cultural inheritance may be compromised or eroded in the future. Whether this manifests itself as the resurgence of national or ethnic identity claims, the spread of religious fundamentalism, the rise of gender politics, or the demands of 'ethnic minorities' for full social inclusion without assimilation, the burning political issue of our time is the requirement to reconcile the facts of cultural diversity with legitimate demands for equal citizenship without sacrifice of personal identity. Arguably, the distinguishing feature of contemporary political life is the insistence that only if those differences which are constitutive of identity – whether differences of race, ethnicity, gender, religion, culture, language, etc. – are given full acknowledgement and respect, not merely in law but in a society's basic institutions, can equal participation for all citizens in a democracy be realised.

The most basic social institution of all in this regard is of course a society's public education system, since it is through education that identity, whether individual or societal, is reflected – validated or discounted – and reconstructed for the future. It is therefore not surprising that concern with identity comes to a head in contestation over the appropriate aims, content, procedures and distribution of public education in pluralist democracies.

It would be hard to imagine any society exhibiting greater diversity among its citizens, on the full range of possible dimensions of difference, than does the 'rainbow nation' of the new South Africa. For evident historical reasons, that diversity has a very tight set of structural relations to social stratification on an exceptionally wide spectrum of unequal access not only to the material benefits of a modern democracy, but to influence in its cultural constitution. These structural relations, inherited by a democratic South Africa from its past, ensure that considerations of 'difference' – ethnic, linguistic, gender, class, cultural – are implicated not only in that inevitable tension between the claims of social equity and the demands for economic development which any society looks to its education system to juggle, but they are also highly significant for any citizen's prospects in the democratic social competition on both dimensions. Each chapter in this section addresses key aspects of the nexus of resulting problems for educational policy and practice.

Whilst South Africa's cultural diversity and associated social divisions can be seen as a especially extreme form of a pervasive modern phenomenon, that society's particular history entrains its own dangers in addressing the issue. Morrow highlights this in his opening analysis of debates around multicultural education in South Africa. In a social context where the fashionable arguments of 'the politics of difference' have very sinister echoes, multicultural education requires a rationale which avoids the mistakes of cultural essentialism and relativism, with their damaging consequences both educational and political.

Morrow mounts an educational case for multiculturalism, on epistemological grounds, laying the foundations for a pluralist understanding of society and education which avoids the twin dangers of hegemony and separatism. In so doing, he insists that only a multicultural approach to education, properly understood, can equip citizens for the complexity and fluidity of personal identity in the modern world. Before that question is further explored in the concluding chapter, two contributions turn directly to one particular dimension of difference – linguistic diversity – bringing the underlying theoretical questions into sharp focus.

Desai and Van der Merwe address the policy tensions which arise from the need to promote English as a global medium of communication whilst validating African languages in a democratic South Africa – tensions which permeate educational debate and seek accommodation in educational practice. They emphasise linguistic inclusion as a prerequisite to full citizenship and argue that such inclusion cannot await the achievement of multilingualism. The primary purpose of language in education policy should be to facilitate learning, and hence access to full democratic participation, for all citizens. Meerkotter is concerned with how this can be achieved in practice, by teachers in under-resourced schools, within the constraints of particular social conditions. She reports a case-study of second language teaching with disadvantaged black learners in a township school. In her analysis of the effectiveness of 'code-switching' as a pedagogical technique, Meerkotter stresses that motivation and identification with the educational process, as well as learning outcomes, are enhanced by an approach in which the teacher shows respect for the learners' cultural identity and includes their cultural resources in a shared educational experience.

The concluding chapter explores the over-arching question of public education's role in promoting and sustaining common citizenship whilst not merely respecting, but celebrating, cultural diversity. Jonathan first sets the matter in its theoretical framework, showing how the liberal democratic ideal, that all should have equal respect for their differing conceptions of the good life and the good society, runs into particular difficulties in that very social practice – education – which is charged with a primary role in the realisation of that ideal. She then contextualises the problem, showing that in the conceptual climate of modernity, exacerbated by contingent conditions of globalisation, personal identity and cultural allegiance are inescapably multi-faceted affairs. That being so, cultural diversity need not be seen as the seed-bed for social division. Understood in all its complexity, as a multiplicity of identifications, allegiances, aspirations and interests which each must accommodate within themselves in modernity, diversity is not so much a problem

230

we must overcome as a predicament we all share. This more positive construal, however, remains so much pie-in-the-sky as long as sources of diversity between persons remain structurally tied to unequal power relations. Thus it is social inequity, not cultural diversity, which threatens social cohesion and paints pluralism as a divisive problem rather than a unifying shared condition.

In beginning with a theoretical analysis, turning then to a key question of related policy, focusing next on the constraints and possibilities offered by practice and then stepping back again to see if the question can be constructively recast, this section aims both to contribute to our understanding of matters of central educational importance and also to demonstrate that theory, policy and practice are interdependent, with each throwing light on the other.

Ruth Jonathan

17

Multicultural education in South Africa

WALLY MORROW

Social justice ... requires not the melting away of differences, but institutions that promote reproduction of and respect for group differences without oppression (Young 1990:47).

The politics of difference

Over the past decades in the liberal democratic world there has been a growing emphasis on the recognition of social diversity. This emphasis is evident in debates on political and social theory and, of course, education, but it is also reflected in the forms of protest which have become prevalent in liberal democratic societies. By now it seems to have become a commonplace that modern societies are 'plural' or 'multicultural' and that their public policy should 'recognise difference', perhaps especially in the field of education in the form of 'multicultural education'.

Advocates of 'multiculturalism' typically understand these developments as a critique of 'liberalism' and its reproductive wing, 'liberal education'. Although this critique takes a variety of forms, central to it are the allegations that 'liberalism' homogenises society – it ignores some of the crucial differences between people which are basic to their identity and its formation – and that the self-understanding of liberalism as 'neutral' is fraudulent. 'Liberalism' is characterised as a form of normalising oppression – more insidious than other forms of oppression due to its benign 'neutral' face – and 'liberal education' is vilified as one of the prime instruments for the maintenance of that oppression.

Defenders of liberalism are understandably shocked by such allegations. In its self-understanding, liberalism has always thought of itself as the primary opponent of oppression, including those forms of oppression which rest on a denial of difference. The ideal of autonomy is one of the defining features of liberalism, and this has been expressed in terms of not merely a tolerance of individual differences but their celebration and promotion, especially in education. Liberalism was always committed to the 'recognition of difference', but, say the critics, it was not the right kind of difference which was recognised.

According to critics, a major flaw in liberalism lies in the way it prioritises individuals in its conceptions of difference and identity. Liberalism is socially 'homogenising' not because it does not acknowledge differences between individuals – that it is committed to doing so is one of its defining characteristics – but because it does not acknowledge, or recognise in its public policies and practices, including education, significant differences between the groups which compose the population. To conceive of identity in individualistic terms, as liberalism does, not only ignores the sources of identity but involves 'abstracting' individuals from the group membership which specifically defines and maintains their identity.

The politics of difference focuses not on differences between individuals but on differences between groups; it refers to what are called 'collective differences'. On this understanding, to talk of a 'diverse' or a 'plural' society is to be referring not to the truism that any society is composed of individuals, who are obviously different from each other in a potentially huge variety of respects, but to differences between the groups that compose the society. The argument is, then, that to fail to recognise collective differences in appropriate ways in public and educational policy is a form of oppression because collective identities are primary. Individual identities, it is claimed, are products and reflections of collective identities, so that to fail to respect collective identities in education, for example, is to undermine the vulnerable individual identities of, particularly, members of traditionally marginalised or oppressed groups, and to fail to provide a nurturing environment in which those identities can develop and flourish.

From the point of view of these debates, South Africa exhibits social diversity in the starkest possible terms. Most of what have been claimed to be salient 'differences' (differences which demand public recognition) in liberal democratic societies are found in South Africa, and frequently in an extreme form. South Africa is the home of a breathtaking range of different languages, religions, ethnic groups, and cultural traditions and practices – the phrase 'the rainbow nation' has been used to highlight this rich and colourful diversity.

From this observation the conclusion can be drawn, so it is thought, that South Africa should enthusiastically embrace 'the politics of difference' and build 'multicultural education' into the heart of its system of public education. South Africa is socially diverse, therefore it ought favour the politics of difference and foster multicultural education. This is the argument I set out to explore in this chapter.

Similarities between Apartheid and 'multiculturalism'

It is understandable why South Africans will approach this argument with some ambivalence. South Africa is a product of an embrangled history of Euro-centric colonialism and its stepchild Apartheid and bitter struggles against these harsh forms of oppression. A defining feature of both colonialism and Apartheid was the identification and maintenance of separate groups in the population. Both the defence of and the struggle against these regimes have deeply entrenched these group differences. Contemporary South Africa, we might say, is not so much 'socially diverse' as 'socially divided'; it is more in need of a 'discovery of commonality' than it is in need of a 'recognition of difference'.

However, there is also a more theoretical kind of reason why South Africans should be anxious about embracing the discourse of 'the politics of difference' and 'multicultural education'. We think of colonialism and Apartheid as so thoroughly unjust and evil that it is difficult for us to imagine that they could once have been plausibly defended, and by people of good will. A constant theme in the official justifications for these oppressive regimes was the need to recognise and respect the differences between the different groups which compose the society, and to protect and perpetuate group integrity. At least in respect to thoughts like this, the discourse of 'the politics of difference' and 'multicultural education' is uncomfortably similar to the discourse of colonialism and Apartheid.

Intellectual apologists for Apartheid would have had little difficulty in agreeing with the statement from Iris Young which I have quoted at the beginning of this paper, and they would have had few problems about agreeing that it is the shortcomings of liberalism which require us to develop a different political philosophy more appropriate for a plural society. They would have agreed that one of the worst forms of oppression is the domination of one group by another, but would have added that this form of oppression is, in practice, impossible to avoid when such groups occupy a common political and geographical space. The only way to avoid such domination and oppression, they said, is for groups to be segregated and provided with the opportunity autonomously to nurture and perpetuate their own distinctive cultures, in their own institutions.

The segregationist position is not unique to Apartheid, as anyone who knows about racial problems in the United States will know. Over the years the defenders of Apartheid pointed to the examples of Ireland, India and Pakistan, and the former Yugoslavia. In Africa itself there have been ongoing problems with 'artificial' colonial boundaries. Nigeria and Rwanda provide brutal examples of the kinds of problems which arise when cultural differences are ignored in public policy. In general terms the problem in all these cases is how to maintain a peaceful and coherent society in a situation of cultural diversity.

The charge that the discourses of Apartheid and 'multiculturalism' are similar to each other is one which the defenders of 'multiculturalism' will find deeply disturbing – their natural response will be passionately to deny it, but what can be their grounds for such a denial? That they see Apartheid as morally obnoxious and 'multiculturalism' as morally virtuous is not sufficient. They need to be able to point to some more substantive differences in order to provide grounds for these moral judgements.

They might, first, think in terms of contrasting goals. Apartheid, they might say, was driven by the goal of oppression; 'multiculturalism' is driven by the goal of alleviating and undermining oppression. But this does little to advance the argument. Here, as elsewhere, good intentions are not enough. I have already indicated that there were some defenders of Apartheid who argued that the goal of the policy was to avoid oppression. Putting aside the suggestion that they were simply lying, we might say that the historical record shows that they were deluded, but if they were deluded, then, given the apparent similarities between the two discourses, perhaps the defenders of 'multiculturalism' are similarly deluded. To rebut this suggestion the defenders of 'multiculturalism' still need to point to substantive differences.

Differences between multiculturalism and Apartheid

There are two closely linked possibilities: one in terms of the underlying theories of social groups, the other in terms of the social/political policy of segregation.

Apartheid was founded on an essentialist account of cultural groups; multiculturalism rejects this account. For Apartheid each cultural group was conceived of as homogenous and self-contained, as having a distinctive and essential nature which needed to be protected from contamination, preserved for the sake of current and future members of the group and perpetuated by means of education. The roots of the view in nineteenth-century evolutionary biology and European racism are clear, and it provides a classical example of the reification of social phenomena. Cultural groups are conceived of on the model of biological species; like species they can suffer extinction or degeneration, and although they can develop gradually over time, such development is guided by a kind of internal dynamic, which, if it is ignored, will lead to the disintegration of the group with the dire consequences of demoralisation and the loss of the natural integrity of the group which is the principal ground of the identity of its individual members. Individual members of a cultural group might, through blindness or ignorance, lose sight of the seminal importance, for their own identities and the significance of their own lives, of maintaining group integrity. This is why group differentiation has, if need be, to be imposed on people for their own benefit, as a matter of political policy.

Multiculturalism rejects the organic metaphor which lies in the roots of such an essentialist account of social groups. The origin and formation of social groups is to be explained in terms of historical, as opposed to organic, processes. For multiculturalism, social groups arise out of the social processes of differentiation and affinity, and, once formed, they shape how people understand one another and themselves; they become, in short, sources of identity for their members. Social groups come into being as an outcome of social encounters and interactions. Thus, the concept of a social group is relational as opposed to essential. In the words of Iris Young (1990:43), 'Groups are an expression of social relations; a group exists only in relation to at least one other group'.

This provides one way of distinguishing between Apartheid and multiculturalism and it leads towards another.

Apartheid insisted that traditional cultural groups needed to be segregated from each other not only to avoid irresolvable conflict but also to ensure the integrity and continued survival of distinctive cultures. In clear contrast to this, multiculturalism holds the view that diverse social groups need all to be accommodated in the same geographical, political and institutional spaces. Indeed the very description of a society as 'plural' or an institution as 'multicultural' implies that the members of diverse social groups share, or should share, common public spaces. 'Multicultural education' implies a form of education which accommodates a variety of 'cultures' in a mutually respectful environment in common institutions.

A policy of segregation harmonises with an essentialist view of social groups and, paradoxically in the light of what happened under Apartheid, one might say that it draws one strand of its inspiration, in the South African context, from a genuine, if paternalistic, concern for the fate of indigenous cultures under the destructive impact of Eurocentric colonialism. Apartheid attempted to minimalise the interfaces between cultures as much, its defenders would have claimed, for the sake of the integrity of indigenous cultures as for the sake of social peace. Multiculturalism is opposed to segregation – it stands for the idea that politics and institutions should generously accommodate culturally diverse groups while avoiding any overt or covert bias in favour of any particular cultural group.

At a formal level this provides a second distinction between the discourses of multiculturalism and Apartheid but, to ground this distinction, we still need to know how multiculturalism can respond to the segregationist claim that it is not possible to maintain social peace and stability without cultural domination, in a situation in which diverse cultural groups inhabit common public spaces and institutions. To distance itself definitively from this view a defence of multiculturalism has to reject a basic theoretical presupposition of the segregationist stance.

Cultural relativism

The segregationist stance – that group domination is unavoidable where diverse cultural groups occupy common political and institutional spaces – presupposes cultural relativism. This is the view that cultures are incompatible with each other, and where they come into conflict there can be only victories and defeats. Cultural relativism is a theory with definite consequences for political and educational policy and practice. If we allow cultures to live together either some will be lost or destroyed as others achieve dominance, or they might all lose their integrity in a kind of bland cosmopolitan homogeneity. Mutual accommodation between cultures is a form of cultural impoverishment, and, far from being desirable, is simply another way of expressing the loss of cultural integrity and a decline in cultural diversity.

Cultural relativism claims that cultures are 'incommensurable' with each other; they each have their own forms of life, and there is no way of 'translating' between cultures. Each culture has its own internally coherent form of rationality – rational deliberation is possible only *within* cultures and there can be no such thing as culturally neutral rational deliberation – rationality does not cross cultural boundaries. The idea that there could be culturally neutral institutions or practices which can accommodate rival cultural groups is seen either as an illusion of liberalism or a fraudulent attempt by one cultural group to maintain cultural and political domination, or perhaps both at the same time. Unless it is merely a form of politically naïve and optimistic romanticism, multiculturalism must oppose this view.

To distance itself definitively from Apartheid's segregationist stance, multiculturalism has to reject the theory of cultural relativism on which it rests.

In order to defend its non-segregationist stance – the claim that cultural diversity can be accommodated in common public space without cultural domination or irresolvable conflict and social chaos – it has to commit itself to the view not only that cross-cultural communication is possible but that there must be some forms of dialogue and deliberation in terms of which cultural conflicts can be resolved or dissolved.

Multiculturalism is incompatible with the kind of dogmatic antagonisms which are a practical consequence of the theory of cultural relativism. Its defence, thus, requires the rejection not only of the theory of cultural relativism but also the kinds of practice underwritten by that theory. Multiculturalism is necessarily committed to the idea that there must be some forms of shared practices which, whatever their origin, are not limited to specific cultures or cultural groups, and which are robust enough to generate mutually acceptable resolutions of inter-cultural incompatibilities and conflicts.

Multiculturalism and liberalism

In distinguishing between multiculturalism and Apartheid we have had to give an account of multiculturalism as having specific characteristics. Multiculturalism needs to be based on a non-essentialist theory of social groups and a rejection of the theory and practice of cultural relativism. There are two important consequences of this result.

One is that this account excludes some accounts of 'multiculturalism' which lead a flourishing life in contemporary populist and polemical debate in this field. Any account of 'multiculturalism' which underplays the social/political sources of the formation of social groups or implicitly or explicitly presupposes cultural relativism is guilty of the charge of being a fellow traveller in the discourse of Apartheid. In spite of self-righteous attempts to distance themselves from Apartheid any defenders of 'multiculturalism' who support the ideas of the intrinsic goodness of cultural diversity, the desirability of ensuring the long-term survival of cultural differences, or of pre-emptively demanding equal respect for all cultural achievements is probably entangled in either an essentialist understanding of cultural groups or cultural relativism or both. Cultural ecology is a contemporary expression of the continuing power of organic and biological metaphors in our social and political theories.

Another is that to the extent that multiculturalism is characterised in terms of a non-essentialist account of social groups and a rejection of cultural relativism, it draws closer to liberalism. It becomes more like a variation within the discourse of liberalism than like a competing discourse. Multiculturalism can still be distinguished from orthodox liberalism in terms of its focus on groups and collective identities rather than autonomous individuals and individual identities, but in other respects it now emerges as a development within liberalism as opposed to a rival to it.

With this understanding of multiculturalism in hand we can now proceed with the exploration of the argument that because South Africa is socially diverse it ought to favour the politics of difference and foster multicultural education. We need to think more directly about multicultural education, and then take into view two major historical characteristics of contemporary South Africa: it is a modernising society engaged in trying to transform itself into a democratic society – on any account a difficult process.

The practice of multicultural education

Bhikhu Parekh (1995) usefully points out that the debate about 'multicultural education' originated in a contrast with what was called 'monocultural education'. Mainstream education in liberal democratic societies was accused of being a form of cultural imperialism, 'monocultural' and 'Eurocentric', which put members of minority cultures at serious social, personal and educational disadvantages. 'Monocultural education' was seen as a form of education which in its 'nature, aims, contents and ethos' consolidated students in one particular culture by implicitly assuming the superiority of that culture and ignoring or marginalising others, or representing them in superficial, uncomplimentary or demeaning terms.

From an educational point of view, 'monocultural education' has serious shortcomings. It is unlikely to awaken students' intellectual curiosity about other cultures or to develop their moral imagination by exposing them to alternative forms of life and enabling them to enter into the spirit of different visions of a good life for human beings. Monocultural education is likely to stunt the growth of students' critical capacities and to breed cultural arrogance, insensitivity and racism.

On this understanding the schooling systems inherited by post-colonial societies were monocultural, as was the schooling system of Apartheid. Under Apartheid, with its separate schooling systems for different cultural groups, what we had was a set of monocultural schooling systems, but we can now add, as Parekh (1995:7) does, that some forms of 'multicultural education' are, paradoxically, 'monocultural', they are '...no less monocultural, and no better, than Eurocentric education'. 'Multicultural education' which draws its inspiration from an essentialist theory of cultural groups and cultural relativism turns out to be *de facto* 'monocultural'. The insistence that various cultures should be accommodated in common institutions is a trivial difference from Apartheid.

Discussions about how we might 'Africanise' the curriculum of South African schools have an important role in the future development of education in South Africa. However, to the extent that they are based on, or move towards, the idea of recommending 'Afrocentric education' to replace 'Eurocentric education' they are simply another form of the monocultural education deeply ingrained in our colonial and Apartheid heritage, and suffer from the same kinds of shortcomings from an educational point of view.

Forms of 'multicultural education' which are, in effect, 'monocultural', foster educational practices which defeat the ideals of multicultural education. To the extent that, in practice, various cultures are merely 'studied' rather than brought into critical dialogue with each other, to the extent that cultures are treated as if they are hermetically sealed from each other and beyond criticism, we have in view a form of educational practice which subverts the real promise of multicultural education.

Running through the whole of this debate, however – and reinforced by the supposed contrast between monocultural and multicultural education – is a misleading assumption about education. Education is understood as embedded in and existing to reproduce and subserve specific cultures. All education is assumed to be a more or less subtle form of indoctrination, which recruits new members for specific cultures.

In opposing this assumption we need to avoid committing ourselves to an unsustainable ahistorical theory of rationality, which is a legacy of pre-Enlightenment religious belief. We need to understand rationality as the practice of reasoning. The practices of reasoning and education are not confined to any particular culture, while nonetheless being in the realm of culture – with all that that implies about how their very existence and their flourishing, corruption or degeneration, is intimately tied to historically variable patterns of theories, institutions and practices. Reasoning is a practice that assumes that no practices are immune from criticism; it is the platform for cultural critique and provides us with the basis for recognising the inevitable partiality and shortcomings of any specific cultures.

As Parekh (1995:7) claims: 'Education cannot transcend the realm of *culture*, but it can and ought to transcend specific *cultures*'. That form of multicultural education which rejects cultural relativism and an essentialist view of cultures is committed to a view of this kind. This has implications for both curriculum content, which is the focus of most of the debate about multicultural education, and for the practice of education, namely, teaching. Multicultural education needs to be underwritten by a characteristic kind of teaching, which might, in fact, be even more important than curriculum content.

For multicultural education to be a live option it needs an educational practice which undermines the temptations of cultural relativism and enables students to become participants in the practices of reasoning. Such a practice is difficult and hazardous – it needs to be porous without becoming merely shapeless. It disrupts the traditional 'cultural' authority of teachers and focuses sharply on their professional judgement. The professional judgement of teachers committed to multicultural education needs to avoid the inauthenticity of pre-emptively favourable judgements of worth, but, at the same time, to be unusually sensitive to possible cultural differences. From this view the teacher is neither a demagogue nor a 'non-judgmental facilitator' – neither a propagandist for a particular culture nor passively 'neutral' between cultures. The professional judgement of a teacher in multicultural education needs to be guided by a positive commitment to fostering the practices of reasoning, and this requires some ironical distance from any particular cultures.

Provided that we interpret it in this way, South Africa must foster the practice of multicultural education, and not merely for the reason that it is a diverse society. Thus interpreted, multicultural education is a kind of education which effectively promotes the capacities, talents and virtues which characterise what it is for a person to be educated as opposed to being merely trained for specified tasks, activities or occupations, indoctrinated into the sentiments or beliefs of a specific culture, or blindly socialised into particular sets of habits and practices. This kind of education disembeds students from myopic immersion in the settled practices of a particular culture and its traditions, and encourages the development of a shared identity across cultural boundaries. The promise of multicultural education is that it can powerfully contribute to such an achievement.

However, the argument about whether South Africa should foster multicultural education also needs to take into view an important feature of contemporary South Africa – it is a society on the trajectory of modernisation.

Multiculturalism and modernisation

Apartheid can be seen as a comprehensive attempt to stem the tide of modernisation but, even during the darkest days, economic developments compelled at least partial 'modernisation'. Modernisation erodes traditional cultures and the stable identities associated with them. Given that Apartheid was based on a commitment to the integrity and continued survival of distinctive traditional cultures, it was right to try to block the processes of modernisation by, amongst other things, protecting traditional cultures in monocultural education systems.

Some of the catalysts and features of modernisation which Apartheid tried to control are urbanisation, the circulation of printed matter and the increasing penetration into everyday life of mass media and new technologies, all of which shrink space and time and disrespect traditional geographical and cultural borders. Such developments expose people to a strong mix of disparate cultural influences and images, increase mutual dependence between people and require the increasing co-ordination of their various activities.

One of the main deficiencies of monocultural education is that it traps students in a traditional culture and, thus, fails to contribute to their access to the modern world; it provides, at best, only limited opportunities for students to develop the talents and virtues needed to cope well in that world of diversity. According to Parekh (1995:10), multicultural education enables '... the student to accept, enjoy and cope with diversity', and being able to do this is at the heart of what is needed to handle the diversity and lack of certainty which characterises a modernising society, especially in the case of South Africa in which the processes of modernisation were kept under such a tight rein during the previous half-century in which modernisation has increased apace in much of the world.

Modernisation and multiculturalism are two sides of the same coin, and multicultural education is a form of education which provides access to modernisation and develops the mobile intellectual and moral capabilities needed to survive and flourish in the modern world. This provides a further reason for South Africa to foster multicultural education.

The politics of difference in an emerging democracy

We can now refocus our attention on the argument that because South Africa is a diverse society it ought to favour the politics of difference and foster multicultural education. The upshot of the arguments of the previous sections of this chapter is that, provided we understand multicultural education in a particular way, South Africa should, of course, foster multicultural education. It is now time to turn our attention to the politics of difference.

On the account of multicultural education developed in this chapter multicultural education and the politics of difference are not the close relatives they are commonly assumed to be; in fact they pull in opposite directions. The argument in support of fostering multicultural education in South Africa is not at the same time an argument in support of the politics of difference. I shall conclude this chapter by arguing that there are good reasons to oppose the politics of difference in South Africa, especially in educational institutions.

A liberal-democratic society is one premised on the view that perfect social justice is unobtainable in the real historical world. Thus we need to establish a polity which remains open to constant attempts to remove injustices which unexpectedly appear, without coming apart at the seams. A liberal democratic society '...makes authority accessible without dissolving it, (and opens) such authority to future deliberation and critique' (Salkever 1990:182).

The politics of difference is a confrontational style of politics which presupposes an established political order and a shared identity. The politics of difference emphasises differences between groups with a view to removing injustices in a political dispensation which is, broadly, just. The risks of the politics of difference are that by generating group hostilities and antagonisms it might lead to social, institutional and political disintegration.

It is significant that the politics of difference has emerged specifically in well-established liberal-democratic societies, in which there is at least some sense amongst their members of a shared identity – a sense of belonging to a common political community. Acknowledging this point, Iris Young writes that, 'Group identification arises, that is, in the encounter and interaction between social collectivities that experience some differences in their way of life and forms of association, *even if they also regard themselves as belonging to the same society*' (Young 1990:43, my emphasis).

The politics of difference is a product of societies which have well-established procedures for resolving conflicts without violence, (relatively) stable public institutions, (relatively) robust traditions of the practice of public deliberation about common interests, (relatively) low levels of poverty and destitution, and (relative) social peace and lack of civil disorder. For those brought up in societies with such characteristics the bitter political compromises and patient collective efforts of which these historical achievements are the outcome are hidden from view and can safely be ignored. The inevitable shortcomings of such historical achievements can be emphasised in the politics of difference with a view to overcoming them and can be treated as a consensual backdrop for the dramatic performances of the politics of difference. The politics of difference is a centrifugal force, parasitic on established institutions and practices.

South Africa has only very recently emerged from a history of oppression underwritten by radical social division. It is in the midst of the difficult process of trying to rebuild itself as a just society – it is too early for the renovators to move in. Many of South Africa's public institutions are fragile, and tainted with the too-easy accusation that they are parts of the historical legacy from which we need to extricate ourselves. The democratic practice of public deliberation about common interests is far from being a well-established tradition, and it is vulnerable to being subverted and distorted by convictions about democracy forged in the abnormal furnace of struggle and shaped by assumptions about structurally induced group hostility and antagonism. South Africa is characterised by high levels of poverty and destitution and plagued by violent crime and a lack of civil security.

Education has an important role in the building and consolidation of a just and cohesive society. South African education and its institutions were dangerously over-politicised during the time of Apartheid education and the protests it evoked. These stances eroded the authority of the professional judgement of teachers and educational institutions. The politics of difference, imported from well-established liberal-democratic societies, aspires to replace these stances, but it is, in effect, merely a continuation of them. It is as corrosively anti-educational a force in contemporary South Africa, undermining the professional judgement of teachers and the educational authority of institutions to the detriment of the education of students.

South Africa, in short, has not yet achieved the kind of secure framework, such as that characteristic of established liberal-democracies, in terms of which it can accommodate the politics of difference with any equanimity. In the historical context of South Africa the politics of difference is more likely to hinder the achievement of a just democratic society than to contribute to its realisation.

At this time in South Africa, the politics of difference is likely to reinforce traditional divisions, rather than to enable us to discover the social cohesion of which we were deprived by colonialism and Apartheid. By contrast, multicultural education (as characterised in this chapter) promises to contribute to the fostering of the shared identity across the divisions of our history, and this is an important dimension of the task of building a just and democratic society to begin to overcome the oppressions of the past.

18

Accomodating diversity in an increasingly global era: reconciling the tension between English and African languages in education policy in South Africa

ZUBEIDA DESAI AND PREVOT VAN DER MERWE

The theme of this section, diversity and social cohesion in education, can be approached from two perspectives – either that diversity and social cohesion are necessarily in tension or that it is only through accommodating diversity that social cohesion can be forged. Although we will be approaching the topic from the latter perspective, we are aware that it is no easy task and that there are many pitfalls along the way.

The focus of this chapter is on ways in which to accommodate South Africa's linguistic diversity.[1] Before doing so, we shall outline the key features of the current language policy of South Africa, as outlined in *The Constitution of the Republic of South Africa*, Act 108 of 1996 (pp. 4–5):

1. The official languages are, in alphabetical order, Afrikaans, English, isiNdebele, isiXhosa, isiZulu, Sepedi, Sesotho, Setswana, siSwati, Tshivenda and Xitsonga.
2. The onus is on the state to create conditions for the development and promotion of particularly the nine African languages.
3. The national and provincial governments must use at least two official languages for the purposes of government.
4. National and provincial governments must regulate and monitor the use of official languages. All official languages must be treated equitably.

5. A Pan South African Language Board established by national legislation must:
   a) promote, and create conditions for the development and use of:
      (i) all official languages;
      (ii) the Khoi, Nama and San languages; and
      (iii) sign language; and
   b) promote and ensure respect for:
      (i) all languages commonly used by communities in South Africa, including German, Greek, Gujarati, Hindi, Portuguese, Tamil, Telegu and Urdu; and
      (ii) Arabic, Hebrew, Sanskrit and other languages used for religious purposes in South Africa.

From the above, we can see that direct government responsibility applies only to the eleven official languages. Promoting the other languages mentioned in the Constitution is the responsibility of the Pan South African Language Board. The new language policy does, however, provide a constitutional framework for building a more multilingual public consciousness and practice.

In this chapter, we shall argue that the accommodation of linguistic diversity depends on reconciling the tension between promoting English and promoting African languages. This tension plays itself out in various forms. For the purposes of this chapter, we are going to focus on some of the tensions in the educational sphere. Firstly, there is the tension between parental preferences and the child's real interests. Given the prominent role that English plays in all aspects of South African life it is understandable that parents would like their children to acquire English, but often the assumption is that the only way to acquire English is through using it as a language of learning. This is often not in the best interests of the child, who struggles to make sense of what she/ he is learning. Secondly, there is the tension between accommodating diversity and building unity. Promoting the use of home language instruction for African language speakers is seen in some quarters as divisive and segregationist – an accusation one can ill afford in post-Apartheid South Africa.

Thirdly, there is the cost factor. Promoting uniformity is presented as being more cost-effective. In fact, we argue in this chapter that it will be difficult to accommodate any diversity in an increasingly shrinking world driven by the imperatives of international capital and World Bank structural adjustment prescriptions (see Mazrui 1997). Pressure to reduce the cost of public education is likely to have a homogenising effect on language in education policies, in a context where, currently, there are minimal resources invested in African languages to make them viable as languages of learning and teaching. Budgetary constraints are likely to reinforce the hegemony of English in education if South Africa is to pursue its GEAR (Growth, Employment and Redistribution) strategy.

In addressing these tensions, we locate our argument in the context of language rights. In debates on rights, the distinction is often made between what Eide (1989, cited in Desai 1994) refers to as 'positive and negative rights'. Political and civil rights are seen as 'negative' rights, the implementation of which is usually cost-free for the state. On the other hand, social and economic rights are regarded as 'positive' and costly. We argue that if the new government wants to give substance to its eleven language policy, it will have to regard language rights as *social and economic rights* rather than political and civil rights.[2] Eide (1989, cited in Desai 1994:195) distinguishes between three levels of state responsibility for human rights: 'The obligation to respect, the obligation to protect, and the obligation to fulfil human rights.'. It is at the level of fulfilling human rights where language rights fit in. There is no getting away from the fact that promoting the use of African languages in domains other than the ones in which they are presently used will require a financial commitment on the part of the state.

In defending our position, we intend to focus on four issues. These are:

- language and national unity;
- the tension between promoting English and promoting African languages;
- language in education policy for schools;
- towards reconciling the tension between promoting English and African languages in language and education.

Language and national unity

The Nigerian linguist Bamgbose has said that 'In the African situation, a person who speaks several languages is to be regarded as a better integrated citizen than one who is only proficient in one language, even if that language happens to be the country's official language' (Bamgbose 1991:3).

The above quotation from Bamgbose raises the point that nations can be, and usually are, multilingual. If we accept Alexander's definition of national unity, that is, a consciousness of the fact of belonging to one South African nation (Alexander 1989:7), what role can language play in facilitating such a consciousness? As Das Gupta (1968 cited in Bamgbose 1991:18) has so rightly pointed out, national unity will be built through acknowledging, not denying, the existence of different languages in a country. There is no getting away from the fact that African languages are the primary linguistic resource of most South Africans. It takes years of concentrated effort to become confident and articulate in a new language, even when the teachers and courses are available. Using education to create a society that is fully multilingual in practice may well provide the best route to long-term empowerment, but it cannot empower very quickly. In the short and medium term, the rights of millions of South Africans will depend on the state's ability to support the use of African languages with the necessary language services, such as interpretation facilities and the use of translation.

National unity can be forged only in a context of national development for all. A society that fosters the development of an élite and exacerbates the divide between rich and poor is unlikely to attain national unity. Skutnabb-Kangas (1990) makes the telling point that the criterion used to divide people into groups that have unequal access to power and resources has shifted from biological 'race' and culture to *language*. Would it be possible for somebody who spoke no English to be elected to the National Assembly in South Africa or to the national executive of, say, the African National Congress (ANC) or the Congress of South African Trade Unions (COSATU)? The answer is not likely to be in the affirmative.

Tension between English and African languages

The question might be asked at this stage whether language issues in South Africa can be discussed without mentioning Afrikaans. We have deliberately decided not to focus on Afrikaans in this chapter for two important reasons. Firstly, very few Afrikaans-speaking people have been denied access to the wider world in South Africa because of their primary language being Afrikaans. There are many reasons for this, the most obvious being that during Apartheid, Afrikaans was actively developed as a language to be used in the public domain. Secondly, as a result of Afrikaans and English being cognate languages, Afrikaans-speakers display a fairly high level of proficiency in English, certainly at the receptive level, and thus have access to the wider global world.

The dilemma of maintaining a balance between globalisation and localisation in the linguistic sphere, however, is more pronounced in the tension between the promotion of English and African languages as reflected in the language policies adopted by many ex-colonial countries. Undoubtedly, a modern state requires for its proper functioning high-level personpower, technology and contacts with the outside world. As Bamgbose (1991:5) quite rightly says, '...whatever they do with their indigenous languages, they will need a major world language for access to higher education, science and technology'. The question Bamgbose proceeds to ask, however, is should these requirements dictate a policy that aims to make everyone function in the imported official language? As we have already stated above, it takes considerable effort and time to master an additional language. Are the voices of the majority of South Africans to remain silent whilst they are mastering this additional language, or do we acknowledge and accommodate their existing linguistic resources? As argued elsewhere (see Desai 1994), not all South Africans have the same requirements for linguistic empowerment. It would be foolish for us to waste time searching for a single approach that would be good for all citizens and all time.

The argument for an English-mainly policy is often based on the premise that we can compete internationally only through the medium of English. It is probably true that most people are conducting their business in a language which, in varying degrees, they have not in fact mastered, but what are the implications of this for productivity and efficiency? How essential is it to master English in order to assemble a motor car, for example? Are there any training manuals in languages other than English and Afrikaans? Might using African languages in training manuals not facilitate greater skills development among speakers of African languages? As stated elsewhere (Trew & Desai 1992:5), 'In a typical post-colonial paradox, the role currently played by English contributes both to national unity and to exclusion of the majority'.

It is now up to people who are committed both to promoting the diversity of our society and to ensuring greater popular participation in all aspects of political life to campaign actively for the wider use of languages other than English. For such a campaign to be effective, however, public resources would have to be invested in the promotion and development of African languages. The importance of this point cannot be sufficiently stressed. We are reminded, of course, of the active way in which Afrikaans was promoted by the National Party when it came into power in 1948.

We now want to look at the proposed language in education policy documents of the Department of Education to reiterate the point made above – that is, policies cannot be mere expressions of ideals; they have to be backed up by realistic implementation plans.

Proposed language in education policy

The documents we will be looking at are the following:

- *Draft Language in Education Policy* published in terms of Section 3(4)(m) of the *National Education Policy Act*, 1996 (Act 27 of 1996) (Department of Education 1997k), and
- *Norms and Standards Regarding Language Policy* published in terms of Section 6(1) of the *South African Schools Act*, 1996 (Department of Education 1996e).

249

Historically, language in education policy in South Africa has two components: language as medium of instruction and language as subject. Before discussing the policy as outlined in the above documents, it would be appropriate to provide a brief historical sketch of language in education policy in South Africa since 1948, the year the National Party came to power. With their election victory, the Nationalist government extended mother tongue instruction to cover the entire period at primary school. Both English and Afrikaans, the two official languages nationally, became compulsory subjects at high school level and one or the other had to be used as medium of instruction at that level. Mother tongue instruction became a key instrument for keeping South Africa's children apart and segregating schools. At the high school level, the policy was to entrench the position of Afrikaans. It was this issue which sparked the Soweto student uprising of 16 June 1976 (see Desai & Taylor 1997).

Although the requirement to learn through the medium of Afrikaans at high school level was subsequently dropped, and English was used as a medium of instruction from Grade 5 (Std 3), the language in education policy remained one which frustrated rather than facilitated learning. This policy continued to privilege those whose home language was either English or Afrikaans by enabling them to be taught through the medium of their first language throughout their years at school, and beyond. This was a right that, in practice, was denied to speakers of African languages. As a general rule, African children began their schooling in their home language but then shifted rather abruptly to English in their fifth year at school – a transition that was, in French's words (1990) 'deeply disabling for millions'.

Current policy

With regard to *language as medium*, the documents state that 'The right to choose the language of teaching is vested in the individual. This right has, however, to be exercised within the overall framework of the obligation on the education system to promote multilingualism' (Department of Education 1997 k:1). Learners will, of course, choose a language as medium from the eleven official languages. Any attempt to move away from the official bilingualism of the past (that is, Afrikaans and English) is dependent on the number of learners choosing such an option (a minimum of 45 learners in a particular grade) and the cost of such a move in both human and material terms.

As far as *languages as subjects* is concerned, the following recommendations apply (Department of Education 1997k:2–3):

a. All learners shall choose at least one approved[3] language as a subject in Grade 1 and 2.

b. All learners shall choose at least two approved languages, of which at least one shall be an official language, from Grade 3 onwards.

c. All language subjects shall receive equitable time and resource allocation.

d. The following promotion requirements apply to language subjects:

   (i) In Grade 1 to Grade 4 promotion is based on performance in one language and Mathematics.

   (ii) From Grade 5 onwards, one language must be passed.

   (iii) From Grade 10 to 12 two languages must be passed, one at first language level, and the other on at least second language level. At least one of these languages must be an official language.

   (iv) Subject to national norms and standards as determined by the Minister of Education, the level of achievement for promotion shall be determined by the provincial education departments.

Reconciling the tension: our response to the language policy documents

Firstly, we outline what we see as the main problem in current language in education policy and, secondly, we look at recommendations to address the problem.

The main problem

As we have already stated above, it is the first component (medium of instruction) that is the main problem in language and education. The majority of learners in schools are currently learning through a language that is not their home language nor their teachers'. We would like to give a concrete example of such a situation. At School X in Khayelitsha where Desai is conducting primary research, the Grade 4 learners all have Xhosa as their home language. So does their teacher. The medium of instruction, however, is English. A writing task given to pupils by Desai illustrates the problem facing learners very graphically. Pupils were given a series of six pictures in an envelope. They had to arrange the pictures in such a way that they told a story. Pupils were then asked to write two stories, one in Xhosa and one in English, based on the six pictures. The Xhosa stories were obviously linked to the pictures and were in narrative mode. The English stories were without exception incomprehensible and not linked to the pictures. On being asked in Xhosa how they experienced the task, all pupils said that they simply did not have the proficiency in English to express themselves clearly. This class is officially taught all subjects in English. The effect of such a policy can only lead to learning being frustrated.

Our conclusion is that the primary aim of a new language in education policy has to be the *facilitation of learning* for all pupils. At times, it is not clear whether this aim, or the *promotion of multilingualism*, is pre-eminent in the documents (see 'Statement of Aim' in Department of Education 1996e). Whilst we would readily acknowledge that one of the aims of a new language policy should be to promote multilingualism, it should not take precedence over the facilitation of learning. It is in the context of this duality that our comments on additive bilingualism need to be seen.

On additive bilingualism

Our working definition of additive bilingualism would be reasonably good competence in two (or more) languages. One can become additively bilingual in various ways. The documents still tend to privilege a particular way of achieving additive bilingualism – that is, using two or more languages as languages of learning. However, one can become equally additively bilingual by using only the home language as the language of learning and learning an additional language as a subject. We acknowledge that this option is mentioned in the documents, but it is not presented as a real alternative.

South Africa, as we all know, is a diverse country with gross inequalities entrenched in various domains of life. Education is no exception in this regard, so, for any language in education policy to work, it has to take into account that the context varies from area to area. A model that might work for one context could be hopelessly inadequate in another. The particular context in which it is implemented will determine its success or failure. In a context where a particular language is hardly used outside of the school and teachers themselves are not proficient in that language, the chances of it succeeding as a language of learning are slim, regardless of the fact that it might be the learners' choice – as is illustrated by work in School X. This is irrespective of whether it is used in conjunction with the home language or not. In such a context, what would be more effective is to extend the use of the home language as a language of learning beyond the initial years at school. The linguistic strengths of learners, the linguistic strengths of teachers and the linguistic environment in which the institution of learning is located are important factors that need to be taken into account. What works in a former white English-speaking suburb is not necessarily going to work in the African township like that of School X. It is important that we do not privilege a model that is more likely to work in a former white school. We would expect a Department of Education in the new South Africa to use the majority perspective as its starting point.

As far as choice is concerned, it is clear that the Department of Education is accommodating diversity, but unless that choice is backed up by a massive injection of human and material resources, such choice is meaningless – as is amply illustrated by the current position with regard to language as medium. English remains the 'popular' choice.

Having said that, we are mindful of the fact that the history of language in education policy in South Africa has led to a perception that only certain languages are capable of serving as languages of learning. Challenging such perceptions needs to be a part of affirmative action for African languages. In this regard, it would be useful to mount a programme of public education around issues in language and education. The focus of such a programme should be ways in which a language in education policy can facilitate rather than frustrate learning. It could start by exposing people to glimpses of what is possible. People's attitudes, which are often presented as the main obstacle, are not static, for it needs to be borne in mind that often there is a disjuncture between people's attitudes and their actual linguistic practices.

Some recommendations
- We would therefore recommend that learners' home languages need to be actively promoted as languages of learning – there is no guarantee that one might become more bilingual by being taught through two languages. Good language subject teaching can also achieve full bilingualism.
- In order to achieve this, resources (both material and human) need to be developed in African languages so that learners can make real choices.
- The teaching and learning of African languages as subjects needs to be given serious attention to realise their use as languages of learning.
- The learning of an African language needs to be made compulsory for all learners. Besides promoting multilingualism, this can result in the teaching and learning of African languages being taken more seriously. The better-resourced former white schools are likely to agitate for and provide more resources for African languages if they have to be learnt by all learners. Such a move is also likely to lead to a changed complexion in the teaching corps as more African language speakers are employed as teachers.

Finally, we would like to say that linguistic discrimination in education is felt most acutely at the level of languages of learning rather than languages as subjects. This is where the thrust of the proposed policy needs to be. There is no suggestion in any recent policy documents about how to prevent the status quo from continuing, albeit now because of choices exercised by learners and their parents.

Conclusion

It will be some time before a truly post-Apartheid language policy evolves. A twin-pronged thrust is needed in evolving such a policy – it is not a question of either guaranteeing access to skills in English or guaranteeing rights to use African languages. We must do both. However, such a policy is likely to emerge only if all the forces involved play an active role in striving for it. The next few years are going to be crucial if South Africa's language policy is not to go the Organisation of African Unity (OAU) route – that is, remain an un-achieved ideal more than a decade later.

Endnotes

1. We are indebted to Dr Hugh Trappes-Lomax of the Institute for Applied Language Studies, University of Edinburgh, for his valuable comments on an earlier draft of this chapter.

2. In November 1997 the South African state's commitment to social and economic rights was put to the test when a terminally ill patient, Mr T. Soobramoney, who could not afford the kidney dialysis treatment he needed to keep him alive, was refused such treatment at a state hospital because of lack of funds. He took the matter to the Constitutional Court, which ruled that he did not have the constitutional right to free dialysis treatment. He died on the 30 November 1997. There has been a public outcry against the Court's decision in the local press and many commentators have hinted that it could 'set an analytical framework for determining the extent of all of the socio-economic rights in the Constitution, including housing, sufficient food and water, social security and education' (*Cape Times*, 4 December 1997). It is our opinion that if pushed to provide resources in African languages, the government might again use the lack of funds as a reason for not extending the use of African languages as languages of learning.

3. In the glossary to the September 1996 Draft Language Policy, the Department of Education distinguishes between approved languages and official languages in the following way: 'As a general rule (exceptions include certain foreign languages which are examined by the University of Cambridge Examinations Syndicate as A Level subjects) only those languages for which syllabuses have been approved as part of national policy are called *approved languages* and may be offered in schools and recognised for the Senior Certificate. *Official languages* constitute a subset of the approved languages' (Department of Education, 1996f:10–11).

19

Linguistic practices in the classroom: code-switching as a communicative resource[1]

SUZETTE MEERKOTTER

The new Constitution of the Republic of South Africa (1996) advocates a policy of multilingualism, which not only strives to develop the home language of learners, but also gives them the opportunity to appreciate other languages and cultures in the multicultural setting in the country. This policy is an attempt to confront past injustices in the educational system. The multilingual setting is not regarded as a hindrance to learning, but, indeed, as a resource for learning.

The proposed Language in Education Policy subscribes to the 'additive bilingualism model', which in effect means the gaining of competence in a second language while the first language is maintained. The primary language of the child is sustained and both languages (and their cultures) are valued and reinforced, which positively affects the child's development. Desai & Van der Merwe take the concept of additive bilingualism further by regarding it as a means to achieve '... reasonably good competence in two (or more) languages' (see Chapter 18 of this volume). Peires (1994:16) says in this regard that '... It is necessary for an individual to make use of all his/her linguistic skills in order to achieve full understanding and full confidence'.

With the above statement of Peires in mind, this chapter is a reflection by a teacher, and particularly a language teacher, on certain principles which emanated from her own education as a student teacher in languages and the actual teaching situations experienced thereafter in South African schools. When presented with the teaching of English and Afrikaans as second languages (regarded as such by the previous Department of Education) in a black school, which are in reality often the third languages of the learners, the author was often surprised by the unrealistic expectations which departmental officials (such as subject inspectors) had of teachers, given the particular teaching and learning situations with which they are confronted.

Student teachers were made aware of the fact that a language teacher was to strive for the 'pure use' of the language to be taught in the class, and learners were to be encouraged to arrive at a communicative use of the target language (that is, the second language which one is aiming to learn) themselves. However, in the actual classroom setting the new teacher was faced with the situation that learners often stared blankly at the teacher's attempts to use the target language as a means to teach the intricacies of a language, which they hardly experienced outside the terrain of the school. A subject inspector visiting the school in question in 1989 made the remark that although he was satisfied with this author's teaching of Afrikaans (as second language), he felt that the use made of English to facilitate the understanding of Afrikaans was to be avoided, and only Afrikaans should be used.

The use of more than one language in the classroom and beyond is referred to as 'code-switching'. This means '... the alternate use of two or more languages in a single piece of discourse: thus a sentence may begin in one language and end in another, several sentences or phrases may be in one language which may then be followed by sentences or phrases in another' (Peires 1994:14).

Peires (1994:15) underscores the point that code-switching has often been met with resistance and was disapproved of or even proscribed by school or education department rules. This is in spite of the fact that code-switching is a phenomenon that is extremely widespread, normal and useful in the discourse of bilingualism. Code-switching, it can be shown, actually enhances learning. By preventing it, learning is inhibited.

By observing the classroom practices of colleagues teaching English and Afrikaans to black learners coming from disadvantaged backgrounds, the aim of the study reported here was to look at the measures which were taken by them to facilitate the teaching and learning process when working under conditions which were often not conducive to any teaching and learning at all.

This chapter then deals with an actual case-study that was carried out in a secondary school setting in a black township. It documents the attempts of a teacher and learners to challenge the above-mentioned constraints and limitations, thereby enhancing pedagogic influences to create a conducive learning atmosphere in the classroom.

From observations made, the conviction emerged that student teachers need to be made aware of the realities in which they would operate. Aspirant teachers need to acknowledge and accommodate the linguistic resources which the learners already have, and use those as resources in the teaching of the new language. Code-switching can be a valuable resource not only in the language classroom, but also in subjects across the curriculum.

Code-switching in a secondary school in Guguletu: A case-study

The case-study was performed in 1994 during the first two terms of the school year at a secondary school in the black township of Guguletu in Cape Town. Afrikaans, English and Xhosa are the three official languages of the province of the Western Cape. The home language of the residents in Guguletu is predominantly Xhosa. English is used as the language of learning and instruction. Xhosa is used, officially that is, only in the instruction of Xhosa as subject in the secondary school. In practice Xhosa is used across the curriculum, especially where both teachers and learners are Xhosa-speaking.

The instruction of Afrikaans as a subject takes place from the fifth year of schooling. At this particular school, it was compulsory up to Grade 9 (the ninth year of schooling) for all learners except those doing technical subjects (due to their full curriculum). At the end of the ninth year, the learners are given the option to continue with the subject. Before the amalgamation of all the education departments in 1996, Afrikaans was a compulsory subject until the end of schooling in the matriculation year (Grade 12). Some schools, however, offered different subject combinations with no Afrikaans, but at this particular school, Afrikaans was generally offered as one of the subjects at matriculation level.

For this case-study, the chosen focus was an analysis of code-switching in a language class, in particular an Afrikaans class at a secondary school in Guguletu. The population in Guguletu has increased considerably in recent years, especially with people moving in from the rural areas in search of better living conditions in and around the metropolitan area. However, the rate of unemployment remains exceptionally high and many residents in the townships battle for survival in the most desperate conditions.

The school itself is regarded as a comprehensive school, in other words a school where academic, commercial and technical subjects are taught. It is a recently established school, and thus better equipped generally than older schools in the vicinity.

Guguletu is geographically situated adjacent to areas where Afrikaans is used as home language by the residents, such as 'coloured' areas like Manenberg, Heideveld and Rylands. It is thus possible for learners in Guguletu to come into contact with mother-tongue speakers of Afrikaans in their daily lives – it would therefore be useful for pupils to acquire the language and, in the current scenario where multilingualism is emphasised, its acquisition can thus be considered of particular value.

The classes observed for the study were Afrikaans classes at Grade 9 level. Classes at the junior secondary level are generally quite large. The Afrikaans teacher under observation was responsible for eight Grade 9 classes. Her teaching load was enormous, as she had to teach 48 periods out of a possible 49 teaching periods per week. Her learners varied in the different classes, but class sizes of 40 to 50 learners were no exception. It should be noted that the language teachers in general at this particular school carried heavy teaching loads. It is thus clear that the teachers and learners were obliged to employ many alternative measures to facilitate the teaching and learning situation, which at the stage of political uncertainty and school turmoil in the country were tasks not that easily performed.

Because teachers were overburdened with so many teaching periods, less time could be used for 'other' activities to promote the use of Afrikaans, like visits to other schools to meet speakers of Afrikaans, library integration periods, etc. Since Afrikaans is offered on a 'second language'[2] basis to Xhosa-speaking learners, it was possible for code-switching to be used as a resource to mediate the teaching and learning situation. English, as the 'official' language of learning and instruction in these schools, would probably emerge in the Afrikaans classes as well, and as the language of the majority of learners was Xhosa, code-switching between three languages was probable.

The nature of code-switching will be considered before an analysis of code-switching in the Afrikaans classes is undertaken.

Code-switching is regarded as a communicative resource for managing interactions in the teaching and learning situation (Zentella 1981:119). According to Enright (1984 cited by Martin-Jones 1993:19) classroom events are seen as units of interaction, in the sense that they represent the teacher's own conceptualisation thereof. The teacher her/himself is responsible for the division of interaction in the classroom and also for the manner in which such interaction is conducted. Code-switching is a strong reflection of the endeavours of the teacher and the learners to mediate the communicative demands of the curriculum in practice (Martin-Jones 1993:9).

According to Martin-Jones (*ibid.* p. 2), the communicative functions of code-switching in teacher discourse and the use of certain languages to perform different functions were particularly emphasised in earlier research projects, whereas recent studies have rather considered the flow of discourse in the classroom and the manner in which code-switching contributed to the interaction between the teacher and learners when two languages are used.

Guthrie (1984) and Milk (1981; 1982) (cited by Martin-Jones 1993:6) were among the first researchers who paid particular attention to the functions of classroom discourse. In their analyses of code-switching in the teaching and learning situation, they considered the type of communicative actions that were identifiable; the language in which certain actions were performed; the frequency and consistency thereof; and the values which were carried over by the teacher's pattern of bilingual communication to the learners.

The use of code-switching further influences the succession of the teaching and learning events, since the flow thereof is continuously negotiated. Teachers and learners exploit the contrasts between the codes by defining different types of discourse, repeatedly negotiating joint frames of reference and exchanging meaning on the spur of the moment (Martin-Jones 1993:13). Gumperz (1982) has referred to this meaningful way of communication as 'contextualization cues' while Tannen (1985) has called them 'meta-messages' (both cited in Moyo 1996:21). Contextualisation cues do not convey meaning in themselves, except when they are used in conjunction with verbal cues in particular moments of interaction.

Code-switching is thus regarded as a resource similar to the use of punctuation marks in a written discourse: it constitutes a resource conveying pragmatic information to interlocutors with regard to the manner in which a specific utterance should be 'read' in the context (Martin-Jones 1993:14).

The manner in which code-switching can be utilised as a resource to control interaction during the teaching and learning situation will now be considered. It became obvious in the case-study undertaken that the learners had a minimal command of the language (Afrikaans) taught as a 'second language' in this particular setting. This placed considerable limitations on communication. The case-study focused on the bilingual or multilingual interaction that could be identified by the use of Afrikaans, Xhosa and English in the classroom. The observer was at the outset under the impression that English would be used to mediate or facilitate the teaching and learning situation in the Afrikaans class. Surprisingly, however, both English and Xhosa were used to facilitate language use in the Afrikaans class – in other words, three languages were actually used by the teacher and the learners as resources in the Afrikaans class.

The four classes observed were one class of boys and three classes of boys and girls. The duration of the periods was 45 minutes. The language use in these classes was personally observed and further illuminated by conversations with the particular teacher. Transcriptions were made of each and every utterance of the teacher and learners. The examples given of code-switching have been selected to exemplify the phenomena, but are just a sample of the material that is available from the teaching and learning events which were recorded during a specific lesson.

As noted before, English is 'officially', though not necessarily in reality, the language of learning and instruction (with Xhosa generally used 'more than frequently'). The mother tongue of the learners is predominantly Xhosa. Afrikaans is offered at 'second language' level, and it is expected that Afrikaans should also be used in the classroom to facilitate the mastery of Afrikaans. However, from the data collected, it became evident that code-switching had to be employed – particularly to illuminate concepts in Afrikaans. Without the resource of code-switching, the learners would definitely have been disempowered in the teaching and learning situation.

Martin-Jones justly says in this regard that '…what is taught and its linguistic expression is a mediation between the constraints inherent in the learning situation and the perception and volition of the teachers' (1993:8). She further states the necessity for looking at the way in which the individuals, namely the teacher and the learners, are coping in the circumstances where limitations are present. One of the ways in which these strategies could be looked at is to consider the use of different codes in their communicative settings. Gumperz (1976 cited by Moyo 1996:21) stated that the nature of code-switching is in most circumstances a meaningful way of communication which must, however, '…be subject to some linguistic constraints'. Code-switching then becomes a powerful reflection of the ways in which the teacher and the learners mediate the communicative demands that are encountered in the implementation of the curriculum.

The particular teacher observed teaching Afrikaans wanted to impress upon the learners the use of verbs. She made use of a number of sentences that dealt with a visit to a station. It was obvious that the learners did not understand all the verbs in Afrikaans. To facilitate the process of understanding the teacher demonstrated the verbs in actions – in other words she wanted to show the learners the meaning of particular words. The learners had to respond to her actions and say what action she was performing. In subsequent lessons the teacher used the equivalent of the Afrikaans verbs in Xhosa sentences, which meant that the learners had to think in Afrikaans to arrive at the correct word.

It did not appear as though the learners first constructed the word in English from the Xhosa sentence that the teacher had given and then supplied the Afrikaans word, but that the learners indeed wanted to construe the correct Afrikaans word from the Xhosa sentences. In this instance, it clearly seems evident that the code-switching with regard to this particular part of the lesson fluctuated between Afrikaans and Xhosa. The communicative function of the above-mentioned events pointed to the fact that vocabulary items were illuminated by switching between the Xhosa and Afrikaans codes. An example of this is would be the exchange in which the teacher asks:

Drink? (Afrikaans for 'drink'). *Sela?* (Xhosa for 'drink'). *Ndiphunga ikofu.* (Xhosa for 'I drink coffee'). *Ndisela iCoke.* (Xhosa for 'I drink Coke'), and the learner responds:
Ek drink koffie. (Afrikaans for 'I drink coffee'). *Ek drink 'n beker koffie.* (Afrikaans for 'I drink a mug of coffee').

When it became important to determine the learners' understanding of the verbs, the question was put in English or again explained in English and Afrikaans. Any comments on the behaviour of learners were made in English, but also in Afrikaans. 'Doing an aside' was also done in English. When the reaction of a learner was evaluated, English was predominantly used.

The teacher made a point of constructing sentences in Xhosa for the benefit of the students to assist them in the understanding of the verbs. At the outset of the study, it was expected that only some code-switching between English and Afrikaans would be observed. It was surprising and encouraging to find more complex interaction in which the teacher (mother tongue Afrikaans) also used Xhosa to support the teaching and learning events in the Afrikaans classes.

The teacher in question reported that she had also embarked on a course to acquire the mother tongue of the learners, namely Xhosa. She further indicated that by her making references in their language, the learners were definitely better motivated and she could even observe significant improvements in their results. An example of references to the learners' mother tongue can be seen in the following exemplary exchange:

TEACHER: I am crying. *Ek huil.* (Afrikaans). *Lila.* (Xhosa). *Ek huil.* (Afrikaans). *Loop.* (Afrikaans). *Walk.* (English). *Hamba.* (Xhosa).
Hardloop. (Afrikaans). *Run.* (English). *Baleka.* (Xhosa).
Die kondukteur waai die vlag. (Afrikaans for 'The conductor waves the flag').
Wenza ntoni? (Xhosa for 'What does he do?') *Waai.* (Afrikaans for 'waves').

It is clearly evident from observation and experience of this and relevantly similar learning situations that the learners often have difficulties in understanding concepts in the 'second language'. If the teacher then explains the concept in the mother tongue of the learners, it serves to motivate them positively. In other words, the learners want to acquire the new language and are appreciative of the teacher's willingness to acquire their mother tongue. The understanding of the language (in this case, Afrikaans) which is taught is therefore enhanced.

Some classroom activities regarding the use of the language were dealt with as follows. Revision was done by using Afrikaans, because the learners already had knowledge of 'verbs'. However, it became necessary at times to explain the concepts in English. With the presentation of new material, more code-switching could be observed. For the new Afrikaans verbs, the Xhosa equivalents were also given and only in exceptional cases were the equivalents in English supplied. The reinforcement of the acquisition of the subject material was done in Afrikaans and also explained in Xhosa and English if problems were experienced. This practice could perhaps be ascribed to the teacher's assumption that the learners would not be able to comprehend the utterance adequately in Afrikaans.

The teacher made considerable use of code contrast and employed it as a communicative resource. An item could, for example, be introduced in Afrikaans, be subsequently explained in Xhosa, and perhaps even English, and in closing again in Afrikaans. Learners often asked questions in English if they wanted to say something that did not relate to the subject material. However, the learners were aware of the language that the teacher would expect in the classroom and therefore often tried to put the question in Afrikaans. Remarks on the discipline in the class, in other words the smooth running of events, were mostly given in English. The teacher also utilised Afrikaans, Xhosa and English in the same discourse. Attempts were made to illustrate the facts, to simplify them, to elaborate and to relate them to the experiences of the learners to promote the involvement of the learners with the lesson proceedings.

One of the most prominent characteristics in the classes observed was the fact that the learning events were positively influenced by the personal teaching style of the particular teacher. She praised the learners in Afrikaans as well as Xhosa when they answered correctly. She had, in the words of Martin-Jones (1993:24), '...a personalized style, a style characterized by *carino* – a close and caring relationship'. This strongly emerged in the subsequent class when the learners had to construct sentences and one of the learners spontaneously remarked that she loved the teacher, to which the teacher charmingly replied that she loved her too.

From the above-mentioned teaching and learning events in a particular class, where a 'second language' was taught, it is clear that the phenomenon of code-switching had considerable impact on the learners. The positive learning atmosphere created by the teacher in the class was further enhanced by the freedom allowed to the learners to switch between different codes, in this case Afrikaans, Xhosa and English. Difficult concepts were better understood, and learners felt at ease to put questions to the teacher. If the lesson had been conducted only in Afrikaans, it seems apparent that learners might well have been inhibited from taking part in the discourse of the classroom.

The positive influence of code-switching that emerged from the case-study at this particular school is underscored by Adendorff's view (1993 cited by

Gough 1996:15–16) of code-switching, namely that '...switches are viewed as guiding the participants' interpretation of academic goals and intentions as well as guiding their interpretation of social relationships in the class'. Adendorff, according to Gough (1996:16), advocates that teachers be given instruction in the value of code-switching in their training.

It is thus important that student teachers and teachers be sensitively alert to the advantages of code-switching, when it becomes evident in an educational setting that learners need assistance in the learning process of a second or third language. However, if teachers themselves are not fully conversant in the language they are teaching to the learners, and then switch codes when their own knowledge is lacking, it may be a cause for concern, '...if the other language is used to fill in the teachers' gaps' (Gough 1996:16). Then code-switching is not used as a facilitative resource, and not '...directed towards [the] hearer's needs' (*ibid.* p. 16).

Thus, there are clearly sound linguistic justifications for employing code-switching to promote language learning. What is also clear from this study, however, is that linguistic cognitive progress cannot be divorced from affective considerations. By the switching of codes employing the learners' mother tongue, the teacher demonstrates respect for the learners' identity and loyalties and shows herself also to be a willing learner. In so doing, motivation and understanding are enhanced, and the classroom learning experience becomes a collaborative enterprise in which more than linguistic facility is encouraged and learned.

Endnotes

1. This chapter is dedicated to Chrissie du Preez, a teacher whose commitment to those learners in her charge was an inspiration to all. The positive and supportive learning atmosphere created by her in the classroom should be the essence of all teaching in a multilingual setting – a respect for one another, and an intense desire to communicate and share with others.

2. A 'second language' denotes a language that is acquired or learned after gaining some competence in a first language. Usually it is not used in the learner's home, but it is used in the wider society in which the learner lives. According to the NEPI document, *Language* (1992:xi), there are, however, vast discrepancies in the extent to which different learners are exposed to a 'second language'. In some cases, what is termed a 'second' language may in effect be a 'foreign language', because the learner has no exposure to the language outside the classroom.

20

Cultural diversity, common citizenship and public education

RUTH JONATHAN

In this chapter, I shall not attempt to cover the broad range of issues that arise for policy and practice, as well as for any justifying theory, when public education is to serve a society characterised by 'pluralism' or 'diversity'. That would require a very large volume in itself. Nor shall I explore variants of 'multiculturalism' to compare or contrast their recommendations with either separatism on the one hand or monocultural hegemony on the other, although today these are burning issues in educational policy debate in South Africa. I shall focus rather on how the reconciliation of cultural diversity with common citizenship bears on a related important area of political and educational dispute. For what is often referred to as a tension in educational policy between the claims of equity and the demands of development is exacerbated in practical politics by the problems of pluralism. I shall try to show that with analysis deployed on a broader canvas than that which is typically considered, headway can be made in the understanding of both tensions: between diversity and citizenship, and also between equity and development.

The latter tension is and always has been present, acknowledged or not, in the public education policies of liberal democracies. For historical reasons, it presents itself in South Africa today in perhaps its most acute form, precisely because that new democratic polity exhibits, as a society, radical diversity on all possible dimensions. By analysing related pluralism issues theoretically, we can advance understanding of the general problem as it applies to all liberal democracies, South Africa among them, and by situating that analysis in the circumstances where it presents itself most starkly, a clearer understanding may help to ground a defensible basis for policy positions not only in that particular context but by extension elsewhere, with relevant variation. Thus the difficulties which South Africa must unavoidably confront today can illuminate a perennial and pervasive 'can of worms' which has long bedevilled public education in liberal democracies.

Briefly stated, the intractable problems referred to, and elaborated on later, arise from the dual functions of any system of education which is simultaneously charged with meeting the aspirations of citizens as persons – goals which vary with their different backgrounds and self-understandings – and the aspirations of citizens as citizens – goals for a common future in which all expect equally to share. To home in on these concerns, we must bring to the fore a key locus of dispute in contemporary political philosophy, since this lies behind many debates about the appropriate political and educational response to 'the problem of pluralism', in whatever guise – class, gender, race or ethnicity – these present themselves.

Diversity and citizenship: the issue

The framework of debate can be sketched straightforwardly. In a democracy which is liberal and constitutional, all are entitled to common citizenship. That citizenship is more than a matter of universal suffrage: it encompasses equal rights of access to whatever goods are commonly provided for all, together with an equal voice in how such goods are constituted and distributed. Without the former, democracy would be purely formal; without the latter, it would have no point. Common citizenship thus requires that before the law, or in relation to social opportunity or the fulfilment of personal goals and commitments, no individual is to be either privileged or discriminated against on 'morally arbitrary' grounds, such as membership of particular class, gender, racial, ethnic, religious or other groupings. Simply, each citizen is an individual person deserving of equal respect. The rights and responsibilities of each are on equal footing with those of any other citizen.

Of course, a glance at the world would remind us, if a reminder were needed, that that simple ideal is 'more honoured in the breach than the observance'. However, in principle the ideal itself is straightforward. To be sure, even in the most just, ordered democracy, conflicts of interest between citizens will arise where social opportunities are scarce and must be competed for or where the chosen priorities of some conflict with those of others. In such cases the measure of liberal justice is not that there be no losers, but that none have the cards stacked against them so that their desires and efforts are at a discount. Nonetheless, in the citizen's relation to the judicial system, to the economic system, to 'public goods', from policing to highway standards, and to social provision, from health care to welfare benefits, the only obstacles to even-handedness between individuals, irrespective of their relations or allegiances to others, are obstacles of political will and practical arrangements.

Unfortunately, there is one arena of social life where the straightforwardness of this ideal cannot be maintained, even in principle. Even more unfortunately, that offending arena is the one most crucial to the good health of both the polity and the society in question. The problematic arena is public education.

Diversity, citizenship and public education: the problem

In relation to public education – by contrast with, say, the judicial system, the economic system or the welfare system – the obstacles to the democratic ideal of even-handedness between citizens in a culturally plural society begin at the level of principle and pervade every issue of policy and practice. Why this social practice should be so problematic can be briefly outlined. The nub of the matter is that education is not just one social practice (still less one public service) among others: it is the practice through which a society operationalises its aspirations for the development of persons and the evolution of the social future. Clearly, in a society that is not homogeneous, there will be a plurality of such aspirations – a diversity of understandings about what constitutes a worthwhile life for the individual and a proper ordering of society. (It scarcely need be said that whilst societies differ markedly in the extent of their internal heterogeneity, homogeneity could only obtain in a society where individuality was suppressed as absolutely as equality was enforced. Heterogeneity, to some degree, is a social given.) Given that the hallmark of a liberal democracy is that none of such diverse 'conceptions of the good' be privileged over others in its social arrangements, then education would seem at first glance to be a social practice which should take as many different forms as there are differing conceptions of the good – of what is worthwhile and important in the past and for the future – in the society in question.

However, it is public education that is at issue: the practice which serves the continuation and renewal of social as well as personal life, and the very existence of a democratically ordered polity presupposes a degree of commonality in the values and aspirations of its members. An enabling commonality is thus at a high premium in that social practice – education – which plays a key role in ensuring the maintenance and good health of polity and society. However, at the same time and on the basis of the very same political principles, this practice more than any other must be scrupulous in its respect for diversity, for otherwise the values and aspirations of some, for themselves and for the social future, are placed at a discount. That a whole series of difficulties and disputes must arise from this conundrum is readily apparent.

Some of these have been much discussed in the literature. Political theorists focus on the nature and scope of liberal toleration, trying to resolve the puzzle that ideally we should 'let a hundred (educational) flowers bloom' except where a particular flower is, in liberal terms, an (educational) weed, compromising the development of rational or moral autonomy in the pre-autonomous young. A weed in those terms would be any programme which aimed to inculcate a particular world-view or conceptual scheme unreflectively and to the exclusion of competitors. The deadlock here is apparent. Liberals are committed to tolerance of whatever presents itself as open to contestation and revision; non-liberals respond that this boils down to liberalism only tolerating a range of versions of itself. It is then charged with being just one ideology among others, with no more right than competitors to draw up the rules of the competition. Real-life cases of this theoretical puzzle range from disputes about public support for programmes of religious or political teaching whose intent is the adherence of learners to their tenets, or for institutions whose orthodoxy denies equality between the sexes, to the complaints of particular groups within society who seek to ensure the survival of their own cultural traditions which they see as both superior to and threatened by the cultural and value agnosticism of liberalism.

The deadlock seems hopeless. It would appear that there are only three ways forward, none of them compatible with an inclusive, democratic polity. If liberals triumph by failing or refusing to respect those who do not share their prioritising of individual autonomy and the parameters for personal and social development it implies, they stand accused of imposing liberal values, to the detriment of dissenters among their fellow-citizens and – more fatally still – in contravention of their own most cherished ideals. Where an alternative world-view (one with a determinate set of commitments it aims to preserve or proselytise) seeks or gains the ascendant, then unless all members of the polity share this world-view from the outset, we have the previous set of problems at best recreated or at worst compounded. The replacement of the first hegemony by the second is thus only a solution where there is no problem. Hence the face-value appeal of what seems the only other option: let a hundred flowers bloom. That third possibility brings us right round in a circle to where we began: the failure to provide, just where it is most needed, that seed-bed for shared social meanings which is constitutive of any society and a prerequisite for any democratic polity.

Dealing with the deadlock

So far, all this is very abstract. I have not attempted to do justice to the subtlety of argument which can be deployed on these questions, nor to the complexity of the issues at stake. Even if the space were available to do so, however, I am unconvinced that we can do more at this level of abstraction than get the problem clear. Educational thinkers, for whom of necessity the problem presents itself with urgency, are impelled to search for pragmatic means, not of resolving the conundrum but of finding the least socially unfair and most educationally sound way of coping with it. Contributions on linguistic diversity to this book survey one important aspect of this task. The renegotiation of curricula, whether to redress gender and social role stereotyping in many affluent societies, to revisit the pre-eminence of 'dead white males' in the literary 'canon' of the United States, to show (token?) respect to immigrant cultures in European countries, or to reclaim local language, history, culture and values in previously colonised societies is another aspect of the task. In addition, to take on aspects of the task, in its many guises, is part of today's recognition that what masqueraded yesterday as homogeneity was actually hegemony.

Too often, however, in the theorising and polemic associated with that pragmatic enterprise, dialogues of the deaf are as apparent in educational debate as they are in political argument. They are compounded by the temptation to suppose that pragmatic coping strategies which seem plausible in one set of conditions could be transposed to a quite different set of conditions. 'On the ground', of course, it matters what exactly is at stake and how the diversity in question came about. Clarity about the general problem is essential, but so is sensitivity to the situation in which any particular instance of it manifests itself, as Morrow makes very clear on both counts in Chapter 17 of this volume.

A third element should be added to understanding of the general issue and sensitivity to particular situations. That is an awareness of structural features of modern societies and systems of public education. I shall focus here on only one such feature, of central importance both for the conduct of public education and also for the understanding of citizenship and pluralism in contemporary democratic societies. This is the dual duty of public education to foster both personhood and citizenship, a dual function which in the actual conditions of today's world magnifies the equity/development tension. As with the statement of the general problem in the previous two sections of this chapter, I can only offer here the outlines of an argument. (I hope to show that contextualising the analysis gives leverage both on the general conundrum and on those real-life instances of it which present themselves most urgently in education.)

Diversity and citizenship contextualised

There is something odd to be noted about much educational debate on identity, pluralism and citizenship. The debate itself is fuelled by the (previously neglected) insight that education is inseparable from its cultural freight: that there is no essentialist 'good' or 'best' education. It has become a truism that the practice of education cannot but be socially constructed and historically located, as are conceptions of identity and citizenship. Despite this guiding insight, constantly deployed within such debates, the problem itself remains often uncontextualised. We might get some leverage on the deadlock at key points if we set in their historical context the ideas underpinning it and the circumstances surrounding it.

For example, the 'monocultural education' repudiated today stands guilty as charged of tending towards hegemonic consequences, and in many societies was indeed embedded in a larger hegemonic political project. Contextualising the issue shows, however, that it would do violence to history to infer hegemonic intent for the education in question. In the days when, in essentialist fashion, it was believed that one could specify an approximation to 'the best that has been thought and said', then wherever such was offered, it could not but be a colonising process, whether across the boundaries of class, gender or ethnicity. Given that process, where access to it was denied (by exclusion or the provision of programmes thought more apt to the ethnicity, class or gender of those deemed unsuited to 'the best'), then denial became a process of disempowerment. The point to be stressed here is that, given an essentialist conception of education, there could be no benign solution. (That is no apologia either for past practice or its political consequences.)

Rejection of essentialism – not to be confused with acceptance of any relativist position – removes one obstacle to a benign solution. It follows, then, that no alternative solution which re-introduces essentialism (such as educational separatism, whatever its motives) can lay claim to being a benign solution. It is clear, furthermore, that essentialism could only have risen to prominence in a society with unequal power relations. That it is in retreat is not unconnected to a shifting of power relations in those societies where it has come under attack. To restructure educational practice on an alternative essentialist basis would therefore be simply to replace one set of inequalities in power relations with another, and to forego the potential of educational practice to mitigate such inequalities.

This point serves as just one example of how we can clarify our thinking by setting in their context the powerful ideas which have constructed the problems we face. We can further clarify it by considering how our current historical circumstance frames the problem now and constrains what could be candidates for defensible response. Thus, for example, recent times have brought geo-political changes which have significantly speeded up 'globalisation' in its cultural and political as well as its economic aspects. This speeding up exacerbates both the problems of pluralism and the long-standing educational tension between equity and development. Worse still, it leads each problem to compound the other. Why this should be so is worth sketching.

Two motors of change are evident. In many liberal democracies over the past two decades, the forces of the market have been unfettered from earlier controls, with the retreat of the state creating a more individualised conception of citizenship in which personal identity is at an increased premium. In formerly authoritarian regimes, emerging democracy (whether by the break-up of previous hegemony, as in the former communist world, or by the enfranchisement of previously excluded populations, as in South Africa) is characterised by contestation over the relation between citizenship and differing identities – contests which shape the nature of democracy and the distribution of life-chances in those societies.

Both types of change turn up the heat under the long-simmering stew of 'cultural diversity' issues. The first makes the citizen-as-consumer sovereign by extending the market across social life. It vaunts individual choice, ignores structural features which make such sovereignty worth more to some than others and thereby fragments citizen-solidarity and common understanding. The ensuing social polarisation moves questions of identity and equal citizenship firmly up the agenda. The second set of conditions, where the polity is being structurally reconstituted, brings identity and citizenship into more direct collision. This is not a straightforward matter, as in earlier days, of competing identities vying for supremacy or seeking mutual accommodation within the boundaries of a state, for the two change-conditions I am highlighting interact with each other.

This can be seen most starkly in the second type of 'new democratisation', where the franchise is radically extended at the same time as an earlier hegemony is dissolved. In this historical case competing identities are not today on equal footing with each other in a majoritarian competition or consensus-building process to develop the complexion of the state. With free market principles unfettered in 'established' democracies at the same time as change elsewhere has globalised them, the viability of states themselves, and hence the value of citizenship within them, does not depend, as the abstract problem suggests, on internal agreement between citizens about goals and values.

Now the wider, global context places a premium on certain personal characteristics and values which are unevenly prized (that is, identified with, exhibited by and encouraged) in differing ethnic, religious, class or gender groupings. This is clearly especially problematic where the state in question is both undergoing reconstitution and is characterised by radical diversity in the composition of its citizenry. (What makes South Africa the starkest current instance of both the theoretical and the practical problem, for politics and for education, is that it is subject to all of the operative variables, in strong form.)

That this combination of historical circumstances reframes the problem of reconciling cultural diversity with common citizenship is not difficult to see. These are not observations about realpolitik, but about relations between agency and structure. Simply put, 'globalisation' superimposes inter-state constraints on pre-existing intra-polity conundra. The agency of states is constrained in a globalised world of unequal power relations, just as the agency of citizens within a polity is constrained by structural conditions. In the social world, whether in so-called 'stable' or 'transitional' democracies, both citizenship and identity are continually reflected, reproduced and modified by personal agency and social structure, and both agency and structure are mediated through the policies and practices of education, since it is through the preparation of the rising generation that the future is constructed. It should not surprise us, therefore, that all of these complex issues come to a head in public education.

The education of persons and of citizens: the theoretical problem in context

In public education a further set of complexities enters the picture, for the expectations which individuals and the state (or in a democracy, persons as persons and persons as citizens) have of public education are often at odds with each other. These conflicting expectations complicate still more the relations between citizenship, identity and public education, for 'public education' is a multi-layered affair. On one level, it is the education of the public, in which all members of the public, as citizens, have a stake since they all collectively have a legitimate interest in the maintenance of those shared cultural understandings, values and allegiances which provide internal stability and those skills and attitudes which will ensure prosperity through global competitiveness. Moreover, in a complex social and economic structure in which social roles are functionally interrelated but differentially rewarded, the maintenance of a range of skills and a diversity of attitudes and personal characteristics is required from any system for the education of the public, as is common allegiance to the existence of that range and the purposes it serves. Citizens look for policies which promote these ends.

Democratically constituted public education, however, is also an education for the public, and the public is made up of individuals and communities who have aspirations and expectations, not for the good of the polity, but for themselves, and which they look to public education to help them realise. Similarly, they have commitments which they expect that education to respect but which may not be shared by fellow citizens with equally legitimate demands.

At this point we must remember that for each individual, (or each combination of individuals bound by commitment to mutual obligation) education has two kinds of value: intrinsic and exchange. In contemporary societies, educational experience and credentials are exchangeable for economic role, social position and associated life-chances. Whereas the public *collectively* endorses a system of education which efficiently produces an appropriate range of role-occupants, each person or bonded group naturally seeks for themselves a position at the more rewarding/desirable end of the range. Even given this conflict of interest for members of the polity, had education a purely instrumental (or even more narrowly, a purely economic) purpose, whether for the individual or the state, this would present no more of a problem than the 'not in my backyard' clash of public and private interest which characterises many social issues.

However, despite recent rhetoric, education is not just a (particularly costly) social service, either provided paternalistically for its clients by an interventionist state or competed for by its consumers in a social market. Rather, it is a fundamental social practice, saturated with value – in aims, content, process and effect – whose hallmark is the reflection, reproduction and modification of personal identity and cultural climate. This being so, each individual, given common citizenship, can expect society not merely to tolerate but to validate, in and through public education, the identities they cherish, the traditions they value, the culture they prize and the personal aspirations they hold for the realisation of their conception of a worthwhile life.

The rub, of course, is that a plurality of identities, traditions, etc. is almost a defining characteristic of contemporary life. Where society privileges some identities over others in education, injury is added to insult, for whatever the intrinsic value of differing identities, whether from the perspective of those who inhabit them or from some objective standpoint, some identities have higher currency than others in the competition for educational exchange value. Thus through the 1960s and 70s, demands for equal respect in education were motivated by the desire to revalidate the intrinsic value of a plurality of identities and also to thereby gain equal access to education's exchange value.

This is the perspective of the disenfranchised, the disempowered and the discriminated against. Prior to democratic conditions of equal respect, there are painful practical dilemmas for individuals (and communities in which they share bonds of identity). Where some loyalties, values and aspirations are educationally privileged, hard personal choices present themselves, as migrants to affluent societies know only too well. With the reconstitution of a polity, however, where that is designed precisely to include the previously disempowered, these hard personal choices are compounded by hard citizen choices, for in that new, happier state, all citizens have, in principle, an equal interest in the internal social cohesion of the polity and in the internal economic efficiency and external economic competitiveness of their society. It now becomes not in their interests as citizens to prosecute their private interests where that might compromise either social cohesion or the economic developments in which they expect to share. Democratisation, on the other hand, is a hollow prize unless the identities of citizens as persons gain equal respect.

'Globalisation', it needs scarcely be said, makes these already difficult matters still worse, for under the conditions which ensue, certain attitudes, values and skills are once again at a premium, with individual societies then having limited autonomy in determining what those high-value attitudes, values and skills will be. A benevolent tyrant running a society characterised by diversity and pluralism (or indeed by a relative homogeneity at odds with global endorsements) might feel obliged to override the wishes of some subjects, paternalistically, in their broader interests. The same society, once democratic, requires of its citizens that in some areas of great personal significance, they voluntarily adopt a self-denying ordinance. Moreover, the self-denial required from some will be greater than that from others. As so often occurs, the crunch is felt most keenly in education – the vehicle for cultural identity of both persons and societies, the seed-bed for value, knowledge and skill, and the means of socio-economic development both of individuals and of polities.

The education of persons and citizens: one practical dilemma

For brevity the practical dilemma in the education of persons and citizens can be illustrated by focusing on the question of language. Language is a vehicle of identity and a key means for its preservation and reconstruction. Linguistic inclusion is a basic demand of citizens in any mulitilingual polity (a normal state-of-affairs too easily overlooked by Anglophone monoglots). To be educated in the medium of one's own language, as has been urged since the Reformation, is both a public endorsement of the worth of the cultural heritage of its speakers and a democratisation of power relations.

It is also, in the modern world, the means to competition for life-chances of those speakers on equal terms with others. Should we then have schools with whatever 'media of instruction' correspond to significant citizen groups in a society? Alternatively, if this were logistically or financially impossible, should we proceed through different media in the early years to a democratically agreed common medium – perhaps the one with the most shared allegiance or the fewest opposing factions? What should be stressed here is that this is not a matter over which either persons, privately, or citizens, collectively, have the luxury of the kind of reflected 'free choice' that both liberal theory and free market democracy vaunt. Rather, structure constrains agency in proportion as agency seeks to discount structure.

This is well illustrated by the South African case in which language diversity is merely one of the full range of relevant issues present. In South Africa we see diversity in a range of dimensions – racial, ethnic, cultural, linguistic, religious, gender and class as well as rural/urban or traditional/modern patterns of life. There is also a wide spectrum of life-chances historically associated with particular constellations of those sources of diversity that interact in the construction of individual identity; there is an emerging democracy seeking substantive content for recently granted formal citizenship rights; and there is a public education system under reconstruction which is now asked to provide the key to fulfilling three goals.

These goals are, firstly, the emancipation of individuals, through popular access to education's intrinsic and exchange value (a project in which both equity and development are promised to individuals); secondly, the building of an equitable, democratic polity in which citizenship is of equal value to all and to which all can reasonably give their allegiance (the project of social cohesion, equity and justice); and thirdly, the efficient production of a skills base and skills mix appropriate to serve an economy which must be internationally competitive (in order to realise the project of social development). Given the internal complexity of modern societies, the first project contains internal contradictions, as argued here. Under globalisation, the last of these projects constrains the first two. The second, overarching project requires the resolution of those contradictions and the accommodation of those constraints.

The question of language policy in South Africa today presents all of the citizenship/identity issues in their most complex practical form. It also illustrates the complexity of educational value and the conflicting dimensions of education's benefit to persons, citizens and states. With eleven official languages the ideal solution might seem to be many media of instruction, as vehicles for personal and cultural identity and their development. Perhaps more realistically, for reasons of logistics and finance, a solution might be at least a rainbow plurality of media of instruction, respecting the identities, recognising the cultural differences and levelling the competitive playing field for significant concentrations of population groups. Unease with such solutions goes beyond resistance to new forms of separatism in the post-Apartheid settlement, for they do not meet the multiple aspirations of citizens. That the full range of media of instruction should be confined to the early years, and that its purpose would be not just to respect a plurality of identities but to get later learning in common media off to a fair start for all is a strategic necessity, both for national policy and for individuals seeking personal emancipation, educational and social. This is not a simple triumph of instrumental over intrinsic valuations, nor of economic over cultural considerations.

It is true that 'minority' linguistic groups worldwide, from Finns to Maori, accept the pragmatic and economic necessity for facility in globally dominant linguistic media and that this is reflected in curricular decisions, but there is more to it than this. For monoglots from historically dominant cultures, it is tempting to think of individuals as inhabiting one of a series of relatively homogeneous linguistic and cultural worlds, for such is theirs. (Interestingly, this is a perspective shared by 'traditional' societies protected or excluded from the developments of modernity.) For persons other than these, however, identity, like language use and its inescapable cultural concomitants, is a more complex matter. For the state, language policy has both internal, political, significance and external, economic, importance, with the latter setting limiting parameters for the former. For citizens within states, there are four kinds of benefit sought from public education, and their interaction precludes the plain contest between 'minority/disadvantaged' and 'dominant/hegemonic' identities, whether in language policy or more generally, which polemic (and too often the theoretical literature) portrays.

In this instance, as one of the collectivity of providers, each citizen requires that sufficient linguistic commonality be assured for the state's internal social cohesion, intercultural understanding and stability. What form that commonality should take, however, is not just a contest of cultural worth, numerical superiority or political dominance, since the imperative of international economic competitiveness makes some candidates stronger contenders than others, on the collective prosperity grounds which are of interest to all citizens. On the other hand, each also seeks sufficient specificity to ensure that their identities are not culturally eclipsed, that the traditions they value are respected and preserved for those who share them and also recognised and understood by those who initially do not. At the same time, though, they require enough commonality for these understandings to be interculturally mutual, for reasons of cultural enrichment as well as social cohesion.

Here, it is not simply that participants in education are citizens as well as private persons and that as such they echo collective demands for national prosperity in which they hope to share. It is rather that the wider society, national and international, is one which they also inhabit, with many of its features – cultural, technological, political – forming part of their complex cultural identities. The complexity of identity under modern conditions is evidenced by conflicts of interest within each person as well as between them as citizens.

Citizenship, identity and public education

That the focus on language in that example could be exchanged for one on cultural content or tradition is clear. Perhaps less obvious is its applicability to 'stable' democracies (including nation-states which globally are culturally and economically dominant), where the equity/development tension in public education, associated with citizen diversity whether class, gender, race or ethnicity based, has long been present. It should be stressed that resulting 'hard choices' for citizens (harder of course for some than for others) are seldom just matters of a regretted pragmatic trade-off between the private claims of personal identity and strategic aims for equal opportunities in a competition between citizens for life-chances. More than this, they reflect the fact that all of us under contemporary conditions have complex sources of identity which give rise to a plurality of interests. Two exempt ostensible categories might be members of 'traditional' groups protected or excluded from cultural change and members of the dominant subcultures of dominant cultures. (It may be that interesting co-incidence which brings synergy to deadlock in theory and dogma in practice.)

In this brief analysis, I have only touched on the complexity of the problems involved in reconciling cultural diversity with common citizenship, in and through the medium of public education, to the benefit of the polity as a whole and of individual citizens and citizen-groups within it. When contextualised, the issues of principle in political theory are sharpened and multiplied. When particular circumstance is mapped onto that framework we see the need to bring into play more subtle conceptions of culture, identity and citizenship than are often deployed. It is also evident we must bring into the analysis the conflicting demands made of public education and the role of the process of societal modernisation, for both good and ill, in setting parameters for what education can achieve.

I have only hinted at that latter process here. It is not to be confused with the spread of powerful economic or political forces, or the 'shrinking world' scenario of globalisation, though that speeds it up. Societal modernisation denotes rather the development of a new kind of pluralism, inseparable from the modern condition. Standardly, the problem of pluralism focuses on diversity *between* persons: it overlooks the inescapable and growing pluralism *within* persons and citizens. The more complex the world becomes, the more each of us inhabits a series of overlapping and fluid identities. This plural structure of the self, moreover, is not associated simply with contingent cultural collisions or social transitions: it is endemic to any but the pre-modern condition. Any educational response to the problems of pluralism, diversity and identity must take account of this new dimension, with all that it implies. Indeed, unless education of and for the public confronts this issue in all its complexity, it is failing in its task, for modernity itself has been fuelled by the very processes of critical reflection and cognitive emancipation which claim to be the hallmark of public education in open, democratic societies.

We thus see that a society such as today's South Africa, exhibiting diversity and pluralism in all its manifestations and pursuing the three goals noted above, does not represent a set of aberrant conditions for which the 'successful' procedures of established democracies need to be adapted. Nor do its cultural and social conditions present a task for public education which elsewhere has been successfully accomplished, for where homogeneity and stability have seemed cosily to reign, it is not so much that all voices have sung the same tune as that some have been less easily heard. So, what is called for is not a solution to a recently arisen problem, seen in perhaps its most acute in South Africa. What is sought for public education is rather a solution to a problem still unresolved in 'established' democracies, in which South Africa may lead the way precisely because it can neither evade nor disguise the issues.

Bibliography

Adelman, H. S. (1992) 'LD: the next 25 years' *Journal of Learning Disabilities*, Vol 25 No 1.

Alexander, N. (1989) *Language Policy and National Unity in South Africa/Azania.* Cape Town: Buchu Books.

ANC (1994) *A Policy Framework for Education and Training* (discussion document), ANC Education Department.

ANC/COSATU (1993) *Framework for Lifelong Learning: A Unified, Multi-path Approach to Education and Training.* Johannesburg: ANC/COSATU.

Apter, S. (1982) *Troubled Children: Troubled Systems.* London: Pergamon Press.

Arnove, R. (1986) *Education and Revolution in Nicaragua.* New York: Praeger.

Aronowitz, S. & Giroux, H. A. (1986) *Education Under Siege: The Conservative and Radical Debate over Schooling.* London: Routledge and Kegan Paul.

Arons, A. B. (1979) 'Cognitive level of college physics students' *American Journal of Physics*, Vol 47 No 7.

Arons, A. B. (1983) 'Students' patterns of thinking – Part 2' *The Physics Teacher*, Vol 21 No 9.

Arons, A. B. (1990) *A Guide to Introductory Physics Teaching.* New York: John Wiley.

Ausubel, D. P. (1968) *Educational Psychology: A Cognitive View.* New York: Holt, Rinehart & Winston.

Badat, S. (1991) 'Democratising education policy research for social transformation' Unterhalter, E. *et al.* (eds) *Education in a Future South Africa: Policy Issues for Transformation.* London: Heinemann.

Badsha, N. (1992) *Access to University Education: The Case of the University of the Western Cape.* CINTSA Admissions Symposium Proceedings, October 1992.

Baird, J. R. & Northfield, J. R. (1992) *Learning from the PEEL Experience.* Victoria: Monash University.

Ball, S. (1990) *Politics and Policy Making in Education: Explorations in Policy Sociology.* London: Routledge.

Ball, S. (1993) 'Education markets, choice and social class: the market as a class strategy in the UK and USA' *British Journal of Sociology of Education*, Vol 14 No 1.

Ball, S. (1994) *Education Reform: A Critical and Post-structural Approach.* Buckingham: Open University Press.

Ball, S. (1995) 'Towards a global core curriculum' (unpublished paper presented at the Oxford Conference on Globalisation and Learning, September 1995).

Bamgbose, A. (1991) *Language and the Nation.* Edinburgh: Edinburgh University Press.

Beaty, E., Gibbs, G. & Morgan, A. (1997) 'Learning orientations and study contracts' Marton, F. *et al.* (eds) *The Experience of Learning* (2nd edn). Edinburgh: Scottish Academic Press.

Bengu, S. M. E. (1997) Address from the steps of Parliament on the occasion of the launch of Curriculum 2005, 24 March.

Benner, P. (1985) *From Novice to Expert.* London: Addison Wesley.

Bernstein, B. (1994) 'Discourses, knowledge structures and fields: some arbitrary considerations' (unpublished paper presented at a seminar in the School of Education, University of Cape Town).

Biggs, J. B. (1987) *Student Approaches to Learning and Studying.* Melbourne: Australian Council for Educational Research.

Biggs, J. B. (1989) 'Does learning about learning help teachers with teaching? Psychology and the tertiary teacher' *The Gazette* Vol 26 No 1, University of Hong Kong.

Biggs, J. B. (1993) 'What do inventories of students' learning processes really measure? A theoretical review and clarification' *Educational Psychology* Vol 63.

Biggs, J. B. (1994) 'Student learning theory and research. Where do we currently stand?' Gibbs, G. (ed.) *Improving Student Learning: Theory and Practice.* Oxford: The Oxford Centre for Staff Development, Oxford Brookes University.

Bird, A. & Gamble, J. (1996) 'National standards and qualifications: a South African perspective' *Inter-Ministerial Working Group Proceedings of the Conference on the National Qualifications Framework* Pretoria: HSRC.

Blaug, M. (ed.) (1968) *Economics of Education 1.* Harmondsworth: Penguin.

Bloom, B. S. (1976) *Human Characteristics and School Learning.* New York: McGraw-Hill.

Bloom, B. S. (1984) 'The search for methods of group instruction as effective as One-to-One Tutoring' *Educational Leadership* 4–17.

Bot, M. (1988) *Training on Separate Tracks.* Johannesburg: SAIRR.

Botha, A. (1998) 'Baptism of Fire for new Education MEC' *Cape Argus*, 24 February 1998.

Bourdieu, P. (1973) 'Cultural reproduction and social reproduction' Brown, R. (ed.) *Knowledge, Education and Cultural Change.* London: Tavistock.

Bourdieu, P. (1986) 'The forms of capital' Richardson, J. E. (ed.) *Handbook of Theory of Research for the Sociology of Education.* London: Greenword Press.

Bowe, R. & Ball, S. (1992) *Reforming Education and Changing Schools. Case Studies in Policy Sociology.* London: Routledge.

Breier, M. (1996) 'Whose learning? Whose knowledge? Recognition of prior learning and the National Qualifications Framework' Unpublished paper presented to the Kenton Education Conference, Wilgespruit.

Breier, M., Taetsane, M. & Sait, L. (1996a) *Reading and Writing in the Minibus Taxi Industry* SoUL Research Report No 6, CACE, University of the Western Cape and Department of Adult Education, University of Cape Town.

Breier, M. & Sait, L. (1996b) *Literacy, Communication and Worker Health in a Cape Factory* SoUL Research Report No 3, CACE, University of the Western Cape and Department of Adult Education, University of Cape Town.

British Government (1903–5) *South African Native Affairs Commission Report* (SANAC).

Brookes, E. G. (1930) *Native Education in South Africa.* Pretoria: Van Schaik.

Brown, H. (1995) *Education, Culture and The State.* Oxford: Oxford University Press.

Brown, P. & Lauder, H. (1997) 'Education, globalisation and economic development' *Journal of Education Policy* Vol 11 No 2.

Campion, J. (1985) *The Child in Context.* London: Methuen.

Candy, P. (1991) *Self-direction for Life-Long Learning.* San Francisco: Jossey Bass.

Cape Argus (1998) Saturday 24 January 1998.

Cape Times (1997) 3 December 1997.

Cape Times (1997) Leader Page, 4 December 1997.

Cape Times (1997) 10 December 1997.

Cape Times (1997) 16 December 1997.

Cape Times (1998) 13 January 1998.

Carneson, J. (1996) 'Investigating change in classroom practice: a fresh approach' Robertson, S. A. (ed.) *In Pursuit of Equality.* Cape Town: Juta.

Carr, W. & Kemmis, S. (1986) *Becoming Critical.* Brighton: Falmer Press.

Center, Y. (1987) 'Integration – historical perspectives' Ward, J. *et al. Educating children with Special Needs in Regular Classrooms: An Australian Perspective.* North Ryde: Macquarie University Press.

Chambers, R. (1983) *Rural Development: Putting the Last First.* New York: Longman.

Chambers, R. (1997) *Whose Reality Counts: Putting the First Last.* London: Intermediate Technology Publications.

Chiseri-Strater, E. (1991) *Academic Literacies: The Public and Private Discourses of University Students.* Portsmouth, US: Boynton/Cook Publishers.

Chisholm, L. (1984) 'Redefining skills: black education in South Africa in the 1980s' Kallaway, P. (ed.) *Apartheid and Education.* Johannesburg: Ravan Press.

Chisholm, L. (1997) 'The restructuring of South African education and training' Kallaway, P. *et al.* (eds) *Education After Apartheid.* Cape Town: University of Cape Town Press.

Christie, P. (1986) *The Right to Learn.* Johannesburg: Ravan Press.

Christie, P. (1997) 'Globalisation and the curriculum: proposals for the integration of education and training' Kallaway, P. *et al.* (eds) *Education After Apartheid.* Cape Town: University of Cape Town Press.

CINTSA (1992) Admissions Symposium Proceedings, Badsha, N. *et al.* (eds) October 1992.

Clark, C., Dyson, A., Millward, A. & Skidmore, D. (1997) *New Directions in Special Needs.* London: Cassell.

Clark, J. (1997) *Proceedings of the 4th Annual conference of the South Association for Research in Science and Mathematics Education*, University of the Witwatersrand, January 1997.

Clark, J. (1998) *Proceedings of the 5th Annual conference of the South Association for Research in Science and Mathematics Education*, University of South Africa, Pretoria, January 1998.

Clarkson, A. (1994) *The History of the Western Cape Education Department.* Cape Town: Western Cape Education Department.

Cleaver, K. (1997) *Rural Development Strategies for Poverty Reduction and Environmental Protection in Sub-Saharan Africa*, Directions in Development Series, World Bank.

Code, L. (1991) *What Can She Know? Feminist Theory and the Construction of Knowledge.* Ithaca, New York: Cornell University Press.

Cohen, D. (1991) 'Revolution in one classroom' Fuhrman, S. H. & Malen, B. (eds) *The Politics of Curriculum and Testing.* London: Falmer Press.

Collins, A. *et al.* (1989) 'Cognitive apprenticeship: teaching the crafts of reading, writing and mathematics' Resnick, L. (ed.) *Knowing, Learning and Instruction: Essays in Honor of Robert Glaser.* Hilldale, N.J.: Lawrence Erlbaum.

COMSEC (Community Self-Employment Centre), brochure, CSIR, Pretoria.

Coombs, P. H. & Ahmed, M. (1974) *Attacking Rural Poverty: How Non-formal Education Can Help.* Baltimore: World Bank/John Hopkins University Press.

COSATU (1993) *Consolidated Recommendations on Adult Basic Education and Training.* Johannesburg: COSATU.

Cross, J., Abraham, C., Kirkaldy, B., Hill, S. & Smith, E. (1994) *The Dimensions used in Records of Needs* Final report to the Scottish Office Education Department, Mimeograph: University of Dundee.

Cross, M. & Chisholm, L. (1990) 'The roots of segregated schooling in twentieth-century South Africa' Nkomo, N. (ed.) *Pedagogy of Domination.* Trenton: World Press.

CSIR (undated) 'Technology for development: CSIR Track Record: Small, Medium and Micro Enterprise (SMME) Development' brochure, Pretoria.

CSIR (1996) *CSIR Technology Impact 1996.* Pretoria: CSIR.

Dahlgren, L. O. & Marton, F. (1978) 'Students' conceptions of subject matter: an aspect of learning and teaching in higher education' *Studies in Higher Education* Vol 3 No 1.

Dale, R. *et al.* (1981) *Schooling and the National Interest.* Lewes: Falmer Press.

Das Gupta, J. (1968) *Language Diversity and National Development* as cited in Bamgbose 1991.

Davidoff, S. & De Jong, T. (1997) 'Slipping through the gaps: understanding and monitoring OD interventions in schools as a strategy for change'. Unpublished paper, Kenton-at-the-Gap conference, Hermanus, October 1997.

Dearing Committee (1997) National Committee of Inquiry into Higher Education, *Higher Education in the Learning Society.* London: HMSO.

De Clercq, F. (1997) 'Effective policies and the reform process: an evaluation of South Africa's new development and education macro policies' Kallaway, P. *et al.* (eds) *Education After Apartheid.* Cape Town: University of Cape Town Press.

De Lange, J. (1981) *Report of the Work Committee: Education for Children with Special Educational Needs.* HSRC investigation into education, Pretoria: HSRC.

Department for Education (DFE) (1994) *Code of Practice on the Identification and Assessment of Special Educational Needs,* London: HMSO.

Department for Education and Employment (UK) (1996) *Skills Audit,* London: HMSO.

Department of Arts, Culture, Science and Technology (1996) *White Paper on Science & Technology: Preparing for the 21st Century.* Pretoria: Government Printer.

Department of Education (RSA) (1992) *Educational Renewal Strategy.* Pretoria: Government Printer.

Department of Education (RSA) (1994) *Draft White Paper on Education and Training.* Government Gazette No 15974, Pretoria.

Department of Education (RSA) (1995a) *White Paper on Education and Training in a Democratic South Africa: First Steps to Developing a New System.* Government Gazette Vol 375 No 16312, 15 March 1995.

Department of Education (RSA) (1995b) *National Qualifications Framework Bill.* Pretoria: Government Printer.

Department of Education (RSA) (1996a) *Lifelong Learning Through a National Qualifications Framework,* Report of the Ministerial Committee for Developmental Work on the NQF, Pretoria, February 1996.

Department of Education (RSA) (1996b) *Green Paper on Higher Education Transformation.* Pretoria: Government Printer.

Department of Education (RSA) (1996c) *National Education Policy Act No 27.* Pretoria: Government Printer.

Department of Education (RSA) (1996d) *South African Schools Act.* Pretoria: Government Printer.

Department of Education (RSA) (1996e) *Norms and Standards Regarding Language Policy.*

Department of Education (RSA) (1996f) *Draft Language Policy* 11 September 1996.

Department of Education (RSA) (1997a) 'Preliminary Report' National Committee on Further Education, Pretoria.

Department of Education (RSA) (1997b) *Curriculum 2005: Lifelong Learning for the 21st Century* Pretoria: Absolutely Media Marketing.

Department of Education (RSA) (1997c) *Curriculum 2005: Lifelong Learning for the 21st Century, A User's Guide,* March 1997.

Department of Education (RSA) (1997d) *Curriculum 2005: Discussion document.*

Department of Education (RSA) (1997e) *Outcomes Based Education in South Africa: Background Information for Educators* Discussion Document, March 1997.

Department of Education (RSA) (1997f) *Policy Document on Adult Basic Education and Training.* Pretoria: Government Printer.

Department of Education (RSA) (1997g) *A Framework for the Transformation of FE and Training in South Africa* (Report of the National Commission on Further Education). Pretoria: Government Printer.

Department of Education (RSA) (1997h) *Curriculum 2005: Specific Outcomes, Assessment Criteria, Range Statements, Grades 1 to 9* Discussion document, March 1997.

Department of Education (RSA) (1997i) *Curriculum 2005: Lifelong Learning for the 21st Century,* March 1997.

Department of Education (RSA) (1997j) *Draft White Paper on Higher Education* Government Gazette No 17944. Pretoria: Government Printer.

Department of Education (RSA) (1997k) *Draft Language in Education Policy* 28 January 1997.

Department of Education and Science (DES) (1978) *Special Educational Needs* (The Warnock Report) London: HMSO.

Department of Labour (1997) *Green Paper: Skills Development Strategy for Economic and Employment Growth in South Africa.* Pretoria: Department of Labour.

Department of Native Affairs (1951) *The Report of the Native Education Committee (Eiselen Report).* Pretoria: Government Printer.

Department of Public Service and Administration (1997) *The Provincial Review Report.* Pretoria, August 1997.

Department of Trade and Industry (1995) *White Paper on National Strategy for Development and Promotion of Small Business in South Africa,* Government Gazette Vol 357 No 16317, Cape Town.

Desai, Z. (1994) 'Privileged tongues: on language rights in South Africa' Da Costa *et al.* (eds) *Let the Voices be Heard.* Cape Town: Wyvern Publications.

Desai, Z. & Taylor, N. (1997) 'Language and education in South Africa' Coulby, D *et al.* (eds) *World Yearbook of Education 1997: Intercultural Education.* London: Kogan Page.

Die Burger (1998) 10 January 1998.

Dodd, A. D. (1938) *Native Vocational Training.* Alice: Lovedale.

Donald, D., Lazarus, S. & Lolwana, P. (1997) *Educational Psychology in Social Context.* Cape Town: Oxford University Press.

Donald, D. (1993) 'Reconceptualising the nature and extent of special educational need in South Africa' *Perspectives in Education,* Vol 14 No 2.

282

Donald, D. (1994) 'Children with special needs: the reproduction of disadvantage in poorly resourced communities' A. Dawes & Donald, D. (eds) *In Childhood and Adversity in South Africa*. Cape Town: David Philip Publishers.

Donn, G. (1995a) 'Education policy in the new South Africa: a study of centre-province relations' Occasional Paper No 56, Edinburgh: Centre for African Studies.

Donn, G. (1995b) 'Curriculum innovation in South Africa's post-Apartheid school system' *Science, Technology and Development* Vol 13 No 2.

Donn, G. (ed.) (1996) 'South Africa: education in transition' Occasional Paper No 63 Edinburgh: Centre for African Studies.

Donn, G. (1997) 'Higher education in South Africa: transforming the system' Kallaway, P. *et al.* (eds) *Education after Apartheid*. Cape Town: University of Cape Town Press.

Dore, R. (1976) *The Diploma Disease*. London: George Allen and Unwin.

Dore, R. (1997) *The Diploma Disease* (2nd edn) Institute of Education, University of London.

Du Toit, L. (1996) 'An introduction to Specialised Education' Engelbrecht, P. *et al.* (eds) *Perspectives on Learning Difficulties*. Pretoria: Van Schaik.

Duvenage, G. D. J. (1973) Undergraduate class lectures, University of the Western Cape.

Dworkin, R. (1993) *Life's Dominion*. London: Harper Collins.

Education Policy Unit, UWC (1997) *The Enhancement of Graduate Programmes and Research Capacity at the Historically Black Universities,* University of the Western Cape, October 1997.

Education, Training and Development Practicioners Project (1997) Phase 2: Systems Building, Johannesburg: ETDP Project.

Eizenberg, N. (1988) 'Approaches to learning anatomy: developing a programme for preclinical medical students' Ramsden, P. (ed.) *Improving Learning: New Perspectives*. London: Kogan Page.

Ensor, P. (1997) 'School mathematics, everyday life and the NQF: a case of non-equivalence?' (unpublished paper presented to the Fifth Annual Meeting of SAARMSE, University of the Witwatersrand).

Entwistle, N. & Ramsden, P. (1983) *Understanding Student Learning*. London: Croom Helm.

Entwistle, N. (1995) 'The use of research on student learning in quality assessment' Gibbs, G. (ed.) *Improving Student Learning: through Assessment and Evaluation*. Oxford: Oxford Centre for Staff Development.

Entwistle, N. (1997a) 'Improving university teaching through research on student learning' UWC Education Faculty Seminar, March 1997.

Entwistle, N. J. (1997b) 'Improving teaching through research on student learning' Forest, J. J. F. (ed.) *University Teaching: International Perspectives*. New York: Garland (in press).

Entwistle, N. J. (1997c) 'Contrasting perspectives on learning' Marton, F. *et al.* (eds) *The Experience of Learning* (2nd edn) Edinburgh: Scottish Academic Press.

Entwistle, N. J. (1997d) 'Motivation and approaches to studying: motivation and conceptions of teaching' Thompson, G. *et al.* (eds) *Motivating Students*. London: Kogan Page (in press).

European Commission (1997) *Accomplishing Europe through Education and Training*. Brussels: A Report by the Study Group on Education and Training.

Ewart, G. D. (1991) 'Habermas and education; a comprehensive overview of the influence of Habermas in educational literature' *Review of Educational Research* Vol 61 No 3.

Fenstermacher, G. D. (1986) 'Philosophy of research on teaching: three aspects' Wittrock, M. C. (ed.) *Handbook of Research on Teaching* (3rd edn). New York: Macmillan Publishing Co.

Field, J. & Schuller, T. (1997) 'Norms, networks and trust' *Adults Learning* Vol 9 No 3.

Foster, P. (1966) 'The vocational school fallacy in development planning' Blaug, M. (ed.) (1968) *Economics of Education 1.* Harmondsworth: Penguin.

Foster, P. (1969) 'Education for Self-Reliance: a critical evaluation' Jolly, R. (ed.) *Education in Africa: Research and Action.* Nairobi: Heinemann.

Freire, P. (1970) *Cultural Action for Freedom.* Massachusettes: Harvard Educational Review.

French, E. (1990) 'English: medium of instruction or enemy of instruction' *Language Projects' Review* Vol 5 No 3.

Fuhrman, S. H. & Malen, B. (eds) *The Politics of Curriculum and Testing.* London: Falmer Press.

Fullan, M. (1982) *The Meaning of Educational Change.* New York: Peoples' College Press.

Fullan, M. (1993) *Change Forces.* London: Falmer Press.

Furlong, A. & Raffe, D. (1989) *Young People's Routes into the Labour Market,* University of Edinburgh: Centre for Educational Sociology.

Garrick, J. (1996) 'The dialectic of informal learning'. Unpublished paper delivered to the International Conference on Experiential Learning, University of Cape Town, 1996.

Gee, J. (1990) *Social Linguistics and Literacies: Ideology in Discourses.* Hampshire: The Falmer Press.

Geertz, C. (1983) *Local Knowledge: Further Essays in Interpretive Anthropology.* New York: Basic Books.

Geidt, J. (1996) 'Distance education into group areas won't go?' *Open Learning* Vol 11 No 1.

Geidt, J. (1997) *Research Methods for Adult Educators* CACE, University of the Western Cape.

Gelderbloem, N. O. (1996) 'The role of the university in post-apartheid South Africa' M.Phil mini-thesis, University of the Western Cape.

Gerwel, G. J. (1991) 'Intellectuals in a changing South Africa' Second David Webster Memorial Lecture, University of the Witwatersrand, Johannesburg.

Gibbons, M. (1997) 'Research and the governance of science'. Unpublished paper presented to the *Running, Reporting and Researching Africa* Conference, Centre of African Studies, University of Edinburgh, October 1997.

Gibson, D. (1996) *Farmworkers, literacy and literacy practices in the Bree River Vallley* SoUL Research Report No 4, CACE, University of the Western Cape and Department of Adult Education, University of Cape Town.

Giroux, H. (1983) *Theory and Resistance: A Pedagogy for the Opposition.* South Hadley, MA: Bergin and Garvey Publishers.

Gordon, I., Lewis, J. & Young, K. (1993) 'Perspectives on policy analysis' Hill, M. (ed.) *The Policy Process: A Reader.* London: Harvester, Wheatsheaf.

Gough, D. (1996) 'Thinking in Xhosa and speaking in English: the theory and practice of contrastive analysis' *Southern African Journal of Applied Language Studies (SAJALS)* Vol 4 No 1.

Govender, V., Greenstein, R., Greybe, S., Mokgalane, E., Samson, M. & Vally, S. (1997) 'Conflict and development in education policy' *Wits EPU Quarterly Review of Education and Training in South Africa* Vol 4 No 3.

Government of Kenya (1992) *Sessional Paper No 2 of 1992 on Small Enterprise and Jua Kali Development in Kenya.* Nairobi: Government Printer.

Gray, B. V. (1990) 'The Science Education Project in KwaZulu 1980–4: Enhancing Teacher Involvement in Educational Change'. Mini-thesis submitted in partial fulfilment of an M.Ed. University of the Western Cape.

Gray, B. V. (1997) 'Towards a more relevant and exciting science curriculum: the trialing of the Science Through Applications Project curriculum materials' *Proceedings of the 4th Annual conference of the South Association for Research in Science and Mathematics Education,* University of the Witwatersrand, January 1997.

Gray, B. V. & Ramahlape, K. (1997) 'Wakening the sleeping giant: a critical look at the process of involving teachers in curriculum and materials development through the Science Through Applications Project (STAP)' *Proceedings of the 4th annual conference of the South Association for Research in Science and Mathematics Education,* University of the Witwatersrand, January 1997.

Green, L. (1991) 'Mainstreaming: the challenge for teachers in South Africa' *Support for Learning* Vol 6.

Green, L., Donald, D. & MacIntosh, I. (1992) 'Indirect service delivery for special educational needs in South Africa: a comparative study of five consultative interventions' *International Journal of Special Education,* Vol 7 No 3.

Greenstein, R. (1996) 'The making of education policy: documents, experts and popular constituencies'. Unpublished paper, Kenton Conference, Broederstroom, October 1996.

Greenstein, R. (1997a) 'Education, identity and curriculum policies in the new South Africa' Kallaway, P. *et al.* (eds) *Education After Apartheid.* Cape Town: University of Cape Town Press.

Greenstein, R. (1997b) 'New policies and the challenges of budgetary constraints' *Wits EPU Quarterly Review of Education and Training in South Africa* Vol 4 No 4.

Grierson, J. & McKenzie, I. (1996) *Training for self-employment through vocational training institutions,* ILO, Turin.

Groener, Z. L. (1997) '*Adult education and training in the South African transition (1990–1994): A study in policy making'.* Unpublished PhD dissertation, University of California.

Gunstone, R. (1992) 'Constructivism and metacognition: theoretical issues and classroom studies' Duit, R. *et al.* (eds) *Research in Physics Learning: Theoretical Issues and Empirical Studies,* IPN.

Habermas, J. (1976) *Legitimation Crisis.* London: Heinemann.

Habermas J. (1984) *Theory of Communicative Action Vol 1, Reason and the Rationalisation of Society.*

Habermas, J. (1991) *Communication and the Evolution of Society.* London: Polity Press.

Hargreaves, A. (1993) *Curriculum and Assessment Reform.* Milton Keynes: Open University Press.

Harris, J., Saddington, T. & McMillan, J. (1994) *Recognition of Prior Learning (RPL): International Models of Assessment.* Pretoria: Report presented to the National Training Board.

Hart, P. E. & Shipman, A. (1991) *Financing Training in Britain,* National Institute Economic Review, May 1991.

Helm, H. (1996) 'The physics lecture: the medium and the message'. Paper presented at the annual South African Institute of Physics Conference, Pretoria, July 1996.

Herman, H. D. (1995) 'Schoolleaving examinations: selection and equity in higher education in South Africa' *Comparative Education* Vol 31 No 2.

Hewitt, P. G. (1983) 'The missing essential – a conceptual understanding of physics' *American Journal of Physics* Vol 5 No 1.

Hilborn, R. (1988) 'Redesigning college and university introductory physics' *American Journal of Physics* Vol 56 No 1.

Hodgson, V. (1997) 'Lectures and the experience of relevance' Marton, F. *et al.* (eds) *The Experience of Learning* (2nd edn). Edinburgh: Scottish Academic Press.

Holiday, A. (1996) Article in *The Cape Times*, 10 January 1996.

Hood, D. (1995) 'New Zealand's qualifications framework' Broadcast, August 1995.

HSRC (1981a) *Provision of Education in the RSA.* Pretoria: HSRC.

HSRC (1981b) *Report of the Main Committee of the HSRC Investigation into Education (De Lange Report).* Pretoria: HSRC.

HSRC (1987) *Education for the Black Disabled.* Pretoria: HSRC.

HSRC (1995) *Ways of Seeing the National Qualifications Framework.* Pretoria: HSRC.

Hyland, T. (1994) *Competence, Education and NVQs: Dissenting Perspectives.* London: Cassell.

ILO (1986) *Youth Employment and Youth Employment Programmes in Africa.* Addis Ababa: JASPA.

Ilon, L. (1994) 'Structural adjustment and education: adapting to a growing global market' *International Journal of Educational Development* Vol 14 No 2.

Jansen, J. (1997) 'Why OBE will fail'. Unpublished paper, March 1997.

Jantjes, E. M. (1987) *A Discussion of Research on Teaching and its Evaluation.* Unpublished Masters thesis, Northwestern University, Illinois, USA.

Jessup, G. (1991) *Outcomes: NVQs and the Emerging Model of Education and Training.* Brighton: Falmer Press.

Johnson, R. W. (1995) 'Campuses in chaos' *The Times*, 9 January 1995.

Johnson, B. (1998) 'Gear hurts education', *Sowetan* 19 February 1998.

Jolly, R. (ed.) (1969) *Education in Africa: Research and Action.* Nairobi: Heinemann.

Joyappa, V. & Martin, D. J. (1996) 'Exploring alternative research epistemologies for adult education: participatory research, feminist research and feminist participatory research' *Adult Education Quarterly* Vol 47 No 1.

Kallaway, P. (1997) 'Reconstruction, reconciliation and rationalization in South African politics of education' Kallaway, P. *et al.* (eds) *Education after Apartheid.* Cape Town: University of Cape Town Press.

Kallaway, P., Kruss, G., Fataar, A. & Donn, G. (1997) *Education After Apartheid: South African Education in Transition.* Cape Town: University of Cape Town Press.

Khosa, M. (1991) 'Capital accumulation in the black taxi industry' Preston-Whyte, E. & Rogerson, C. (eds) *South Africa's Informal Economy.* Cape Town: Oxford University Press.

King, K. (1971) *Pan-Africanism and Education.* Oxford: Clarendon Press.

King, K. (1974) *Pan-Africanism and Education.* Oxford: Oxford University Press.

King, K. (1991) *Aid and Education in the Developing World.* London: Harlow, Longman.

King, K. (1993) 'Education policy in a climate of entitlement: the South African case' *Perspectives in Education* Vol 14 No 2.

King, K. (1996) *Jua Kali Kenya: change and development in an informal economy.* Oxford: James Currey.

King, K. & McGrath, S. (1996) 'The methodological challenge of researching education, training and enterprise in the age of globalisation' Papers on Education, Training and Enterprise No 2, December 1996, CAS, Edinburgh.

Kirp, D. (1982) 'Professionalisation as policy choice: British special education in comparative perspective' *World Politics*, Vol 34 No 2.

Kohn, A. (1991) 'Caring kids: the role of the schools' *Phi Delta Kappan* Vol 72 No 7.

Kolb, D. (1984) *Experiential Learning*. New Jersey: Prentice-Hall.

Kreel, L. & Low, T. C. C. (1995) *Analysis of First Year Pass Rates for the University of the Western Cape* Deptartment of Statistical Sciences, University of Cape Town.

Kriegler, S. M. & Farman, R. (1995) 'Redistribution of special education resources in South Africa: beyond mainstreaming towards effective schools for all' Engelbrecht, P. *et al.* (eds) *Perspectives on Learning Difficulties*. Pretoria: Van Schaik.

Kriegler, S. M. & Skuy, M. (1996) 'Perspectives on psychological assessment in South African schools' Engelbrecht, P. *et al.* (eds) *Perspectives on Learning Difficulties*. Pretoria: Van Schaik.

Kruss, G. 'Educational restructuring in South Africa at provincial level: the case of the Western Cape' Kallaway, P. *et al.* (eds) *Education After Apartheid: South African Education in Transition*. Cape Town: University of Cape Town Press.

Kuhn, T. (1970) *The Structure of Scientific Revolutions*. Chicago: University of Chicago Press.

Lange, D. (1988) *Tomorrow's Schools: The Reform of Education Administration in New Zealand*. Wellington: Government Printer.

Lauder, H. *et al.* (1994) *The Creation of Market Competition for Education in New Zealand*. Wellington: New Zealand Ministry of Education.

Lauglo, J. & Lillis, K. (eds) (1988) *Vocationalising Education: An International Perspective*. Oxford: Pergamon

Lave, J. (1988) *Cognition in Practice*. Cambridge: Cambridge University Press.

Lave, J., Murtagh, M. & De La Rocha, O. (1984) 'The dialectic of arithmetic in grocery shopping' Rogoff, B. & Lave, J. (eds) *Everyday Cognition: Its Development in Social Context*. Cambridge: Harvard University Press.

Lave, J. & Wenger, E. (1991) *Situated Learning: Legitimate Peripheral Participation*. Cambridge: Harvard University Press.

Lazarus, S. & Donald, D. (1995) 'The development of education support services in South Africa: basic principles and a proposed model' *South African Journal of Education* Vol 15.

Leach, J., Ryder, J. & Driver, R. (1996) 'A perspective on undergraduate teaching and learning in the sciences' Working Paper 1 Undergraduate Learning in Science Project (ULISP). Leeds: University of Leeds.

Levin, H. M. (1982) 'The dilemma of comprehensive secondary school reforms in Western Europe' Altbach, P. G. *et al. Comparative Education*. New York: Macmillan.

Levin, R. (1991) 'People's Education and the politics of negotiation in South Africa' *Perspectives in Education* Vol 12 No 2.

Lin, H. (1982) 'Learning physics vs passing courses' *The Physics Teacher* Vol 20.

Linder, C. J. (1992) 'Is teacher-reflected epistemology a source of conceptual difficulty in physics?' *International Journal of Science Education* Vol 11.

Linder, C. J. (1993) 'Undergraduate science students' conceptions of learning' Reddy, V. (ed.) *SAARMSE 1993 Proceedings* Natal: CASME.

Linder, C. J. & Hillhouse, G. (1996) 'Teaching by conceptual exploration' *The Physics Teacher* Vol 34 No 6.

Linder, C. J. & Marshall, D. (1996) 'Introducing and evaluating metacognitive strategies in large-class physics teaching' (paper presented to the annual Improving Student Learning Symposium, University of Bath, UK, September 1996).

Lingard, D., Knight, P. & Porter, S. (1993) *Schooling Reform in Hard Times*. Brighton: Falmer Press.

Lomofsky, L. & Mvambi, N. (1988) 'An exchange programme between pupils and teachers in different ethnic and cultural communities' *SAALED National Conference Proceedings*, University of Natal, Durban.

Loram, C. T. (1917) *The Education of the South African Native*. Oxford: Clarendon Press.

Lundgren, V. (1977) *Model Analysis of Pedagogical Processes* In-house publication, Department of Educational Research, Stockholm Institute of Education.

Macdonald, A. M. (1993) 'Commitments and constraints' *Evaluating the Science Education Project 1977–1988*. Cape Town: Oxford University Press.

Mackie, R. (ed.) (1980) *Literacy and Revolution. The Pedagogy of Paulo Freire*. Great Britain: Pluto Press.

Malherbe, E. G. (1977) *Education in South Africa*. Cape Town: Juta.

Marginson, F. (1993) 'Generic skills and the needs of employment' Focus Occasional Paper on Adult Education, Sydney: Adult Literacy and Basic Skills Action Coalition (ALBSAC).

Martin, E. & Ramsden, P. (1987) 'Learning skills, or skill in learning?' Richardson, J. E. *et al.* (eds) *Student Learning: Research in Education and Cognitive Psychology*. Milton Keynes: SRHE and Open University.

Martin-Jones, M. (1993) 'Code-switching in the classroom: two decades of research' Centre for Language in Social Life Working Paper Series.

Martinius, M. E. (1922) *A Sketch of the Development of Rural Education (European) in the Cape Colony 1652–1910* Grahamstown. Privately published.

Marton, F. & Saljo, R. (1976a) 'On qualitative differences in learning: I. Outcome and process' *British Journal of Educational Psychology* Vol 46.

Marton, F. & Saljo, R. (1976b) 'On qualitative differences in learning: II. Outcome as a function of the learner's conception of the task' *British Journal of Educational Psychology* Vol 46.

Marton, F. & Saljo, R. (1997) 'Approaches to learning' Marton, F. *et al.* (eds) *The Experience of Learning* (2nd edn). Edinburgh: Scottish Academic Press.

Marton, F., Hounsell, D. J. & Entwistle, N. J. (eds) (1997) *The Experience of Learning* (2nd edn). Edinburgh: Scottish Academic Press.

Mathews, J. (1989) *Tools of Change*. Sydney: Pluto.

Mazrui, A. (1997) 'The World Bank, the language question and the future of African education' *Race & Class* Vol 38 No 3.

McDermott. L. (1991) 'What we teach and what is learned – closing the gap' *American Journal of Physics* Vol 4.

McGrath, S. (1996a) 'Learning to work? Changing discourses on education and training in South Africa, 1976–1996'. Unpublished PhD dissertation, University of Edinburgh.

McGrath, S. (1996b) 'Education and training in transition: analysing the NQF' Donn, G. (ed.) *South Africa: Education in Transition* Occasional Paper No 63, Centre for African Studies, University of Edinburgh.

McGrath, S. (1997a) 'Reforming South African TVET: linking national policies and institutional practices' Papers on Education, Training and Development, Centre of African Studies, University of Edinburgh.

McGrath, S. (1997b) 'Reading the NQF: towards an analytical framework' Kallaway, P. *et al.* (eds) *Education after Apartheid*. Cape Town: University of Cape Town Press.

McGrath, S. (1997c) 'Marketing education in South Africa? Education policy discourse in the new South Africa, 1994–6' Brock, C. (ed.) *Education as a Commodity*. London: Cassell.

McGrath, S. (1997d) 'National policies and institutional practices: the credibility gap in South African education and training reform' Papers in Education, Training and Enterprise 3, Centre of African Studies, University of Edinburgh.

McGrath, S. & King, K. (1996) 'Learning to compete: African education, training and small enterprise development in the era of globalisation' Papers on Education, Training and Enterprise No 1, October 1996, Centre for African Studies, University of Edinburgh.

McLaren, P. (1989) *Life in Schools: An Introduction to Critical Pedagogy in the Foundations of Education.* New York and London: Longman.

McNay, I. & Ozga, J. (eds) (1985) *Policy-making in Education: The Breakdown of Consensus.* Oxford: Pergamon Press.

McPherson, A. & Raab, C. (1989) *Governing Scottish Education: A Sociology of Policy Since 1945.* Edinburgh: Edinburgh University Press.

Meerkotter, D. (1993) 'The NECC, People's Education and emancipatory action research at the University of the Western Cape' Davidoff, S. *et al.* (eds) *Emancipatory Education and Action Research.* Pretoria: HSRC.

Michelson, E. (1995) 'The politics of memory: South Africa and the recognition of prior learning'. Unpublished paper presented at the CACE International Conference on Adult Education, Cape Town.

Michelson, E. (1996) 'Taxonomies of sameness: the recognition of prior learning as anthropology'. Unpublished paper presented at the International Conference on Experiential Learning, University of Cape Town.

Mitchell, D. & Ryba, K. (1994), *Students with Education Support Needs* Report to the New Zealand Ministry of Education. Hamilton: Waikato University Press.

Mitchie, J. & Smith, J. G. (eds) (1995) *Managing the Global Economy.* Oxford: Oxford University Press.

Morphet, A. (1997) 'Getting quality into the system' Bensusan, D. (ed.) *Whither the University?* Cape Town: Juta.

Morrow, W. E. (1992) 'A picture holds us captive'. Unpublished paper, October 1992.

Morrow, W. E. (1994) 'Entitlement and achievement in education' *Studies in Philosophy and Education* Vol 13.

Morrow, W. E. (1996a) 'Stakeholders and senates: the governance of higher education institutions in South Africa' *Cambridge Journal of Education* (forthcoming).

Morrow, W. E. (1996b) 'Teacher education, pluralism and the ugly lines of segregation in South Africa' Craft, M. (ed.) *Teacher Education in Plural Societies.* London: Falmer Press.

Mosdell, T. (1991) 'Power, patronage and control' Preston-Whyte, E. & Rogerson, C. (eds) *South Africa's Informal Economy.* Cape Town: Oxford University Press.

Motala, S. (1997) 'From policy to implementation: ongoing challenges and constraints' *Wits EPU Quarterly Review of Education and Training in South Africa* Vol 5 No 1.

Moulder, J. (1991) *Facing the Educational Policy Crisis.* Pretoria: Heinemann.

Moyo, T. (1996) 'Code-switching among competent bilinguals: a case study for linguistic, cultural and group identity?' *Southern African Journal of Applied Language Studies (SAJALS)* Vol 4 No 1.

Muller, J. (1995) 'In praise of virtual thought'. Unpublished paper presented at the Kenton Conference, Grahamstown, October 1995.

Murray, A. V. (1937) *The School in the Bush.* London: Longman Green.

Murray Report (1969) *Commission of Enquiry into Children with Minimal Brain Dysfunction.* Pretoria: Government Printer.

National Commission on Special Needs in Education and Training (NCSNET) and National Committee for Education Support Services (NCESS) (1997) *Education for All from 'Special Needs and Support' to Developing Quality Education for All Learners* Public Discussion Document, August 1997.

National Education and Training Forum (1993) *Founding Agreement.* Johannesburg: National Education and Training Forum.

NEPI (1992) *Language.* Cape Town: Oxford University Press/NECC.

NEPI (1992) *Support Services.* Cape Town: Oxford University Press/NECC.

NEPI (1993a) *The Framework Report.* Cape Town: Oxford University Press/NECC.

NEPI (1993b) *Human Resources Development.* Cape Town: Oxford University Press/ NECC.

NEPI (1993c) *Adult Basic Education.* Cape Town: Oxford University Press/NECC.

NEPI (1993d) *Adult Education.* Cape Town: Oxford University Press/NECC.

NEPI (1993e) *Post-Secondary Education.* Cape Town: Oxford University Press/NECC.

National Training Board (1994) *A Discussion Document on a National Training Strategy Initiative.* Pretoria: NTB.

National Training Board and GTZ (1997) *Education, Training and Development Practices Project: Phase 2 Report* Government to government technical co-operation Project: RSA and Federal Republic of Germany; Cape Town.

National Training Strategy Board (1994) *National Training Strategy Inintiative Document* Johannesburg: National Training Strategy Board.

National Union of Metalworkers of South Africa (1991) 'NUMSA Vocational Training Project' Johannesburg: NUMSA.

New Zealand Ministry of Education (1989a) *Governing Schools.* Wellington: Ministry of Education.

New Zealand Ministry of Education (1989b) *Education Act.* Wellington: Government Printers.

New Zealand Ministry of Education (1993) *New Zealand Curriculum Framework.* Wellington: Learning Media Limited.

New Zealand Ministry of Education (1997) *A Future Qualifications Policy for New Zealand: A Plan for the NQF* Green Paper. Wellington: Government Printer.

New Zealand Ministry of Education (1998) *School Qualifications for 16–19 year olds* Wellington, New Zealand (http://www.minedu.govt.nz).

New Zealand Qualifications Authority (1991) *Designing the Framework.* Wellington: NZQA.

New Zealand Qualifications Authority (1992) *A Qualifications Framework for New Zealand: An Introduction to the Framework.* Wellington: NZQA.

Ngoro, B. (1998) 'Crisis talks on matric failure rates in townships' *Cape Argus* 24 February 1998.

Northedge, A. (1997) 'Teaching understood as discourse initiation: an illustrative case study taken from open learning materials'. Unpublished paper, September 1997.

Novak, J. D. & Gowin, D. B. (1984) *Learning How to Learn.* Cambridge: Cambridge University Press.

Nyerere, J. (1967) *Education for Self-Reliance.* Dar es Salaam: Ministry of Information and Tourism.

Nzimande, B. (1997) 'Foreword', Kallaway, P. *et al.* (eds) *Education after Apartheid.* Cape Town: University of Cape Town Press.

O'Connor, I. (1973) *The State in Crisis*. London: Routledge.

O'Connor, P. (ed.) (1994) *Thinking Work*. Sydney: ALBSAC.

Offe, C. (1985) *Disorganised Capitalism*. Oxford: Polity Press.

Ottoson, J. (1997) 'After the applause: exploring multiple influences on application following an adult education program' *Adult Education Quarterly* Vol 47 No 2.

Parekh, B. (1995) 'Education for a culturally plural society' *Papers of the Philosophy of Education Society of Great Britain* March 31–April 2 1995.

Peires, M. (1994) 'Code-switching as an aid to L2 learning' *Southern African Journal of Applied Language Studies (SAJALS)* Vol 3 No 1.

Phillips, B. (1993) *Towards a Concept for a South African National Qualifications Framework*. Johannesburg: Gencor.

Picot, B. *et al.* (1988) *Administering for Excellence: Effective Administration in Education* (The Picot Report) Wellington: Taskforce to Review Education Administration.

Price, R. F. (1979) *Education in Modern China*. London: Routledge and Kegan Paul.

Prinsloo, M. & Breier, M. (1996) *The Social Uses of Literacy*. Cape Town: Sached Books and Amsterdam and Philadelphia: John Benjamin Publishing Company.

Prosser, M., Trigwell, K. & Taylor, P. (1994) 'A phenomenographic study of academics' conceptions of science learning and teaching' *Learning & Instruction* Vol 4.

Provincial Skills Development Pilot Project (1998) *Report to the Steering Committee*, 31 March 1998, Durban.

Prunty, J. J. (1985) 'Signposts for a critical educational analysis' *Australian Journal of Education* Vol 29 No 2.

Radcliffe, G. (1996) 'Die toelatingsbeleid van Universiteit van Wes-Kaapland'. MEd thesis, University of the Western Cape.

Raffe, D. (1991) 'School leaving and qualifications' Edinburgh: Centre for Educational Sociology, University of Edinburgh.

Ramsden, P. (1981) 'A study of the relationship between student learning and its academic context'. Unpublished Ph.D. thesis, University of Lancaster.

Ranson, S. (1995) 'Theorising education policy' *Journal of Education Policy* Vol 10 No 4.

RDP (1994) *White Paper on Reconstruction and Development: Government's Strategy for Fundamental Transformation* Cape Town.

Reeder, D. (1981) 'A recurring debate: education and industry' Dale, R. *et al. Schooling and the National Interest*. Lewes: Falmer Press.

Reich, R. (1991) *The Work of Nations*. London: Simon and Schuster.

Republic of South Africa (1996) *National Small Business Act 1996* Government Gazette Vol 377 No 17612, Cape Town.

Rheinallt Jones, J. L. & Saffrey, A. L. (1933/4) *The Social and Economic Conditions of Native Life in the Union of South Africa; Findings of the Native Economic Commission 1930–1932* Collated and summarised version in *Bantu Studies* Vol 7 Nos 3 & 4 and Vol 8 Nos 1 & 2.

Richardson, J. E. (1986) *Handbook of Theory for the Sociology of Education*. London: Greenword Press.

Riddell, S., Thomson, G. O. B. & Dyer, S. (1992) 'A key-informant approach to the study of local policy-making in the field of special educational needs' *European Journal of Special Needs Education* Vol 7 No 1.

Ritzer, G. K. (1998) *The McDonaldization Thesis*. London: Sage.

Robinson, P. (1997) 'Literacy, numeracy and economic performance'. Unpublished paper, Centre for Economic Performance, London, September 1997.

Rogan, J. R. & Gray, B. V. (1998) 'Science education as South Africa's trojan horse' Accepted for publication in the *Journal for Research in Science Teaching*. Theme Issue on Science Education in Developing Countries.

Rogoff, B. (1990) *Apprenticeship in Thinking: Cognitive Development in Social Context.* Oxford: Oxford University Press.

RSA (1996) *Constitution of the Republic of South Africa* (Act 108 of 1996) Pretoria: Government Printer.

Saint, W. S. (1992) *Universities in Africa: Strategies for Stabilization and Revitalization* World Bank Technical Paper No 194.

SAIRR (1997) Information bulletin from the South African Institute of Race Relations, RR97/65.

Salkever, S. G. (1990) ' "Lopp'd and Bound": How liberal theory obscures the goods of liberal practices' Douglass, R. B. *et al.* (eds) *Liberalism and the Good.* London: Routledge.

Samoff, J. (1996) 'Frameworks! South African education and training policy documents, 1994–1996'. Unpublished paper prepared for the Macro-Education Policy Unit, University of Durban-Westville, September 1996.

SAQA (1995) South African Qualifications Authority Act.

SAQA (1997) *Regulations governing the activities of National Standards Bodies Appendix B,* Pretoria.

Scottish Office Information Directorate (1995) Press Release on the Education (Scotland) Bill, Edinburgh: Scottish Office 1 December 1995.

SCRE (1994) Scottish Council for Research in Education *Implementing 5–14: a progress report* (Interchange 23) Edinburgh: HMSO.

Sieborger, R. (1997) ' "How the outcomes came out": a personal account of and reflections on the initial process of development of Curriculum 2005'. Unpublished paper, Kenton-at-the-Gap conference, Hermanus, October 1997.

Sietske, W. & Thrupp, M. (1995) 'Choice, competition, and segregation: an empirical analysis of a New Zealand secondary school market 1990–1993' *Journal of Education Policy* Vol 10 No 2.

Skutnabb-Kangas, T. (1990) *Language, Literacy and Minorities.* London: A Minority Rights Group Report.

Skuy, M. & Partington, H. (1990) 'Special education in South Africa' *International Journal of Disability, Development and Education* Vol 37.

Smithers, A. (1993) 'All our futures'. London: Channel 4 Television.

SOED (1979) *16–18s in Scotland: The First Two Years of Post-Compulsory Education.* London: HMSO.

SOED (1987) *Curriculum and Assessment in Scotland: A Policy for the '90s.* Edinburgh: HMSO.

SOED (1993) *The Structure and Balance of the Curriculum 5–14.* Edinburgh: HMSO.

SOED (1994a) *Children and Young Persons with Special Educational Needs: Assessment and Recording Services* (Draft Circular) Edinburgh: HMSO.

Standing, G., Sender, J. & Weeks, J. (1996) *Restructuring the Labour Market: the South African Challenge: An ILO Country Review.* Geneva: ILO.

Starcke, A. (1978) *Survival: Taped Interviews with South Africa's Power Elite.* Cape Town: Tafelberg.

Stewart, F. (1995) 'Globalisation and education'. Unpublished paper presented at the Oxford Conference on Globalisation and Learning Oxford: September 1995.

Strebel, A. (1987) 'Report to the Faculty of Arts concerning student intake and distribution in the faculty'. Unpublished report, University of the Western Cape.

Street, B. V. (ed.) (1993) *Cross Cultural Approaches to Literacy.* Cambridge University Press.

Subotzky, George *et al.* (1997) *The Enhancement of Graduate Programmes and Research Capacity at the Historically Black Universities* Final Research Report, October 1997, Education Policy Unit, University of the Western Cape.

Sunday Times (1998) 11 January 1998.

Sunday Times (1998) 22 February 1998.

Swann, W. (1985) 'Is the integration of children with special educational needs happening? An analysis of recent statistics in special education' *Oxford Review of Education* Vol 11 No 1.

Tandon, R. (1988) 'Social transformation and participatory research' *Convergence* Vol XXI Nos 2 & 3.

Taylor, E. (1983) 'Orientations to study: A longitudinal interview investigation of students on two human studies degree courses at Surrey University'. Unpublished PhD thesis, University of Surrey.

Technology and Human Resources for Industry Programme (THRIP) (1997) 'Draft THRIP Strategic Plan', Pretoria.

The Argus (1995) Various articles in newspaper.

The Guardian (1996) 'Schools Face Exam Revolution' 2 March 1996.

The President's Conference on Small Business (June 1994), Pretoria.

Theron, M. (1996) Personal communication.

Thomas, P. R. & Bain, J. D. (1984) 'Contextual dependence of learning approaches: the effects of assessments' *Human Learning* Vol 3.

Thomson, G. O. B., Riddell, S. & Dyer, S. (1989) *Policy, Professionals and Parents.* Mimeograph: The University of Edinburgh.

Thomson, G. O. B, Ward, K. & Wishart, J. (1995) 'The transition to adulthood for children with Down's Syndrome' *Disability and Society* Vol 10 No 3.

Thomson, G. O. B., Ward, K. M. & Stewart, M. (1995) *The 5–14 Development Programme and Least and Most Able Pupils.* Mimeograph: The University of Edinburgh.

Thorpe, M. & Thompson, J. (1993) *Learning File for Course EH266.* Milton Keynes: The Open University.

Torres, C. A. (1990) *The Politics of Non-Formal Education in Latin America.* New York: Praeger.

Trew, R. & Desai, Z. (1992) 'Language rights in the Draft Bill of Rights' textual suggestions submitted to the ANC's Constitutional Committee in February 1992.

Trigwell, K. & Prosser, M. (1991) 'Relating approaches to study and quality of learning outcomes at the course level' *British Journal of Educational Psychology* Vol 61.

UNESCO (1972) 'Technical and vocational education' *Apartheid: Its Effects on Education, Science, Culture and Information.* Paris: UNESCO.

UNESCO (1961) *Rural Education.* Paris: UNESCO.

UNESCO (1994) *Salamanca Statement* on principles, policy and practice in special needs education.

University of the Western Cape (1982) Mission Statement issued by University Council and Senate, University of the Western Cape.

Van den Berg, O. C. & Gerwel, G. J. (1990) 'Student selections: challenge of the new decade' *UWC News* Vol 1 No 3.

Van Driel, J. H., Verloop, N., Van Werven, H. I. & Dekkers, H. (1997) 'Teachers' craft knowledge and curriculum innovation in higher engineering education' *Higher Education* Vol 34 No 1.

Van Rossum, E. J. & Schenk (1984) 'The relationship between learning conception, study strategy and learning outcome' *British Journal of Educational Psychology* Vol 54.

Walker, M. & Badsha, N. (1993) 'Academic development and the challenge of curriculum change at UWC – an overview', Walker, M. (ed.) *AD Dialogues* Vol 1.

Walters, S. (1996) 'Education, training and development practitioners (ETDPs) within reconstruction and development of South Africa' *Adult Education and Development* 46 (96 Institut fur internationale zusammen arbeit des deutschen Volkschuleverbandes e.v.).

Weideman, E. (1996) 'Trashing their own school: how mob behaviour turns people into animals' *Drum* Vol 3 No 213.

Western Cape Education Department (1997) *What are the Key Issues around Implementing C2005/OBE in the Western Cape?* Curriculum Advisory Services, discussion document.

White, R., Gunstone, R., Elterman, E., Macdonald, I., McKittrick, B., Mills, D. & Mulhall, P. (1995) 'Students' perceptions of teaching and learning in first-year university physics' *Research in Science Education* Vol 25 No 4.

Whitehead, A. N. (1949) *The Aims of Education*. New York: New American Library.

Wilson, A. (1983) 'The promise of situated cognition' Merriam, S. (ed.) *An update on Adult Learning Theory*. San Francisco: Jossey Bass.

World Bank (1971) *Education Sector Working Paper*. Washington DC: World Bank.

World Bank (1995) *Priorities and Strategies for Education*. Washington DC: World Bank.

Young, I. M. (1990) *Justice and the Politics of Difference*. Princeton: Princeton University Press.

Young, M. (1995) 'Modularization and the outcomes approach: towards a strategy for a curriculum of the future' Burke, J. (ed.) *Outcomes, Learning and the Curriculum*. London: Falmer.

Young, M. & Watson, J. (eds) (1992) *Beyond the White Paper: the Case for a Unified System at 16+*. London: University of London Institute of Education.

Zentella, A. C. (1981) 'Ta bien, you could answer me en cualquier idioma: Puerto Rican codeswitching in bilingual classrooms' Duran, R. (ed.) *Latino Language and Communicative Behavior*. Norwood, N.J.: Ablex Publishing Corporation.

Index